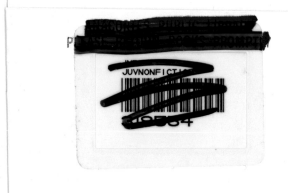

THE Comic Book
READER'S COMPANION

AN A-TO-Z GUIDE TO EVERYONE'S FAVORITE ART FORM

Ron Goulart

HarperPerennial
A Division Of HarperCollins*Publishers*

Designed by George J. McKeon

Library of Congress Cataloging-in-Publication Data
Goulart, Ron, 1933–
    The comic book reader's companion : an a-to-z guide to everyone's favorite art form / Ron Goulart. — 1st ed.
        p.   cm.
    Includes bibliographical references.
    ISBN 0-06-273117-3
    1. Comic books, strips, etc.—United States—Encyclopedias.
I. Title.
PN6725.G633   1993
741.5'0973—dc20   92-18795

93 94 95 96 97 ❖/RRD 10 9 8 7 6 5 4 3 2 1

Acknowledgments

The following people provided material that was helpful in the preparation of this volume, but they are in no way responsible for the uses made of it: Michael Barson, Jon Berke, J. Randolph Cox, Will Murray, Fred Rhoads, Don and Maggie Thompson, and Robert Wiener.

Introduction

Comic books as we know them have been around for close to 60 years. This *Companion* is intended to serve as a sort of encyclopedia, a handy reference book that's also fun to read. The book provides a good deal of information about one of America's favorite forms of reading matter and offers concise yet detailed entries on every type of character and comic book, past and present.

Chiefly you'll find two sorts of entries, those dealing with specific characters and those covering specific comic book titles. In addition, we've included some definitions of general terms, such as Good Girl Art and Silver Age. Included herein are entries on every major superhero, from Superman onward, plus a fair sampling of minor ones. You'll find the best-known animals here, such as Mickey Mouse and Howard the Duck, and, for good measure, Ziggy Pig and Hoppy the Marvel Bunny. There are also entries on such jungle queens as Sheena and Nyoka, masked cowboys like the Lone Ranger and barefaced ones such as Kid Colt, wallbangers and wildmen like the Punisher and Ghost Rider, plus a multitude of others. There are entries on *Famous Funnies*, the book that started the modern comic business six decades ago, *Action Comics*, which gave the world Superman, and dozens of others.

Since this is a reference work, there aren't quite as many pictures as are found in the average comic. You'll find, however, 100 illustrations, many of them shot from original art and some from hitherto unpublished sources.

This is the kind of book I've been wishing someone would do for several years now. When I realized there were no other volunteers, I decided to do it myself. I hope you enjoy the result.

—*Ron Goulart*

A Note on Editorial Quirks

In the course of long and prosperous careers, both DC Comics, Inc. and Marvel Comics have done business under a variety of names. In the days of the pioneering Major Nicholson, DC was known as, among other things, National Allied Publications, Inc. It later took to calling itself Detective Comics, Inc., and for a long stretch was known as National Periodical Publications, Inc. Marvel, especially when the inventive Martin Goodman was in charge, published comic books under an impressive list of names. Overstreet's *Price Guide* lists 60 of them, ranging from Animirth Comics, Inc. and Atlas Magazines, Inc. to Timely Comics, Inc. and Zenith Publishing Co., Inc. For the sake of simplicity and clarity, I refer to DC throughout this book as DC and to Marvel as Marvel, even if they called themselves something else during the period under discussion.

I frequently state that a comic book appeared late in a certain year or in the spring of another year rather than giving a specific month. That's because the cover date of a magazine may be anywhere from a month to four months ahead of the actual publication date.

The Comic Book Reader's Companion

ACTION COMICS Quite probably the most influential comic book ever published, DC's *Action* hit the newsstands in the spring of 1938 and introduced SUPERMAN to the world—or at least introduced him to the increasing number of kids who were discovering funny books. It took the rest of the world, including other magazine publishers, nearly another year to figure out what was going on. Superman triggered the superhero boom of the late 1930s and early 1940s that turned the comic book business into a major industry.

The Man of Steel was showcased on the initial cover of *Action Comics* lifting an auto over his head, and a 13-page adventure by Jerry Siegel and Joe Shuster led off the issue. Backing up Superman were cowboy Chuck Dawson, adventurer Tex Thomson, newsman Scoop Scanlon, and master magician ZATARA. In addition to Shuster, the artists included Bernard Baily, Will Ely, and Fred Guardineer.

Over the years, *Action* featured a variety of backup characters. Among them were the Black Pirate, the Vigilante, CONGO BILL, SUPERGIRL, Tommy Tomorrow, and the Legion of Super-Heroes. In 1988, DC tried *Action* as a weekly, with others—the Secret Six, Nightwing

Action Comics Weekly # 601, Dave Gibbons, © 1988 DC Comics, Inc. All rights reserved.

(see BATMAN), BLACKHAWK, etc.—in the limelight. Before a year was out, however, it was once again a monthly, with Superman the undisputed star.

ADAM STRANGE   *See* Mystery in Space.

ADVENTURE COMICS   The Pioneering Major Nicholson's second title was launched in the late autumn of 1935 and was first called *New Comics*. Although of the same dimensions as the 64-page FAMOUS FUNNIES, it originally provided a fat 80 pages for just one thin dime. A potpourri of mostly one- and two-page features, *New Comics* offered both humor and adventure strips, the majority of them laid out in Sunday-page format. The title became *New Adventure* with #12 (January 1937) and just plain *Adventure* with #32 (November 1938). During the nearly 50 years it was on the stands, *Adventure* showcased a variety of characters, including THE SANDMAN, Hourman, Starman, SUPERBOY, the Legion of Super Heroes, and SUPERGIRL.

On the adventurous side in the early issues were *Castaway Island*, *Slim and Tex*, *Captain Quick*, and *Dale Daring*. Work by Jerry Siegel and Joe Shuster started appearing in the second issue. Their *Federal Men* was a G-man serial starring Steve Carson, whose grim, sharp-featured profile probably made even Dick Tracy envious. Included in the funny stuff were *Dickie Duck*, *Sagebrush N' Cactus*, *J. Worthington Blimp*, and *The Strange Adventures of Mr. Weed*. These last two were by a talented teenage Brooklyn cartoonist named Sheldon Mayer.

With the 12th issue, the magazine began to transform itself. Humor all but vanished from the covers, replaced by action and violence. The interior was overhauled as well. While almost all the adventure strips were still to be continued, they now took up four to eight pages. After Major Nicholson departed in the spring of 1938, several new serious features were added—*Anchors Aweigh!*, *Rusty and His Pals*, *Captain Desmo*, and *Tod Hunter, Jungle Master*.

Next came a wave of costumed crimefighters and superheroes. The Sandman made his debut in #40 (July 1939), written by Gardner Fox and drawn at first by Bert Christman. Next was Bernard Baily's Hour-Man, who got his powers from a superdrug he'd invented. He began in #48 (March 1940). *Adventure*'s next superhero was auspiciously launched in #61, getting the cover and the leadoff position. Starman, whose abilities derived from the radiated starlight he collected by way of his gravity rod, was the joint effort of the prolific Gardner Fox and former sports cartoonist Jack Burnley.

The Shining Knight came on stage in #66, nicely drawn by Creig Flessel. Wearing golden armor and mounted on a winged horse, he'd been frozen for several centuries. Once thawed, he became a sort of Connecticut Yankee in reverse. In issue #69 (December 1941), the Sandman got an updated look—yellow tunic and tights, purple cowl, cape, and boots—and a boy companion named Sandy. Chad Grothkopf was the artist who handled the transition story and Paul Norris did the next two. Then the formidable team of Joe Simon and Jack Kirby took over, and Sandman became the uncontested leading man for the next several years.

In 1946, Superboy, who'd had his origin the year before in MORE FUN COMICS, moved over to *Adventure* and assumed the featured spot. In the late 1950s the Legion of Super Heroes, with such members as Cosmic Boy, Saturn Girl, and Lightning Lad, was first seen. Supergirl entered in the 1960s. *Adventure* continued, a digest-sized publication in its final days, until the early 1980s.

THE ADVENTURES OF ALAN LADD   In their post-World War II efforts to find substitutes for the fading superheroes, some publishers gave movie stars a try. Alan Ladd had been portraying hard-bitten tough guys on the screen since breaking through to stardom in

Paramount's *This Gun for Hire* in 1942. In 1949, deciding he might also prove to be a popular comic book action hero, DC introduced a bimonthly titled *The Adventures of Alan Ladd*.

The first five issues had photo covers of Ladd, some of which look as though they might have been shot especially for the magazine. Copy identified Ladd as "your favorite Hollywood star" and "Hollywood's #1 he-man." The Alan Ladd of the comic book was a combination of the actor's onscreen and off-screen personalities. He appeared as himself in each of the book's 10-page adventures. Sometimes the action developed out of a studio situation, such as when Ladd helped out a director friend by working as a stuntman. Others, such as the one where he worked as a jet test pilot, took place outside the Hollywood milieu. Dan Barry drew the first issue, then Ruben Moreira took over. The magazine, after nine issues, ended its run early in 1951.

During this same period, FAMOUS FUNNIES, and then Lev Gleason, tried a Buster Crabbe comic. Not even some covers by Frank Frazetta and interior work by Al Williamson and Alex Toth could keep the book going. Magazine Enterprises did a Dick Powell one-shot and publisher Victor Fox came out with two issues of a Dorothy Lamour title. None of the actors did anywhere near as well as their cowboy colleagues.

THE ADVENTURES OF BOB HOPE As part of its post–World War II move away from superheroes, DC introduced a comic book devoted to the popular movie and radio comedian. *The Adventures of Bob Hope* hit the stands early in 1950. It lasted through 109 issues, shutting down early in 1968.

The early plots, as *The Comic Reader* points out, "consist of Hope as an unemployed womanizer who tries to meet beautiful women and avoid paying rent. . . . [But later they] began to use many fantasy elements."

The chief artist for most of the first decade

was Owen Fitzgerald. After working anonymously on *Bob Hope*, Fitzgerald went on to ghost the *Dennis the Menace* Sunday page. Later artists included Bob Oksner, Mort Drucker, and superhero specialist Neal Adams. Chief scriptwriters were editor Larry Nadle, Cal Howard, and Arnold Drake.

Among the other comedians to have comic books based on them were Laurel & Hardy, Abbott & Costello, Milton Berle, the Three Stooges (drawn originally by Norman Maurer, the son-in-law of Stooge Moe Howard), Jackie Gleason, Edgar Bergen & Charlie McCarthy, and Dean Martin & Jerry Lewis. After that team split up, the comic book continued with Lewis alone.

AIRBOY   *See* Air Fighters Comics.

AIR FIGHTERS COMICS This was the comic book that introduced not only Airboy but the Heap as well. Hillman Periodicals published the first issue late in 1941, with a lineup provided by the FUNNIES, INC. shop. Although that issue wasn't a hit, they tried a second issue a year later with an entirely different cast of characters. *Air Fighters* now displayed considerable sex and violence, and the revitalized version took off. Among the new characters was Airboy.

Charles Biro, who was under contract to Lev Gleason at the time and was occupied on *Daredevil* and *Boy Comics*, created Airboy and had a hand in the scripting. He drew the first few covers, but never the stories inside, and remained anonymous throughout. Airboy was an orphan lad who flew an experimental plane named Birdie. The plane, which flapped its wings, was acquired by Birdie from the monks who had reared him. In it, he took to the air against both the Nazis and the Japanese, but his most formidable opponent was a striking young lady known as Valkyrie, who had a heart "as black as the devil's." (Actually, she was a good–bad young woman, a more youth-

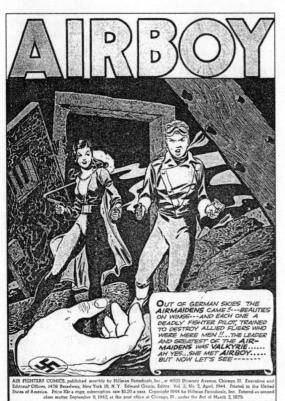

Airboy, Fred Kida, © 1944 by Hillman Publications, Inc.

ful version of the Dragon Lady.) Fred Kida, a gifted disciple of Milton Caniff, drew most of the flying hero's encounters with her and her ruthless gang of Airmaidens.

Airboy dominated the magazine, and late in 1945 its name was changed to *Airboy*. It continued as *Airboy* until 1953. Among the other artists who illustrated his aerial adventures were Dan Barry, Arthur Peddy, and Ernie Schroeder, who worked on the feature during its final years.

The unsuccessful initial issue included such airborne characters as the Black Commander, Crash Davis, and the Mosquito. Backing up Airboy from the second issue onward were Iron Ace, the Bald Eagle, the Black Angel, and Skywolf. Iron Ace was a dual-role character. In everyday life he was a Royal Air Force flyer

named Captain Britain. Donning a full suit of armor, he went aloft in his alternate identity. The Bald Eagle, one of the few hairless heroes of the period, was a skinhead who carried on a one-man air war against the Axis, piloting a black plane he called the Flying Coffin.

The Black Angel was in reality lovely, raven-haired Sylvia Manners, a freelance World War II combat pilot. Wearing one of the tightest-fitting costumes in GOLDEN AGE comics, she had to put up with not only such flying opponents as Baroness Blood, "the Nazi cobra of the skies," but with giant vampire bats, witches, and werewolves. The first artist to draw her was John Cassone. While he was good at depicting the necessary planes and weapons, his real forte was the female form. He was especially fond of showing his heroine from the rear. If Cassone had had a family crest, it surely would've had buttocks in its design.

Skywolf was in the BLACKHAWK mold, leading an independent squad of aviators in air combat against the Germans in World War II. In addition to his paramilitary uniform, he wore a white wolf's head as a hat. In the third issue of the magazine, Skywolf encountered the Heap. During World War I, a flying ace named Baron Emmelmann had crashed in a lonely swamp and been seriously injured. Instead of dying, his body merged with the vegetation. Eventually he became "a fantastic HEAP that is neither animal nor man." A somewhat ambiguous soul, the walking compost pile tended to be anti-Nazi and, when not terrorizing the local citizens, he would rip up German soldiers. The Heap eventually outgrew Skywolf, and the somewhat mellowed monster was given a feature of his own in 1946. Mort Leav drew him first. Among the many other artists who also drew him were Dan Barry, Carmine Infantino, and Leonard Starr.

Eclipse Comics revived Airboy, as well as Valkyrie, Skywolf, the Heap, and others of the old *Air Fighters* gang, in 1986. The revival lasted a bit more than three years.

ALL-AMERICAN COMICS   Begun in the spring of 1939, this was the first title that the enterprising M.C. Gaines put together for DC assisted by the youthful Sheldon Mayer as editor. Gaines was no great believer in superheroes. He initially provided a package that mixed original adventure features and strip reprints, and it wasn't until the 16th issue (July 1940) that *All-American* got around to introducing a true superhero in the person of the GREEN LANTERN.

The early issues offered reprints of such Gaines favorites as *Mutt & Jeff*, *Skippy*, *Reg'lar Fellers*, and *Believe It or Not*. The most successful of the initial batch of original features was Jon Blummer's *Hop Harrigan*. It dealt with a clean-cut young aviator and was later the basis for both a radio show and a movie serial. Blummer was also responsible for *Gary Concord, the Ultra-Man*, which began in the eighth issue. Despite its title, this was futuristic science fiction, and had nothing to do with superheroes.

After the advent of Green Lantern, which Mayer had urged him to add, Gaines opened the magazine to an assortment of other costumed do-gooders. These included THE ATOM, Dr. Mid-Nite, and Sargon the Sorcerer.

Reflecting the changes in the postwar marketplace, the magazine became *All-American Western* with issue #103 (November 1948). In 1952, DC converted it to *All-American Men of War* and as a combat comic book it continued until the summer of 1966.

ALL STAR COMICS   The magazine that introduced the superhero team concept, *All Star* began as a quarterly in June of 1940. It was edited by Sheldon Mayer and initially offered brand new, unrelated adventures of the more popular characters from DC's handful of other titles. The innovation came with the third issue, when Mayer and writer Gardner F. Fox came up with the notion of having all the resident *All Star* heroes join together to form a crime-fighting group called the JUSTICE SOCIETY OF AMERICA (JSA).

The founding members of the JSA were THE FLASH, GREEN LANTERN, SANDMAN, THE ATOM, the Spectre, HAWKMAN, DR. FATE, and Hour-Man. In #4, which was the first bimonthly issue, a single theme ran through all the stories. From then on the Justice Society got together each issue to defend the country against spies, travel to other planets, feed the starving of Europe, and defeat such villains as the Brain Wave, the Psycho-Pirate, and Degaton. All the

The Human Torch™, Carl Burgos, unpublished, 1939.

book-length adventures were the work of the inventive Fox. Initially each hero's regular artists drew the individual chapters.

The title continued, with the membership of the JSA changing along the way, until #57 (February–March 1951). Then, in a good indication of how comic books were changing, it became *All Star Western* and went on for another decade.

ALL WINNERS COMICS Marvel's imitation of rival DC's ALL STAR COMICS came along in the summer of 1941. Initially *All Star* offered an anthology of new adventures of popular characters from other DC titles—THE FLASH, HAWKMAN, the Spectre, the GREEN LANTERN, etc. But when Marvel tried to put together a book that would showcase its hit characters, it could only come up with CAPTAIN AMERICA and Bucky, the Human Torch and Toro, and the SUB-MARINER. Marvel was forced to fill the rest of the slots with such definite second bananas as the Angel, the Black Marvel, and the Whizzer (who came by his superpowers by way of an injection of mongoose blood).

Although *All Star* had introduced the innovative and eventually influential JUSTICE SOCIETY in its third issue late in 1940, Marvel didn't get around to imitating that concept until 1946. *All Winners* #19 saw the birth of the All Winners Squad, Marvel's first superhero team. The key members were, as might be expected, Captain America and Bucky, the Torch, and Toro, and the Sub-Mariner. The Whizzer and MISS AMERICA filled out the roster. The Squad appeared again in issue #21 (there was no #20), that time teaming up to solve "The Riddle of the Demented Dwarf." The magazine then became *All Teen* and featured various youthful characters. *All Winners* had a one-issue revival in 1948, without the Squad, and then was gone for good.

AMAZING-MAN COMICS The creative team behind this title went on to put together MAR-VEL COMICS. Part of the Centaur line, *Amazing-Man* started with issue #5 (September 1939) and ended with #26 (January 1942).

The staff included artists Bill Everett and Carl Burgos and editor Lloyd Jacquet. The star of the magazine was Everett's Amazing-Man, a somewhat mystical superhero who'd picked up his powers in the mountains of Tibet. Burgos's contribution was the Iron Skull, an android in a business suit who fought crime in what was then the future, the distant 1970s. Other heroes were the Shark, a SUB-MARINER type; Mighty Man, who could shrink, grow, and change shape; and Minimidget, a doll-sized gangbuster who was teamed with an equally small lady named Ritty. Other characters came and went. The incomparable Basil Wolverton contributed *Meteor Martin*, a science fiction saga dealing with spaceships and parallel worlds, to the last two issues.

Amazing-Man, Sam Glanzman (Sam Decker), © 1940 by Comic Corporation of America.

ANIMAL COMICS The birthplace of Walt Kelly's Pogo, it was published by Dell and edited by Oskar Lebeck. The first issue appeared at the end of 1941 and the thirtieth and last at the end of 1947. Also featured in *Animal Comics* was the venerable rabbit gentleman Uncle Wiggily.

Kelly's personable possum was first seen in a story entitled "Albert Takes the Cake." Pogo looked rather seedy and was, as the title indicates, upstaged by the cunning and voracious Albert the Alligator. It took Pogo a couple of years to attain his final form, to cease looking like a real possum and become a cartoon character. By that time Kelly, too, had found himself and was telling audacious tales that blended slapstick, burlesque, nonsense, and a touch of cannibalism.

Uncle Wiggily signed on in the second issue (February–March 1942). He had been in business since 1910, when writer Howard R. Garis created him for a bedtime-story newspaper column. Despite his longevity and reputation, the rabbit never managed to become the star of *Animal*. Kelly's crew captured the leading position and held onto it. Even when Uncle Wiggily was featured on a cover, members of

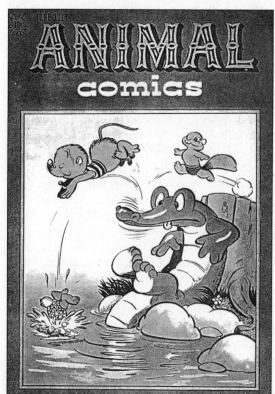

Animal Comics, Walt Kelly, © 1946 by Oskar Lebeck.

the Pogo gang were almost always in evidence there, as well.

Among the others in the book were Cilly Goose, Hector the Henpecked Rooster, and a sheep named Blackie. Kelly sometimes drew them too.

AQUAMAN   Originally DC's answer to SUB-MARINER, he first surfaced in MORE FUN COMICS #73 (November 1941). Unlike many of his GOLDEN AGE contemporaries, Aquaman wasn't sidelined when the popularity of superheroes waned in the postwar 1940s. Never among the most popular characters, he nevertheless managed to hang on. He was a modest star of the SILVER AGE, became a founding member of the JUSTICE LEAGUE OF AMERICA in 1960, and has made several comebacks since. In his 1990s return to comics, in light of all he'd been through over the past half century, DC referred to him as a tragic hero.

Aquaman was a fully clothed underwater hero, wearing a tunic of golden chain mail and sea-green tights and gloves. He was the joint creation of editor-writer Mort Weisinger and artist Paul Norris. In the 1941 origin story, Aquaman explained to a curious sea captain that he was the son of a noted scientist who'd discovered the ruins of an ancient city in the ocean depths, possibly Atlantis. After moving them into a watertight undersea home, his father used the ancient books and records of Atlantis to teach his son how to breathe under water, develop great strength, and swim with tremendous swiftness. For good measure, Aquaman learned how to communicate with fish and other aquatic creatures.

At maturity, Aquaman decided "there is much evil in the upperworld" and that he must leave the sea now and then to punish evildoers. The notion that he could only survive an hour out of water was not mentioned in the early stories. Over the years, his origin has been revised several times. A later version states that he was the result of a union between his lighthouse-keeper father and a woman from Atlantis (this might have been inspired by the old sea chantey "The Eddystone Light," popularized by Burl Ives and others, about the lighthouse keeper who slept with a mermaid). More recent accounts maintain that Aquaman himself is a native of the undersea kingdom and was abandoned as a child.

The feature continued in its modest way in *More Fun* until early in 1946. Then the sovereign of the sea moved into ADVENTURE COMICS for an extended stay. Manly Wade Wellman and Otto Binder were the chief scripters in the 1940s and artwork was by Louis Cazeneuve and John Daly. Early in 1960, when Ramona Fradon was the artist, Aquaman finally got a sidekick. Garth was a young outcast from Atlantis, which was no longer a defunct operation. Upon teaming up, he became known as Aqualad (Aqua-Boy in his first appearance).

In 1962, after nearly 20 years on the job, Aquaman was given his own magazine. It was in the *Aquaman* comic book that his hitherto-placid life took on most of its complexities. He married an exiled undersea queen named Mera, fathered a son who was named (inevitably) Aquababy, and for a time ruled as king of Atlantis. He also discovered that he had an evil half brother Orm, who was known as Ocean Master. The comic book, with the scripts by George Kashden and Steve Skeates and art by Nick Cardy and then Jim Aparo, sank in the early 1970s.

It has been revived several times since. In his most recent return, Aquaman was treated as a tragic figure and Shaun McLaughlin's script explained that "he has never known peace. His half-brother is his greatest enemy. His only son is dead. Murdered by yet another enemy. His wife tried to kill him, then abandoned him." The DC *Who's Who* explains that because of his dense body structure, the undersea hero is able to "withstand great pressure and change in temperature." Due to that density, he currently tips the scales at 325 pounds.

ARCHIE The perennial teenager, redheaded, freckled Archie has been in comic books for over 50 years. He was created, with some outside help, by cartoonist Bob Montana and appeared originally in MLJ's *Pep Comics* #22 (December 1941). He and Jughead, Betty, Veronica, and Reggie have been attending Riverdale High ever since and have appeared in numerous other titles.

Teenagers were coming into their own in the early 1940s, both as a target for manufacturers and as a source of inspiration for entertainment. Henry Aldrich, the well-meaning but bumbling teen who was the prime inspiration for Archie, had first appeared in 1938 in Clifford Goldsmith's Broadway play, *What a Life*. Henry had jumped to radio and then into movies. MLJ decided that a comic book version of Henry Aldrich and the various other wacky teens who were proliferating in the media would appeal not only to teenage readers but to kids who hadn't yet reached their teens but were eager to. Archie Andrews led the same sort of problem-plagued life as Henry Aldrich, Andy Hardy, and the rest, and got entangled with the same sort of pretty girls.

Usually unsung when credit for developing *Archie* is handed out is Vic Bloom, who produced the script for the first story. An editor-writer, he also worked for Dell and nearly two years earlier had been involved with a feature entitled *Wally Williams* in POPULAR COMICS. This was a light adventure strip that mostly dealt with high school athletics. Interestingly enough, Wally attended Riverview High, had a best friend named Jughead, and a blonde girlfriend named Betty. His mentor was his gray-haired Gramps. In Bloom's introductory script for Archie, Betty and Jughead figured again and Riverview became Riverdale. Archie, who looked only about 13, had a full set of parents but turned for advice to his live-in Gramps. In *Pep* and in *Jackpot*, where he was also appearing, Archie quickly grew into an older teenager and acquired a jalopy. Both Gramps and Bloom were soon gone.

The increasingly popular Archie got a magazine of his own in 1942. By that time most of the other regulars, including principal Mr. Weatherbee and all-purpose teacher Miss Grundy, were in place. Eventually Archie also took over *Pep*, ousting such sobersided heroes as Hangman and THE SHIELD. In the spring of 1946, MLJ officially became Archie Comic Publications. Over the years the Archie titles have multiplied and have included *Archie's Joke Book*, *Archie's Girls*, *Betty and Veronica*, *Archie's Pal*, *Jughead*, *Archie Comics Digest*, *Archie's Madhouse*, *Archie's Pals 'N' Gals*, *Jughead's Jokes*, *Betty & Veronica Summer Fun*, and *Little Archie*.

A small army of artists has drawn the Archie material, including Harry Sahle, Bill Vigoda, Al Fagaly, Tom Moore, George Frese, and Dan DeCarlo.

THE ARROW   *See* Funny Pages.

THE ATOM   By the early 1990s DC had used this name for two different characters. The first Atom debuted in the GOLDEN AGE and the second, and much smaller one, during the SILVER AGE. Both have retired and returned several times over the years and have even managed to coexist.

The earlier hero was introduced in ALL-AMERICAN #19 (October 1940) as the Mighty Atom, a name possibly borrowed from that of a real-life, and diminutive, strongman of the day. The Atom was redheaded college student Al Pratt, who stood just over five feet tall. His school chums "constantly kid him about his small size" and have nicknamed him the Atom. Vowing to do something about his 97-pound-weakling status, Pratt undergoes physical fitness training with a down-on-his-luck trainer he's met. He turns into a muscleman, one who "now has a tremendous strength that is unbelievable in one so small." He adopts a secret costumed identity as the Atom and begins a career of crime-fighting. Since nobody treated

his civilian self with any respect even after he became the Atom, Pratt was one of the more anguished heroes of the 1940s.

Writer Bill O'Connor and artist Ben Flinton, journeymen at best, created the character. When they entered the service in 1942, Joe Gallagher became the artist. He didn't take a lyrical approach to drawing adventure material, favoring a gritty, cartoony look. He had a swift, shorthand approach to action, suggesting more than he showed. Gallagher's Atom stories were rich with the props and locations of the meaner edge of big-city life: Ashcans and alleys, street cleaners, pushcarts, junk wagons, tenements and shanties, pool halls, junkyards, mom-and-pop grocery stores, lampposts, and fire hydrants. He stayed with the Atom for several years, also drawing him as a member of the JUSTICE SOCIETY in ALL STAR COMICS.

The Atom moved from *All-American* to *Flash Comics* in 1947. He acquired a new, flashier costume in 1948 and left comics the following year. He has returned on various occasions, for *JSA–JLA* team-ups, to serve on the All-Star Squadron. Along the way he picked up "atomic" strength and became a true superhero.

The new Atom debuted in SHOWCASE #34 (October 1961). Borrowing from Doll Man, editor Julius Schwartz and writer Gardner Fox converted him into a fellow who could shrink at will (see FEATURE COMICS). "I always felt the Atom of the 1940s was misnamed," Schwartz has said. "He was simply called the Atom because he was a short fellow. I got the idea of having him a regular six-footer able to reduce himself to any size he wanted to. It just struck us as we were groping around for a theme that wasn't being done by any superheroes." They gave their hero the civilian name of Ray Palmer, in honor of the longtime editor of *Amazing Stories*. Gil Kane, an admirer of Doll Man's original artist Lou Fine, got the job of drawing the dinky do-gooder.

This Atom was given his own magazine in the spring of 1962. It was retitled *The Atom &*

Hawkman in 1968 and continued under that name until it folded the following year. Among the subsequent revivals have been *Sword of the Atom*, by Gil Kane and writer Jan Strand, involving the tiny hero in sword-and-sorcery adventures in a world where everybody is six inches tall, and *Power of the Atom*, a short-lived series in 1988–89.

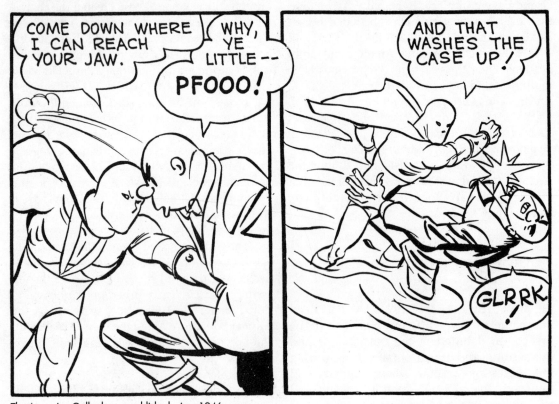

The Atom, Joe Gallagher, unpublished, circa 1946.

BABE Combining two of the country's favorite topics, sex and baseball, the *Babe* comic book ran through 11 issues from the spring of 1948 to the spring of 1950. Published by Prize Publications, it was written and drawn by the incomparable Boody Rogers.

Babe Boone, sometimes known as the Darling of the Hills, was an attractive blonde young woman who resided in "a peaceful little valley in the Ozarks" with her Mammy and Pappy. This little valley didn't seem to be more than a hoot and a holler from Li'l Abner's Dogpatch, and Rogers indulged in a good deal of raucous hillbilly humor. Besides being stupefyingly attractive to men, Babe was an all-around athlete of amazonian proportions.

Frequently she was spirited off to the East to play on the Brookdale Blue Sox—the only woman on the team. The games she played in were usually unorthodox. On one occasion she struck out no less than eight batters at once, and while sliding into home plate she burrowed so deeply into the ground that the opposing player was unable to reach her to tag her out. Babe was also unbeaten at football and boxing.

The Bell Syndicate tried a comic strip version titled *Ivy Green*, but was unable to sell it.

Recently an episode of *Babe* was reprinted in Art Spiegelman's *Raw*.

Babe, Boody Rogers, © 1948 by Feature Publications, Inc.

BATMAN Created by artist Bob Kane and writer Bill Finger, he's one of the longest-running and most successful heroes in comic books. Batman was introduced in DETECTIVE COMICS #27 in the spring of 1939 and he's been on the job continuously ever since. His companion Robin came along in the spring of 1940. There is still a Robin in comics but he's not the original. Several youths have assumed the role over the years.

There was little fanfare preceding the arrival of the new character. A small typeset announcement appeared in *Detective* #26 (April 1939) saying simply, "THE BATMAN! This thrilling new adventure strip starts in the May issue of DETECTIVE COMICS! Don't miss it!" A month later, when #27 hit the stands, there was Batman on the cover. He was swinging over the urban rooftops on a rope, with an arm-lock around the neck of a hood in a green pin-striped suit. He led off the issue in a scant, six-page story. Kane got the sole credit; Finger's name never appeared on the feature. Bruce Wayne, a wealthy young socialite, and Com-missioner Gordon were the only regulars intro-duced in the first episode. The new mystery man was referred to as the "Bat-Man" through-out and it was only revealed in the final panel that Bruce Wayne and the "mysterious and adventurous figure" were one and the same. A dedicated reader of pulp fiction, Finger had been much influenced by heroes such as THE SHADOW.

There was no mention of Gotham City, Bat-man drove a red coupe and not a batmobile, his cowl didn't fit quite right, and its pointy ears were a mite lopsided. Nonetheless it was a sig-nificant debut because it launched one of DC's most valuable properties. Over the ensuing months, Kane and Finger—with considerable help from Gardner Fox, who wrote several of the early scripts—gradually filled in the details. Batman's utility belt was introduced; he acquired not only a batmobile but a bat-plane as well.

The earliest version of his origin appeared in *Detective* #33. In just two pages it was explained that young Bruce Wayne had wit-nessed the sidewalk slaying of both his parents by a stickup man. The boy vowed that he'd "avenge their deaths by spending the rest of my life warring on all criminals." After years of dedicated work and study, the young man emerged as a brilliant scientist and a top ath-lete. While musing one evening that he must have a persona that would "strike terror into their hearts," he was visited by a large bat that flew in the open window: "It's an omen. I shall be a BAT!" And thus was born "this avenger of evil, *The Batman!*"

Robin was added in *Detective* #38 (April 1940). The Boy Wonder was actually Dick Grayson, a circus acrobat who worked with his mother and father as part of the Flying Graysons trapeze act. After his parents were killed in an accident rigged by gangsters, Dick was befriended by Batman and became his pro-tégé. He moved into the socialite's mansion and underwent a training program: "And thus Dick Grayson, by the hand of fate, is trans-formed into that astonishing phenomenon, that young Robin Hood of today, ROBIN THE BOY WONDER!" Robin started a trend. During the months that followed, many established heroes—including THE SHIELD, the Wizard, the Human Torch, and THE SANDMAN—took on boy sidekicks.

Batman and Robin encountered some of the best and most appealing villains in comic books. Topping the list was the Joker, who has been plaguing the caped crusader for over a half century. The white-faced, purple-suited criminal mastermind was inventive and auda-cious. He almost always challenged the team by announcing that he was contemplating a crime and daring them to stop him. He first appeared in *Batman* #1 early in 1940. Among the many other colorful foes introduced in the early years were the Penguin, the Scarecrow, Two-Face, the Cavalier, and Clayface. One of the most important women in Batman's early life was a clever and cunning jewel thief known as the Cat. Later on she was known as Cat-woman and, because of his mixed feelings about her, Batman never quite succeeded in bringing her to justice.

Batman, given his own magazine in 1940, was the first DC hero so honored after SUPER-MAN. Batman and Robin also showed up in the 1940 edition of *New York World's Fair Comics* and thereafter were in its successor, WORLD'S FINEST COMICS. In the mid-1940s, Robin added to his workload and began appearing in solo adventures as well. Beginning in *Star Spangled Comics* #65 (February 1947), a *Robin* feature led off each issue, replacing *The Newsboy Legion*. On occasion Batman would also pop into a story. Robin remained there until the magazine was converted to *Star Spangled War Stories* in 1952. In *World's Finest* #71 (July–August 1954), Batman and Robin entered into a partnership with Superman and started working as a trio in that magazine.

Working without Robin, Batman embarked on a seemingly endless series of team-ups with other characters. Starting in the mid-1960s in THE BRAVE AND THE BOLD, he appeared with a succession of partners that included the GREEN LANTERN, THE FLASH, AQUAMAN, THE GREEN ARROW, Deadman, the TEEN TITANS, SGT. ROCK, and Wildcat. That continued into the early 1980s. Batman has continued to be one of DC's most adaptable characters. Various teams of writers and artists have been able to provide entertaining variations of the contemporary dark knight. Victorian and future versions have also been successful. Several spin-off characters have evolved over the years as well, including Ace the Bat-Hound (launched in *Batman* #92 in 1955), Batwoman (first seen in *Detective Comics* #233 in 1956), Bat-Mite (introduced in *Detective Comics* #267 in 1959), and Batgirl (debuting in *Detective Comics* #359 in 1967).

When Dick Grayson eventually outgrew the part of Boy Wonder, he became a completely different crimefighter known as Nightwing. In 1983, a youth named Jason Todd was trained by Bruce Wayne to take over as Robin. Five years later, as the result of a nationwide phone poll, this new Robin was allowed to die, done in by the Joker. In 1989, yet another Robin was introduced, this time a young man named Tim Drake. In Frank Miller's 1986 Dark Knight series, set in a gritty world some years hence, Robin was portrayed by a red-haired girl named Carrie Kelly.

Among the many artists and writers who've worked on *Batman* are Jerry Robinson, Dick Sprang, Charles Paris, Denny O'Neil, Neal Adams, Dick Giordano, Gil Kane, Jim Mooney, and Brian Bolland.

Batman, Frank Miller, © 1985 DC Comics, Inc. All rights reserved.

BLACK CANARY   This alternate identity is multi-generational and has thus far been used by the original Black Canary and, more recently, by her daughter. In addition, the junior Black Canary had carried on a long-running relationship with the crime-fighting GREEN ARROW. The senior Black Canary was first seen in *Flash Comics* #86 (August 1947). She also became a member of the JUSTICE SOCIETY OF AMERICA.

The first version of the character was created by writer Robert Kanigher and by artist Carmine Infantino. She initially appeared as a mystery-woman guest in *Johnny Thunder*, where she was billed as "the most fascinating crook of all time." The hapless Johnny fell in love with her, little realizing that she would replace him from #92 (February 1948) onward. By that time readers had learned that she was actually dark-haired Dinah Drake, operator of a florist shop. By donning a long blonde wig, a low-cut satin costume, and black net stockings, she became not a crook but a dedicated crimebuster. In the outfit she looked very much like a high-class cocktail waitress. Teamed with the Black Canary, though originally unaware of her dual identity, was a tough private eye named Larry Lance.

She remained in *Flash* until its final issue (February 1949). She started guesting in ALL STAR in #38 and was installed as a full-fledged member of the JSA in #41, replacing the unfortunate JOHNNY THUNDER. She held on until the last issue in 1951. The Black Canary returned in *Justice League of America* #21 in the early 1960s and eventually was initiated into the JLA (see JUSTICE LEAGUE OF AMERICA). SUPERMAN referred to her at the time as the "prettiest member" of the group. She met the Green Arrow at the JLA and he became, according to official DC history, "her lover and business partner."

From the late 1960s she appeared with the archer in many of his magazine appearances. "By now, the passage of time and the pressures of continuity had caused an amoeba-like split in the persona of our hero," pointed out editor Mike Gold in the 1991–92 *Black Canary* miniseries. "It was determined that the Black Canary of the post-World War II period was the mother of the present Black Canary. . . . The older version died several years ago." The current Canary's father was private eye Larry Lance.

THE BLACK CAT She was one of the most formidable lady crimefighters in 1940s comic books. The Black Cat was an expert at judo, boxing, gymnastics, fencing, and marksmanship, and she could handle a motorcycle impressively. In everyday life she worked as a Hollywood movie star.

The Black Cat, first drawn by Al Gabriele, was introduced in publisher Alfred Harvey's POCKET COMICS #1 (August 1941). The comic-buying public was not ready for a digest-sized book and the title ceased after four issues. Black Cat became a regular in *Speed Comics* as of #17 (April 1942), sharing the regular-sized magazine with such characters as Shock Gibson, Captain Freedom, and the Girl Commandos.

Linda Turner, "Hollywood movie star and America's sweetheart," was suffering from ennui in the summer of 1941. When she realized that her director, a Teutonic fellow named Garboil, was a Nazi agent who was slipping pro-Hitler propaganda into her latest film, she decided to do something about it. Designing herself a black cat costume—a skimpy one— she became a spy-smasher. "If this works I'll kill two birds with one stone," the redheaded actress excitedly told herself. "I'll have my thrills and I'll do my duty to my country,"

After exposing the director, the Black Cat went on to catch a wide range of spies, gangsters, crooks, and con men. Among the series regulars were Rick Horne, a handsome, tweedy reporter with the *Los Angeles Globe*; Tim Turner, Linda's gray-haired father and a former cowboy star; and C.B. DePille, a flamboyant director who always wore a beret and dark glasses. Although Horne knew Linda well and worked with the Black Cat on many a case, it never dawned on him that the two were one and the same. That may be why the Black Cat's nickname for the newsman was "Stupid." Her dad, of course, was aware of her dual role. Toward the end of her run, she started working with a boy companion, a former circus acrobat known as the Black Kitten.

Several artists drew the feature, including the team of Pierce Rice and Arturo Cazeneuve, Joe Kubert, Bob Powell, and Jill Elgin. Soon after the Black Cat got her own magazine in 1946, Lee Elias became the chief artist. A gifted illustrator and one of the best of the followers of Milton Caniff, Elias gave the feature a new, slicker look and amused himself by slipping real Hollywood personalities into the stories.

The changes that took place in the *Black Cat* comic book are indicative of those going on in the comic book business during the decade following the end of World War II. Early in 1949, the title was changed to *Black Cat Western* and the costumed crimefighter had adventures only in cowboy locales. At the end of the year, after only four Wild West issues, it was back to just plain *Black Cat*. With #30 (August 1951), the name became *Black Cat Mystery*. Linda appeared on the cover, but not inside, and she remained off the scene for the next several years.

Getting in on yet another trend, Harvey converted to horror. Corpses, monsters, stranglers, and exploding skulls became standard fare on the covers. Then, early in 1955, as the Comics Code was coming into effect, the magazine once again became *Black Cat Western* and Linda Turner, in reprints, was back. That lasted for but three issues. Then came toned-down horror under the eventual title of *Black Cat Mystic*. The magazine sputtered out in 1958.

Harvey revived *Black Cat* briefly in the early 1960s, publishing three issues of a reprint book. In the late 1980s, Harvey began a sporadic series of reprints, mostly in black and white.

BLACKHAWK   He was a freelance soldier for more than a half century. Created by Will Eisner and Charles Cuidera, Blackhawk and his paramilitary group began in MILITARY COMICS #1 in the summer of 1941 and continued to battle the forces of tyranny, under two separate publishers, into the 1990s.

Eisner was editing both *National Comics* and *Military* for Everett "Busy" Arnold's Quality Comics group. As stars for the latter title, he once explained, he wanted "a super-guerrilla group. I liked the idea of a group having an island of its own, outcasts from every nation. I had a fascination with the Foreign Legion then."

The leader of the group was a Polish aviator whose sister and brother were killed in a Nazi bombing raid. He escaped from his country and emerged several months later as Blackhawk. He and his band of flying comrades were based on a mysterious island. Eventually the team, all of whom dressed in dark-blue uniforms and visored caps, included Olaf, Hendrickson, Andre, Stanislaus, and Chuck. Chop-Chop, a broad caricature of an English-mangling Chinese, served as both cook and mascot. Over the years he would change more than any of the other Blackhawks.

Eisner drew the first two covers, and wrote and laid out the first 10 stories. Cuidera provided the finished art. The continuities were somewhat more naturalistic than much current comic book fare, touching on the realities of the war in Europe and even allowing some characters to die. In the 12th issue, Reed Crandall, with a little help from Alex Kotzky, took over the drawing. Crandall was an exceptional craftsman and seemed to relish drawing the nasty Axis villains and sultry ladies that were required. He was also very good at depicting the many weapons, planes, gadgets, engines of destruction, and exotic locales. He remained the chief artist for several years.

Quality added a *Blackhawk* title in 1944 and kept it going until late in 1956. After the end of World War II, *Military* changed its name to *Modern Comics*. To insure that no readers were lost, the line "Formerly Military Comics" ran on the covers for the next two years. In both magazines the postwar Blackhawks went after a variety of international villains. Among the other artists and writers were Bill Ward, William Woolfolk, and Manly Wade Wellman.

When Busy Arnold quit the comic book

business, he licensed several of his characters to DC. Although it didn't continue *Modern*, DC did pick up *Blackhawk* with #108 (January 1957). The artist was Dick Dillin, who'd also worked on the character at Quality. As the number of science fiction stories increased, monsters and robots were seen on the covers more frequently. Toward the end of the Quality run, Chop-Chop had become less of a caricature. The process continued at DC, although he still dressed in Chinese fashion rather than in uniform.

In 1967, succumbing to superhero mania, DC converted the Blackhawks to superpowered, costumed heroes. That phase lasted for 12 issues. Then the Blackhawks became themselves again, but after just two more issues, the magazine shut down with #243 late in 1968. There had been talk that Crandall would return, but that never happened. Pat Boyette drew the final stories.

Early in 1976, DC tried again and came out with *Blackhawk* #244—"Back from the DEAD! The Greatest Fighting Team in the WORLD!" The stories, still set in the contemporary world, featured the old gang. Chop-Chop, however, was now named Chopper. No longer a caricature, he was a martial-arts expert, spoke standard English, and wore the same uniform as his fellow Blackhawks. That uniform had been jazzed up some, featuring the wide red lapels and glimpse of hairy chest favored by Las Vegas singers. Steve Skeates was the writer, George Evans the artist. Evans, who'd put in time assisting on the *Terry and the Pirates* newspaper strip since his memorable days at EC, had a tendency to draw most of the characters with the huge ears that were a trademark of *Terry*'s George Wunder.

That revival lasted exactly a year, then Blackhawk and company were gone again until 1983. This time around, Blackhawk and his group were back in their natural habitat, the World War II years. Chop-Chop was now known as Wu Cheng. With Mark Evanier scripting and Dan Spiegle drawing, the Black-

hawks sounded and looked better than they had in a long while. Despite that, this revival lasted only a little over two years. In 1987, Howard Chaykin did a three-issue miniseries, featuring a solo Blackhawk in a postwar adventure aimed at mature readers. The next year the old soldier showed up in the shortlived ACTION COMICS weekly. In 1989, the Blackhawks were back in a monthly written by Martin Pasko and drawn by Rick Burchett. Set in 1947 and again "suggested for mature readers," the new *Blackhawk* made it through 16 issues before expiring in the summer of 1990.

Blackhawk, Reed Crandall, © 1943 by Comic Magazines.

THE BLACK HOOD *See* Top-Notch Comics.

THE BLACK OWL *See* Yank and Doodle.

BLACKSTONE The famous real-life magician Harry Blackstone (1885–1965) was also a comic book character. Thanks to his friend and ghost-writer Walter B. Gibson, the silver-haired stage illusionist had a second life as a newsstand hero from 1941 to 1948.

Gibson, best known as the creator of THE SHADOW, had started ghosting Blackstone's magic books in the late 1920s. In 1941, he approached Street & Smith, publishers of both the Shadow pulp magazine and the comic book, and suggested a Blackstone comic. What made the deal especially appealing to S & S was the fact that Gibson guaranteed them that the magician would purchase half of each issue's print run to give away at his stage shows. The first issue (dated May 1941) was called *Super-Magic Comics*. With the second, it became *Super Magician*. Blackstone become younger and handsomer for his comic book career and also acquired a pretty assistant named Rhoda. On the covers he was frequently referred to as the "World's Greatest Living Magician."

Gibson wrote all of the Blackstone stories, which usually dealt with the magician touring exotic locales with his stage show and running into spurious wizards and warlocks whom he proceeded to outwit and debunk. Another dependable plot element was Rhoda's changing into a scanty costume. Typical story titles were "Blackstone in Voodoo Valley," "Blackstone and the Gold Amu Zam," and "Blackstone Meets the Pirates of Twin Island."

The early artwork was provided by the Jack Binder shop. Gibson later brought in some of his cronies, including James Hammon and Kemp Starrett. Both men, along with Gibson, had been associated with the Ledger Syndicate in Philadelphia.

When Blackstone's agreement with Street & Smith came to an end in early 1946 he ceased to be the star of *Super-Magician Comics*. He was replaced by Nigel Elliman, a fictitious magician. Gibson also wrote the Elliman scripts until the magazine folded in 1947.

In 1946, Gibson repackaged Blackstone, selling *Blackstone, Master Magician* to an outfit called Vital Publications. That lasted three issues. In 1947 came *Blackstone the Magician Detective*. EC (originally Educational Comics) published one issue and the following year Marvel did three more. After his brief stint as a Marvel hero, Blackstone retired from comics.

THE BLACK TERROR The most interesting thing about him was his costume. One of the numerous superheroes who came along during the boom of the early 1940s, he had little else to distinguish him from his many superhuman newsstand competitors. But his jet-black costume with the gold trim and the skull and crossbones emblazoned across the chest was striking, and it probably influenced latter-day heroes like the Punisher. The Black Terror first appeared in *Exciting Comics* #9 (May 1941) and survived until the summer of 1949.

The Terror was created by prolific writer-editor Richard Hughes and the earliest artist was Elmer Wexler. An early caption explained the hero's origin this way: "Dabbling in formic ethers, Bob Benton, a timid young druggist, chances on a source of mighty powers! With the help of young Tim Roland, he secretly employs his great strength as THE BLACK TERROR . . . Nemesis of Evil!"

The hero's boy companion, by the way, had no other name and, when he donned his junior-sized replica of the Black Terror's costume, he was still known simply as Tim.

Benton's drugstore was located near City Hall, where his girlfriend Jean worked as secretary to the mayor. Through her, the team got leads on all sorts of jobs, involving faulty dams, civic corruption, racketeering, etc. Unlike some crime-busting duos who dropped everything to pursue a crook, the Black Terror and Tim were equally concerned about their business. On one typical occasion, Benton, getting into his costume in the store, told his sidekick, "I'm going to snoop around headquarters, Tim!"

Black Terror, Jerry Robinson–Mort Meskin, © 1948 by Better Publications, Inc.

The lad replied, "I'll watch this end, Bob!" and remained behind the counter. Despite his powers and his flamboyant costume, Tim never lost sight of the fact that he was a kid. Many times he traveled to the scene of a crime on his bicycle.

The Terror and Tim tended to avoid world-class villains, specializing instead in spies, saboteurs, highjackers, black marketeers, and assorted fascists. Throughout the war years, the anonymous artwork on the feature was dull and uninspired. In the final years, however, things improved greatly. George Tuska took a turn drawing some of the adventures, as did the impressive team of Jerry Robinson and Mort Meskin. They saw to it that the Terror twins went out with a bang.

The Black Terror got a book of his own in 1942 and was also a regular in *America's Best*. All of these, along with *Exciting*, folded in 1949. An independent version of the character appeared briefly in 1989 and 1990.

BLAZING COMICS Although produced by FUN-NIES, INC., the same shop that provided art and editorial for *Marvel Mystery*, *Target*, and *Blue Bolt*, this was not a winner. It first appeared in the spring of 1944 and expired, after just five issues, early in 1945. *Blazing* did, however, manage to give the world one of the most unusual costumed heroes of the World War II years—the Green Turtle.

Drawn and possibly written by an artist named Chu Hing, the strip had the Turtle aiding the Chinese in guerrilla warfare against the Japanese invaders. He was a true mystery man who wore a green cowl and a cloak that had an enormous turtle-shell design emblazoned on it. Since readers rarely saw the hero's face—not because of his half-mask, but because he usually kept his back to the camera—it's possible Hing intended him to be Chinese, although the colorist gave him pink skin. He was aided by a sidekick called Burma Boy and flew a turtlish rocket plane.

Blazing also featured a magician-detective known as Mr. Ree, a white goddess called Jun-Gal, and a native American fighter pilot named Red Hawk. There was also a swashbuckling Black Buccaneer, rendered by a youthful Leonard Starr.

Green Turtle, Chu Hing, © 1944 by Rewl Publications.

BLONDE PHANTOM   She was one of several women who Marvel tried to thrust into stardom in the postwar 1940s. Venus and Namora were two others. The prolific Otto Binder seems to have been the initial scriptwriter and Syd Shores was the chief artist. The Blonde Phantom was first seen in *All Select Comics* #11 (Fall 1946) and with the next issue the magazine changed its name to hers.

In the civilian world, she was Louise Grant, mild-mannered secretary to private detective Mark Mason. Around the office Louise dressed conservatively, wore harlequin glasses, and had her hair pulled back in a bun. To become the Blonde Phantom, she let down her hair, changed into a low-cut, bare-midriff scarlet evening gown and traded her specs for a black domino mask.

Although Louise had a crush on her dapper, pipe-smoking boss, she didn't have a very high opinion of his sleuthing abilities. She was continually noticing things he'd overlooked, spotting clues he'd missed. In many instances she became the Phantom in order to clean up a case that Mason was bungling. This was obviously a feature aimed at winning the same girl readers who were buying Marvel's *Millie the Model*, *Tessie the Typist*, and *Patsy Walker* (see TESSIE THE TYPIST). Among its basic assumptions were that most secretaries are smarter than their bosses and that most men are too dense to see beneath the surface to the woman within. However, in order to also attract the pubescent boys who frequented newsstands, *Blonde Phantom* tossed in the traditional props and poses associated with GOOD GIRL ART.

The title survived through its 22nd issue (March 1949). Marvel then converted it to *Lovers*, a romance comic with even more potential appeal to a female audience. America's Lovely Lady of Adventure also appeared, briefly, in *Marvel Mystery*, *Sub-Mariner*, and ALL WINNERS.

THE BLUE BEETLE   A surprisingly resilient superhero, he has been appearing in comic books for more than a half century. He had his humble beginning in Victor Fox's *Mystery Men Comics* #1 (August 1939) and was the creation of an artist calling himself Charles Nicholas and, possibly, Will Eisner. The Blue Beetle's initial run ended around 1950; Charlton brought him back in 1955 and again in the mid-1960s. In 1986, DC revived him yet again, trying him out in a title of his own that lasted just short of two years. Most recently he's been on view in DC's *Justice League International* (see JUSTICE LEAGUE OF AMERICA).

The Blue Beetle started out toward the back of *Mystery Men*, hanging out in short four-page adventures. Until his second appearance, he didn't even have a crime-fighting costume. Eventually he started showing up in the distinctive blue chain-mail outfit and black domino mask that became his trademark. Wisely, he soon abandoned the bug antennae he'd worn on his cowl.

In everyday life the Blue Beetle was an impatient rookie cop named Dan Garrett. He was one of the few superheroes who acquired his powers through attention to his diet. Captions continually reminded readers that he was "given super-energy by vitamin 2X." His chain-mail costume, by the way, made him "almost invulnerable." While later heroes had crack scientists for mentors, the Beetle settled for a druggist. Apparently it never occurred to him to buy 2X in quantity, so every time he wanted to become supercharged he had to drop into the neighborhood pharmacy to get a dose from its inventor, Dr. Franz.

Once powered by 2X, he would rush around for eight or ten pages, cracking skulls and wisecracking as he hunted down such villains as the Wart, Scrag, Mr. Downhill, Countess Belladonna, and a crazed scientist called Doc. The Beetle was especially fond of lying flat on roofs and ledges and then dropping down on surprised thugs. Now and then, he would scare his foes with "the sign of the Beetle," a little blue scarab he'd leave on desks and tabletops or lower into a room on the end of a

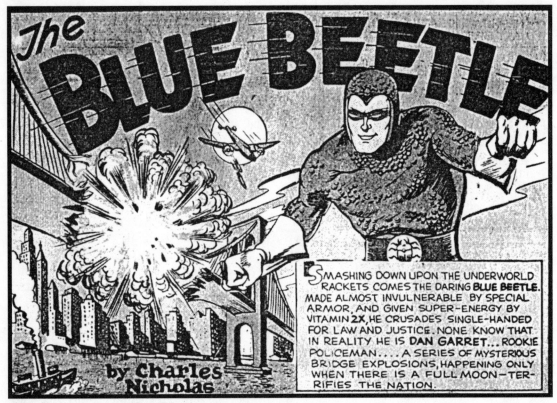

The Blue Beetle, Sam Cooper, © 1940 by Fox Publications, Inc.

string. Sometimes he worked with a beetle projector that flashed the frightening symbol on walls. SUPERMAN had Lois Lane to rescue time and again, and the Beetle had blonde Joan Mason, also a newspaper reporter.

Surprisingly, the Blue Beetle became publisher Victor Fox's most popular character. He moved to the front of *Mystery Men* and was showcased on every cover. He got a second magazine all his own and was also a star of an anthology, *Big 3*.

Nicholas's name remained on the feature, but a great many others drew the Beetle's myriad adventures. These included Larry Antonette, Sam Cooper, Louis Cazeneuve, and Al Carreño. He was portrayed on covers by such artists as Lou Fine, Joe Simon, Edd Ashe, and Ramona Patenaude.

Blue Beetle's knack for survival was first demonstrated late in 1941, when, for financial reasons, Fox abruptly suspended operations and halted publication of all his titles (see WONDERWORLD COMICS.) The *Blue Beetle* comic book, however, was continued by Holyoke Publishing, which had been Fox's printer. Holyoke took over the magazine with #12 (June 1942) and in its first two issues used up all the Fox backlog of material, most of which was drawn by Carreño. Holyoke then brought in its own artists, chief among them Charles Quinlan.

With #14, the Beetle was given a boy companion, a blond lad named Sparkington J. Northrup. He wore a simplified version of his mentor's costume and called himself Sparky. In the 17th issue, he became Spunky and after the 19th he retired and Dan Garrett went solo again. Later, when the Blue Beetle worked as a secret agent in Europe, Spunky returned, but in mufti. During his Holyoke phase, the Beetle had no apparent superpowers and didn't make use of his special vitamin.

In the spring of 1944, Victor Fox returned to comics, launching new titles, reviving old ones, and taking back *Blue Beetle*. "Suddenly Blue Beetle developed strange new powers," comics historian Robert Jennings has observed. "These powers were not uniform or consistent from story to story, or even within the same story. A few of his new talents included the ability to [mentally love objects], to fly and to completely alter his physical appearance by an effort of will power. He also adopted a Beetle-mobile. . . . The most amazing and aggravating of the changes was his sudden ability to expand his size and become a giant."

In the middle of 1946, Jerry Iger's shop began packaging the magazine. Artist Jack Kamen was one of the major contributors. The sex and violence content began to go up. From #52 on, *Blue Beetle* included true crime material and the final issue, #60 (August 1950) had the slogan "True Crime Stories" prominently displayed on the cover. Dr. Fredric Wertham included a panel from #54 among the illustrations in *Seduction of the Innocent*, his 1954 book that attacked comic books for their negative effects on children.

Charlton brought back the character in 1955, first in reprints and then in original stories. The revival lasted just four issues. In 1964 he gave it another try. Dan Garrett was still the Blue Beetle, but now he became a superhero by way of a magic phrase said over a sacred scarab that had been found in an Egyptian tomb. This revised Beetle hung on for 10 issues. Finally, in 1967 Charlton introduced a brand-new Blue Beetle in the person of Ted Kord, who also turned into a crimebuster by using a magic scarab. Steve Ditko was the artist on this five-issue run.

DC acquired Blue Beetle, along with other Charlton properties, in 1986. As written by Len Wein and drawn by Paris Cullins and Dell Barras, the Beetle was Theodore (Ted) Kord again.

In the DC version, though, Kord had taken over the role after Dan Garrett was killed. DC managed a bit better than Charlton and kept its Blue Beetle title afloat for 24 issues. The hero has kept working as a member of the JUSTICE LEAGUE.

BOY COMICS   Published by Lev Gleason and edited by Charles Biro and Bob Wood, the magazine featured "a boy hero in every strip!!" Only the villains were adults. *Boy*—"two years in the making!"—began with issue #3 in the spring of 1942 and lasted until the spring of 1956.

The star of the magazine was Crimebuster, a costumed teenager initially drawn by Biro. For a youth, Crimebuster encountered an abundance of grown-up violence, bloodshed, and sex. His recurring antagonist was Iron Jaw, a vile Nazi agent who'd had the lower portion of his face replaced with wicked-looking metal choppers.

Among the other kid characters were Young Robin Hood, a daring pilot named Swoop Storm, and Dick Briefer's time-hopping wiseguy Yankee Longago.

Boy toned down considerably in the post-

Crimebuster, Norman Maurer, 1983.

war years, with Biro concentrating on such contemporary social problems as civic corruption and juvenile delinquency. In his final years, Crimebuster switched to civvies and went by his everyday name of Chuck Chandler. Later artists on CB included Norman Maurer, a boy himself when he started working for Biro, William Overgard, and Joe Kubert.

THE BRAVE AND THE BOLD   When it was introduced in the summer of 1955, DC's *The Brave and the Bold* was devoted to swashbuckling adventure tales in a historical setting. Later on, it served a more important function, as a launching pad for such SILVER AGE heroes as the TEEN TITANS, Metamorpho, the JUSTICE LEAGUE, and the renovated HAWKMAN.

The early SA issues had offered such characters as the Golden Gladiator, the Silent Knight, Robin Hood, and Joe Kubert's Viking Prince. Then with issue #28 (February–March 1960), the Justice League of America, an updated version of the old JUSTICE SOCIETY, was introduced for a tryout run of three issues. With #34 (March 1961) began three issues showcasing a new, improved Hawkman, with scripts by his creator Gardner Fox and art by Kubert. Hawkman tried out again in three more issues in 1962 and 1963. In 1964 the Teen Titans auditioned and the following year brought the changeable Metamorpho.

Later in its life, *The Brave and the Bold* took to featuring a wide variety of team-ups between BATMAN and an assortment of others, including Deadman, GREEN ARROW, and SGT. ROCK. DC revived the title in 1991.

BUGS BUNNY   *See* Looney Tunes and Merrie Melodies.

CAPTAIN AMERICA The undisputed champ of patriotic superheroes, he has been defending his country against Nazis, Communists, monsters, and every conceivable threat to democracy for more than half a century. There have been lean years, and periods of forced retirement, and for an extended spell he was frozen in an iceberg. But the star-spangled defender has always managed to bounce back. He was created for Marvel by Joe Simon and Jack Kirby. On the cover of the first issue of *Captain America Comics*, dated March 1941, he can be seen in all his red, white, and blue glory socking Adolf Hitler.

Until the advent of Captain America, characters who got whole comic books of their own first had to have a successful tryout elsewhere—SUPERMAN in ACTION COMICS, CAPTAIN MARVEL in WHIZ, and the Human Torch in MARVEL. Simon and Kirby's creation was an exception.

"Captain America was created for a time that needed noble figures," Kirby once said. "We weren't at war yet, but everyone knew it was coming. That's why Captain America was born; America needed a superpatriot."

As to their hero's appearance, Kirby explained, "Drape the flag on anything and it looks good. We gave him a chainmail shirt and a shield, like a modern-day crusader. The wings on his helmet were from Mercury. . . . He symbolized the American dream." A few years later, publisher Martin Goodman let it be known that he, too, had had a hand in the invention of the character. In Stan Lee's *Secrets Behind the Comics*, he had himself depicted in comics format saying, "I must create a comic character who will represent freedom's battle against fascism!" and hitting his desk with sufficient force to produce a *Bam!*

The origin story showed blond Steve Rogers trying to enlist in the service but being turned down "because of his unfit condition." It isn't clear in the introductory episode whether he willingly took an experimental injection from the noted scientist Professor Reinstein or whether he was forced into it, but he did seem to go along with Reinstein's scheme to create a super-soldier. The "strange seething liquid" worked like a magical Charles Atlas course, turning Rogers from a 97-pound weakling into a superhuman. Reinstein had envisioned a "corps of super-agents whose mental and physical ability will make them a terror to spies and saboteurs!" But the prof was gunned down by a Gestapo agent after creating just one superman, who then took the name Captain America.

It would seem that carrying on a double life while a private in the United States Army would be extremely difficult, but that's what Rogers tried to do. He pulled it off and even met Bucky Barnes, an energetic, fearless youngster described as the "mascot of the regiment." The two teamed up against the "vicious elements who seek to overthrow the U.S. government!" Chief among those vicious elements was the Red Skull, a Nazi agent who wore a crimson death's-head mask and was to Cap and Bucky what the Joker was to Batman and Robin. First surfacing in the initial issue, he returned twice more in the first year, then came back to plague them numerous times over the years.

When not battling enemies of democracy, the duo ran into some other rather spooky foes, including a phantom hound, Oriental zombies, the Hunchback of Hollywood, the Black Talon, and the Black Witch. As comics historian Mike Barson has pointed out, these early horror tales are "a crazy combination of 1930s movies, pulps, and detective fiction." One of the decent characters introduced early on was Betty Ross, "special investigator for the U.S. government," whose cases often put her in need of rescue.

Although the credits for the stories in the first 10 issues read "art and editorial by Joe Simon–Jack Kirby," much of the artwork was by others. There was help from Al Avison, Al Gabriele, Charles Nicholas, Syd Shores, Al Liederman, and Reed Crandall. The innovative splash panels, often stretching across two pages, were almost always Kirby's work. "Movies were what I knew best," Kirby once explained, "and I wanted to tell stories the way they do." When Simon and Kirby were lured over to DC, the Captain and Bucky were taken over by Avison, Shores, Gabriele, and, eventually, a host of others.

The Captain and Bucky flourished during the World War II years, appearing not only in their own title but in *All Winners, U.S.A.*, and *All Select*. In addition, Bucky moonlighted as part of THE YOUNG ALLIES. A great many of their covers were drawn by the estimable Alex Schomburg, who designed numerous intricate battle scenes.

In 1946, Steve Rogers and Bucky became civilians and it was revealed that Rogers had once been a schoolteacher. He became a teacher at the Lee School in Manhattan and Bucky lived with him as his ward. They began, as George Olshevsky notes in *The Marvel Comics Index*, "serving their country in a different way—by fighting thieves, black marketeers, gunrunners, murderers, swindlers, extortionists, blackmailers, and all the other reprehensible types who prey upon society." *Captain America* also became part of *Marvel Comics*, starting with #80 (January 1947). As part of Marvel's postwar move to add more women characters, Bucky was retired in 1948—after having been wounded—and replaced by a costumed lady called Golden Girl. She was Cap's old government agent friend, now calling herself by the more patriotic name of Betsy Ross. The two remained together until late in 1949. *Marvel Comics* turned into *Marvel Tales*, a horror comic, in the spring of 1949. The *Captain America* book survived until late that same year, and was called *Captain America's Weird Tales* its final two issues.

Editor Stan Lee, who continued to have faith in the sales potential of the Marvel superheroes, tried to revive the top three of the 1940s—The Human Torch, SUB-MARINER, and Captain America—in the mid-1950s. The trio appeared in individual adventures in the revised YOUNG MEN, starting with #24 (December 1953), and then each was given a title of his own. *Captain America* #76 picked up the old numbering and was dated May 1954. Teamed again with Bucky, the superpatriot now performed as a dedicated cold war crusader and was billed as "Captain America . . . Commie Smasher!" In some of the stories, Steve Rogers was a professor at the Lee School, while in others he was once again in the Army. John Romita was the artist.

The rejuvenated hero specialized in Russian plots. As one Red official expressed it, "He has been the democracies' strongest foe of fascism . . . and now of our own cause . . . International Communism." Copy emphasized that Communism was "the worst threat America has ever known!" The Captain and Bucky tackled such dangers as an electricity-charged monster named Electro, who was green and had a red hammer and sickle on its chest, a plot to smuggle "a million dollars of dope . . . Enough to move the South Africans to revolt," and a scheme to blow up the United Nations headquarters. After thwarting that one, Captain America remarked to Bucky that "Americans play not to win, necessarily, but for the sake of good sportsmanship and fair play . . . which Nazis and Reds know nothing about at all!" While seemingly in tune with many of the right-wing politicians of the period, Captain America failed to win the hearts and minds of comic book readers, and his magazine collapsed after just three issues.

Eventually the SILVER AGE revival came along, and when Captain America returned—without Bucky—he fared considerably better. He's been on the scene ever since. It was the old, original Cap who showed up in *Avengers* #4 early in 1964 and joined a group that included THOR, Iron Man, and THE HULK. A headline on the cover announced that "Captain America Lives Again!" Inside it was revealed that as a result of a long-ago battle with a villain named Baron Zemo, Bucky was killed and the Captain ended up being frozen in an Arctic ice floe for twenty years. Beginning with #58 (October 1964), Captain America also started sharing *Tales of Suspense* with Iron Man. In 1968, with #100, the magazine became *Captain America*—"Cap, in his own magazine at last!" Jack Kirby had returned to drawing the super-patriot and he continued to do so in the new title. Stan Lee wrote the scripts. In 1971 Cap got a new, temporary sidekick in the person of the Black Falcon.

Over the years, the 1940s Captain America, along with Bucky, has reappeared from time to time. The contemporary Captain has continued to flourish. Like that of many another mythical figure, the story of Captain America's origin and early days has been retold and revised many times. It has been explained, too, that the right-wing red-baiter of the 1950s wasn't Cap at all but an impostor.

Among the many writers and artists who've worked on the legend are Steve Englehart, Roy Thomas, Steve Gerber, Fabian Nicieza, Sal Buscema, Mike Zeck, Frank Robbins, Gil Kane, John Byrne, and Kevin Maguire.

Captain America®, Kevin Maguire–Terry Austin. All Marvel characters and the distinctive likenesses thereof are trademarks of Marvel Entertainment Group, Inc. and are used with permission. © 1992 Marvel Entertainment Group, Inc.

CAPTAIN FUTURE Although working for the same publisher, this Captain Future was not related to the planet-hopping, pulp science fiction hero of the same name. This was a rather dull fellow who debuted in *Startling Comics* #1 (June 1940) and was billed as the "Man of Tomorrow." His costume, only slightly more imaginative than what he might've worn at the YMCA, consisted of blue shorts, blue shoes, and a red T-shirt with a yellow lightning bolt on the chest.

Like many another superhero, he'd come across his powers by chance—"Accidently crossing the gamma-ray with the infra-red band, Dr. Andrew Bryant, studious young research worker, discovers a miraculous source of power, enabling him to perform feats impossible to all others. Determined to use his great prowess in the aid of mankind, he becomes Captain Future, nemesis of crime!" The captain could perform all the feats that SUPERMAN was capable of, and in addition he could generate lightning bolts out of his hands to hurl at crooks.

With the 10th issue, *Startling* introduced the Fighting Yank, who pretty much nudged Captain Future out of the leading spot. About this time Bryant became enamored of Grace Adams, "pretty young would-be detective." In partnership with her Aunt Agatha, Grace founded the Agatha Detective Agency. Most of the captain's exploits after that centered around his pulling Grace and her aunt out of the messes their sleuthing got them into. He left *Startling* in 1946 and was last seen in *America's Best* the following year. Kin Platt was the initial artist.

CAPTAIN MARVEL He was the most popular superhero of the 1940s, in his prime outselling all the competition. Created by editor-writer Bill Parker and artist C.C. Beck, Captain Marvel was introduced in the first issue of Fawcett's WHIZ COMICS early in 1940. He thrived for well over a decade and it took a lawsuit to put him out of business.

Late in 1939, Roscoe K. Fawcett sent out a promotion piece to magazine distributors across the country. It announced the impending debut of *Whiz Comics*, which would star Captain Marvel, "another character sensation in the comic field!" Until then, the Fawcett

organization had been known for such magazines as *Mechanix Illustrated*, *Motion Picture*, *Real Life Story*, and *Captain Billy's Whiz-Bang*. Now they were promising wholesalers a comic book, one that was "here to stay." The forthcoming title would lead the parade and bring "permanent profits." Many comic book publishers would make similar claims and fail to live up to them, but in the case of Fawcett, all the advance hyperbole turned out to be true.

The original name for the superhero was to be Captain Thunder, and he was going to be the leader of a group of heroes. But the group notion and the name were discarded. And Parker, perhaps with suggestions from the Fawcett staff, came up with a variation on the dual-identity theme. Captain Marvel was really a teenager named Billy Batson. By uttering the magic word "SHAZAM!" (revealed to him by a mysterious wizard in a long-forgotten section of subway tunnel), Billy could transform himself into the red-clad Captain Marvel, the World's Mightiest Mortal. Despite the fact that the captain was invincible, it was Billy who quietly dominated the stories. Captain Marvel was the one who tangled with the villains, but he always returned to his true identity of Billy, by again shouting "Shazam!" once the danger had passed.

There was a great visual appeal to the early adventures. "The basis I go on is never to put in a single line that isn't necessary," Beck once said. "Don't try to show off." His pages exemplified his philosophy and were models of simplicity, clarity, and design. They were fun to look at as well as to read. He based the captain's face on that of movie star Fred MacMurray and the costume on that of a typical soldier in a light opera.

The captain was fortunate enough to have Sivana, billed as the World's Maddest Scientist, as his frequent opponent. The small, bald, bespectacled evil genius—who wore the same sort of white medical jacket as the neighborhood druggist Beck modeled him after—appeared in the first story and recurred with gratifying frequency. He was a clever fellow, cunning and intriguingly circumlocutory in his schemes. Only Rube Goldberg equaled Dr. Thadeus Bodog Sivana in constructing complex devices for performing simple chores. It often seemed that IQ point for IQ point, he was probably smarter than Cap, whom he was fond of calling the Big Red Cheese. Captain Marvel's early career was complicated by Beautia, Sivana's lovely blonde and good-hearted daughter. The young lady had a crush on him and at times he found himself looking on her with favor.

Unlike the average comic book villain, Sivana was well aware of his opponent's dual identity. He soon realized that if he could keep Billy from saying "Shazam!" he'd be rid of Captain Marvel. He never succeeded in that goal, but that didn't keep him from being a world-class villain. In an early issue of *Whiz*, Sivana was sentenced to "77 consecutive prison terms, totaling 9,000 years, at hard labor" as "punishment for your innumerable crimes." Anybody who got 9,000 years in jail had to be impressively bad.

The idea of Captain Marvel leading a team finally got put to use in *Whiz* # 21. That issue was dated September 5, 1941, since by then the increasingly popular title was coming out every four weeks. In a continuity that was not completely serious, three other Billy Batsons showed up—Tall Billy, Fat Billy, and Hill Billy. Sivana and his confused minions kidnapped them all. In trying to help the authentic Billy, the others yelled "Shazam!" along with him. Four flashes of zigzag lightning followed and the entire quartet was transformed. Modest, the newcomers decided to be "kinda Second Lieutenant Marvels." The lieutenants returned from time to time.

As the demand for Captain Marvel stories increased—the captain was appearing in *Captain Marvel Adventures* and *America's Greatest Comics* in addition to *Whiz* in the early 1940s— Fawcett first went to outside artists and then had Beck set up a shop of his own. Among the

outsiders were Joe Simon and Jack Kirby, who produced a somewhat hurried-looking first issue of *Captain Marvel Adventures*, and George Tuska, who drew the second and third. Employed by Beck were Pete Constanza, Morris Weiss, Chic Stone, Kurt Schafenberger, Dave Berg, Al McClean, and Marc Swayze. Otto Binder, an established pulp science fiction writer, joined the team to do scripts in the second year. He was responsible for several hundred stories, including just about all those dealing with time travel, space travel, and other sci-fi staples. He also invented the popular Mr. Tawny, the talking tiger.

Whiz Comics was selling nearly half a million copies a month before its first year was out. By 1943, *Captain Marvel Adventures* was selling about a million copies per issue, and in 1946 the figure approached a million and a half. And that was the year when the magazine was appearing every two weeks. Life was not exactly a bed of roses for Cap, however, because in 1941 DC had taken legal action against Fawcett. It was their contention that Captain Marvel was so close to Superman that he infringed on the copyright. The lawsuit was fought throughout the 1940s and into the 1950s. Finally, when the ultimate ruling went against them, Fawcett quit publishing Captain Marvel in any shape or form. The final issue of *Whiz* was dated June 1953, the last *Captain Marvel Adventures* November 1953.

DC, who'd put him out of the business in the first place, arranged for the return of the Big Red Cheese in 1973. They even hired C.C. Beck to draw the new comic book. It was called *Shazam!* because in the interim Marvel Comics had introduced a completely different Captain Marvel of its own and trademarked the name. Beck, unhappy with the scripts and the working conditions, didn't remain with the project long. The magazine limped along until 1978, having inspired a relatively successful kids' television show.

DC has tried to revive the once-popular captain now and then, having him drawn in a

Captain Marvel, C.C. Beck, © 1941 by Fawcett Publications, Inc.

much more serious and contemporary style, but he hasn't succeeded in a book of his own. He has, however, served as a member of the JUSTICE LEAGUE in recent times.

CAPTAIN MARVEL, JR. Sensing that there were potential profits in spin-offs, Fawcett Publications began adding to the Marvel Family less than two years after the introduction of the increasingly popular CAPTAIN MARVEL. The first

addition was Captain Marvel, Jr., a teenage superhero who was introduced in the senior captain's WHIZ COMICS #25 (December 1941). He took up residence in MASTER COMICS as of #22 (January 1942) and added a book of his own late in 1942. Never as successful as his brawnier predecessor, Junior nevertheless had a long and lucrative career that lasted until 1953.

His coming was preceded by the arrival of the man who would be his primary antagonist over the next year or so. Captain Nazi, "World Enemy No. 1," showed up in *Master* #21. He was Hitler's own personal superhero, a vicious fellow in a green-and-yellow costume with a swastika on the chest and epaulets on the shoulders. He wore his blond hair in a crew cut and his face was "marked with a Heidelberg dueling scar." In his maiden visit to America, he was matched against Bulletman, but Captain Marvel dropped in from *Whiz* to lend a hand. Captain Nazi managed to escape at the end of the story, but left a note warning he'd be looking up Captain Marvel next month in *Whiz*.

One of the side effects of that encounter was that young Freddy Freeman was crippled and left for dead by the German superman. Captain Marvel, however, carried Freddy to his old mentor Shazam and the bearded wizard saved his life by granting him the ability to turn into a superhero at will. Freddy had to say "Captain Marvel!" to turn into Captain Marvel, Jr. Unlike Billy Batson, he wasn't converted into an adult, but into a superteen. His costume was similar to that of the senior hero, but it was blue instead of red. In his civilian identity, the crippled Freddy worked as a street-corner newsboy.

Captain Marvel, Jr. went to *Master* in the next issue to aid Bulletman in his return match with Captain Nazi. In #23, the young hero was given a spot of his own and became the star of the magazine. He battled the German superhero through eight different issues in 1942, in both American and European locales. After that, the villain faded away. He also did several turns in the *Captain Marvel, Jr.* magazine. Other early villains were Mr. Macabre and Captain Nippon. Later the blue-clad superboy frequently tangled with Sivana, Jr., the nasty son of the elder Marvel's favorite foe.

The initial artist, and also the first to draw the vile Captain Nazi, was Mac Raboy, who also did the *Master* covers for several years. An exceptional artist, he was notoriously slow, and often had help. In some stories, entire pages are by other hands. In Càptain Marvel, Jr.'s own

comic, Al Carreño was the chief artist. Raboy did the covers for this magazine, too. Further along, Bud Thompson, who'd previously drawn a newspaper panel about Hollywood stars, became the artist for both titles. Among the scriptwriters were Ed Herron and Otto Binder.

Fawcett started *The Marvel Family* late in 1945. In this eventual monthly, the two captains and MARY MARVEL, along with the spurious Uncle Marvel, joined together to form a sort of clannish Justice Society. They also had separate adventures in some issues. The final number was 89, dated January 1954, and it was there that Captain Marvel, Jr. made his final appearance of the era.

DC revived him twice as a backup in the *Shazam!* book, first from 1973 to 1978 and again, briefly, in 1987.

Captain Marvel, Jr., Mac Raboy, © 1942 by Fawcett Publications, Inc.

CASPER   The friendly little ghost, sweet-tempered and innocuous, started off on movie screens in November of 1945. He branched out into comic books, television, and merchandising, and became a multi-million-dollar property. Not bad for someone who had the disadvantage of being dead.

The Casper character was developed by animator Joe Oriolo, with some help from artist-writer Sy Reit. Oriolo sold all rights to Paramount's Famous Studios animation division and the first cartoon short, titled "The Friendly Ghost," reached the cinema palaces of the nation late in 1945. Though the sweet little boy ghost didn't make a tremendous impact, Famous decided to give him another shot in 1948 in "There's Good Boos Tonight." That was followed by one more in 1949 and yet another in 1950.

The following year, though, the studio turned out five of the cartoons. Casper had arrived, which was a considerable achievement for a character Leonard Maltin has called "the most monotonous character to invade cartoonland since Mighty Mouse." For Maltin, there was an annoying sameness to the cartoons. "Casper is forever in search of a friend, but wherever he goes, the people he meets take one look and shriek," he's said. "It's children or young animals who welcome his friendship."

Casper first materialized in comic books in St. John's *Casper the Friendly Ghost*. Alfred Harvey took over the title in 1952 with the sixth issue and has stuck with the amiable spook, with some lapses, ever since. The Casper of the comics wasn't the outcast of the movies, and he acquired a circle of chums and antagonists. He also enjoyed many encounters and adventures that didn't involve his fruitless efforts to win friends and influence people. Among the other characters introduced in the *Casper* titles were Wendy the Good Little Witch and Spooky the Tuff Little Ghost. A great many artists and writers have contributed to the Casper saga over the years, but the publisher has never allowed credits to appear on any of the material.

The Casper cartoons began appearing on television in the early 1950s, adding to his popularity with very young children. In the early 1960s, after Famous Studios had sold a goodly portion of their animated backlog to Harvey, a series of new Caspers was created for airing on TV.

The character's increased popularity spawned a host of other titles, including *Casper's Ghostland, Casper and Nightmare, Casper and Spooky, Casper and Wendy, Casper in Space*, and the *Casper Digest*. The subsidiary characters also branched out, resulting in Wendy and Spooky titles.

CAT-MAN COMICS   A comic book with a roster of rather odd characters, it was inaugurated in the spring of 1941 and lasted until the summer of 1946. The leading hero was the nine-lived Cat-Man. Also to be found in the magazine were a crimebuster who dressed like a priest and another who dressed like a hobo.

The Cat-Man was first seen in the fourth issue of *Crash Comics*, and when that magazine folded an issue later, he graduated to a title of his own. In everyday life he was David Merryweather, an American who'd been raised in Burma by tigers after bandits slaughtered his parents. "By constant association he acquires the attributes of the cat family," a caption explained. "Most important of all, he is endowed with the fabulous nine lives!" Once full-grown and back home, Merryweather became a crimefighter. His costume was somewhat like that of Batman, except the cowl was catlike and the color scheme included orange, blue, and red.

Merryweather joined the Army late in 1941 and also became the guardian of a tough little blonde girl of ten or eleven. She became his costumed sidekick Kitten and by the mid-1940s had blossomed into a teenager. Charles M. Quinlan drew the majority of the feline team's adventures. Bob Fujitani became the artist for the final phase.

Cat-Man Comics, Charles M. Quinlan, © 1944 by Helnit Publishing Co., Inc.

The Deacon was a reformed crook who operated "from a secret hideout in the Marshland church." His costume consisted of a priest's suit, complete with clerical collar, that he'd found in the abandoned church when he first sought shelter there. He was assisted by a blond young man named Mickey. The Rag-Man was "a wealthy New York Columnist" whom the underworld thought they'd rubbed out. He assumed a derelict disguise to prey on crooks and gangsters and was assisted by a large black man named Tiny. Both these unusual heroes were the creations of Allen Ullmer, who'd apparently fallen under the spell of Will Eisner's SPIRIT.

Other characters in *Cat-Man* included the Pied Piper, the Hood, Blackout, and the Little Leaders. This last represented a teaming up of Cat-Man's Kitten and the Deacon's Mickey.

CHALLENGERS OF THE UNKNOWN The first important hero team to emerge in the SILVER AGE, they possessed no special powers and had to rely on their wits and diversified abilities to wage their campaign against odd and unusual villainy. Created by Jack Kirby, the Challengers debuted in DC's SHOWCASE #6 (February 1957). They moved into their own magazine in 1958 and continued to challenge the unknown, with time out for a couple of extended leaves, over the next 20 years.

The group consisted of Ace Morgan, fearless jet pilot, Prof Haley, master deep-sea diver, Red Ryan, famed mountain climber, and Rocky Davis, Olympic wrestling champ: "Four strangers who escaped death when their plane crashed on the way to a ceremony honoring them for individual acts of heroism," as the copy once explained. "Knowing that they were living on borrowed time, the four men banded together to form . . . a group dedicated to exploring things that other men dare not." The Challs decked themselves out in purple jumpsuits when in their team phase. During the early years, they were joined by June Robbins, "a young adventuress and computer expert," who worked alongside them but was never an official member.

Kirby obviously had been influenced by the pulp fiction magazines of the 1930s and 1940s. What he fashioned was a gang of adventurers resembling the groups assembled by such pulpwood stalwarts as Doc Savage, THE SHADOW, and the Avenger. The team, like their pulp predecessors, faced an unsettling succession of unusual challenges. One issue they'd be captured by aliens who'd stick them in a space circus, the next they'd travel back in time and get dragooned into helping build the pyramids. In commenting on Kirby's creation, Will Jacobs and Gerard Jones in *The Comic Book Heroes* praised the notions that poured from his imagination and added that his "art, very tight and forceful in action sequences, [was] highly inventive with alien landscapes and machinery." Kirby, ever restless, abandoned the *Challengers* after the eighth issue of their magazine. On Kirby's last five issues, Wally Wood served as inker. Various scripters followed and Bob Brown provided the artwork after Kirby's departure.

The title continued until late 1969, returning in 1973 and again in 1979. During one phase the Challs took to appearing in red-and-gold costumes that made them look more like superheroes. Later they returned to their purple togs, but added an hourglass symbol on the tunic. They continued to make occasional comebacks in subsequent years.

CLASSICS ILLUSTRATED An attempt to give comics-reading kids some acquaintance with great books, the magazine began in the autumn of 1941 under the less erudite title of *Classic Comics*. For about the next 20 years, it turned out funnies-format adaptions of over 150 works, including *Moby Dick*, *Don Quixote*, *Great Expectations*, *Hamlet*, *Crime and Punishment*, and *Faust*.

Albert Kanter had been a real-estate broker, a traveling salesman, and a manufacturer of toy telegraph sets. In 1941 he was doing business in Manhattan as Elliot Publishing. Later publicity releases explained that Kanter had been impressed by the "furor in newspaper editorials and from Parent-Teacher organizations about the terrible effect that the so-called 'horror' and 'blood and thunder' comics were having on juvenile minds." He thereupon conceived the notion of adapting literary classics in comic book format. Meyer Kaplan, who worked as a bookkeeper and later as an editor for Kanter, has said, "I think it was purely a brilliant business decision. Comics were taking hold. . . . I'm sure Albert Kanter had looked at it and said, 'What can we do in this format—which is growing like wildfire—that is different from what anyone else is going?'" What Kanter did, after taking on two partners to provide additional financing, was to start publishing *Classic Comics*.

The first title was *The Three Musketeers*, drawn by Malcolm Kildale. It appeared in October of 1941. The initial print run was 200,000 copies, a relatively modest one for those days.

Just about all the artists who drew for *Classic Comics* during its first years were affiliated with Lloyd Jacquet's FUNNIES, INC. shop. Jacquet didn't provide his top artists—no doubt because Kanter was not paying top page rates. Men like Kildale, Allen Simon, and Louis Zansky were second-rate at best and, when rushing the way they obviously were here, the results were far from compelling. The adaptions, which Kaplan has said were by Evelyn Goodman, "art director, secretary, script director," were not impressive. *Huckleberry Finn*, for example, was told in the third person in the *Classic Comics* version. *Ivanhoe*, *A Tale of Two Cities*, and *Moby Dick* also suffered.

Even so, the line caught on, possibly because kids had discovered they could base book reports on the adaptions, as bad as they were, and thus save considerable time. The overall look improved in the mid-1940s, when Jerry Iger's shop took over production. The first title Iger packaged was *Oliver Twist*, #23 in the series and originally published in the summer of 1945. Artists such as Bob Webb and Matt Baker, who'd been drawing somewhat sexier material in the pages of *Jumbo*, *Fight*, etc., now started doing *Two Years Before the Mast*, *Frankenstein*, and *Lorna Doone*. Henry Kiefer, one of the busiest hacks of the 1940s, also drew many of the adaptions. Ruth Roche wrote most of the scripts. In the mid-1950s, Iger ended his association with the series and from then on Kanter relied on freelancers, including such former EC regulars as Joe Orlando, George Evans, and Graham Ingels.

Unlike other comic books, these were kept in print and each title went through several editions. An account in a 1946 issue of *Publishers Weekly* stated that by that time the company had sold "about one hundred million of its 28 titles." The name of the line was changed in 1947 to *Classics Illustrated*, when the adaption of *The Last Days of Pompeii* was issued. Under that title, new adaptions were issued regularly until 1962.

Kanter never had much competition. Dell tried its own line of adaptions in 1942. Called *Famous Stories*, the series lasted only two issues, doing just *Treasure Island* and *Tom Sawyer*. In the late 1940s, *Fast Fiction*, later calling itself the

The Last of the Mohicans, Ray Ramsey, © 1942 the Gilberton Company, Inc.

more stately *Stories by Famous Authors Illustrated*, began. It made it through 13 issues, doing adaptions of such works as *Beau Geste*, *Scaramouche*, and *Macbeth*. Kiefer worked for this line, too. In the 1970s Marvel had a brief fling with good books and did three dozen *Classic Comics* of its own.

Late in 1989, a partnership between First Comics, Berkley Books, and the Classics Media Group launched a new series of *Classics Illustrated* titles. These were in trade paperback format and sold for $3.95 in comic shops and bookstores. The early adaptions included *Great Expectations*, *The Scarlet Letter*, *Moby Dick*, and *Treasure Island*. A great deal better-looking than most of what had previously appeared under the *Classics Illustrated* umbrella, these comics boasted artwork by Bill Sienkiewicz, Dan Spiegle, Rick Geary, and Gahan Wilson. The line did not succeed, however, and by 1991 had ceased publication.

THE CLAW   The quintessential sinister Oriental, he loomed into view in the first issue of *Silver Streak Comics* (December 1939). "A monster of miraculous powers who is out to dominate the universe," the Claw had all the attributes of the better-known Dr. Fu Manchu. What gave him an extra edge was the fact that he could grow several stories high at will. Seeing the Claw come swelling up out of a midnight sea smack into the path of an unsuspecting ocean liner, or watching him squeeze a disloyal minion to death in one huge hand while chuckling, "Die, swine!", were awesome experiences indeed.

Completely evil, the Claw lived but to kill, plunder, and ravage. In his earliest forays against humanity, he was opposed by various business-suited civilians, but the Claw easily upstaged them. What was needed was a hero to match him. This was taken care of in *Silver Streak* #7, when Jack Cole, who'd created him, put the Claw up against the DAREDEVIL. Their monumental battle stretched over several issues.

The Claw, Jack Cole, © 1940 by Your Guide Publications, Inc.

The Claw, billed as "the World's Worst Villain," next showed up in *Daredevil Comics* #2 (August 1941), again starring in his own feature. Drawn now by Bob Wood, he was opposed by a mysterious hero who wore a white costume and a skull mask and called himself the Ghost. The Ghost, who in real life was Brad Hendricks, dropped out after *Daredevil* #20. The Claw went on until #31 and was then knocked off.

CLIP CARSON   Not all the good guys in GOLDEN AGE comics wore costumes and quite a few had nary a superpower. Some were crusading reporters, some were hard-boiled private detectives, and some were soldiers of fortune following in the footsteps of *Captain Easy* and *Jungle Jim*. One of the latter was Clip Carson. The creation of artist Bob Kane and writer Bill Finger, he first showed up in ACTION COMICS #14 (July 1939), just two months after BATMAN had debuted in DETECTIVE COMICS.

Carson had a broad daredevil grin, wore jodhpurs, boots, and a gun belt, and smoked a pipe. His early adventures, as depicted by Kane with help from teenage assistant Jerry Robinson, involved him with murderous Arabs, tiger men who prowled the jungles of India, and a hazardous trek in search of ivory in Africa, "whose jungles teem with insects, beasts, snakes, fever, and wild natives."

After winding up the safari adventure and besting a bewhiskered villain with the somewhat redundant name of Wolf Lupo, Clip lost the services of Kane. The next artist was Sheldon Moldoff. Moldoff's work was rich with homages to his favorite artists, including Hal Foster, Alex Raymond, Milton Caniff, and Burne Hogarth. During this phase of his career, Clip went around looking like Jungle Jim, Flash Gordon, Secret Agent X-9, TARZAN, and Pat Ryan. George Papp took over in November of 1940 and stayed on until the end. The last nine adventures ran in MORE FUN COMICS. By the time of his last go-round (February 1940), Clip had become less devil-may-care and was working in China as a "foreign correspondent for a large New York paper."

THE CLOCK   Although his adventures were badly drawn and poorly written, he was an important character. The Clock was the first masked hero created directly for comic books. The dapper crimefighter made his debut late in 1936, appearing at about the same time in two different magazines, and went on to be part of several others during his eight years as a mystery man. The Clock was the invention of artist-writer George E. Brenner.

The Clock was in reality Brian O'Brien, "wealthy young sportsman" and amateur criminologist. In his crime-fighting phase he wore a tuxedo, fedora, and a black silken mask that covered his face. Brenner's source of inspiration was the mystery men of the pulps, such as THE SHADOW, the Spider, and the Phantom Detective. After cleaning up a criminal mess, the Clock left his calling card behind. It showed the face of a timepiece and bore the line, "The Clock has struck."

Brenner's pioneering masked man was introduced in the November 1936 issues of both *Funny Pages* and *Funny Picture Stories*. He next showed up in *Detective Picture Stories* and at the end of 1937 he moved into *Feature Funnies* as of the third issue. He remained there for another 28 issues and then switched to *Crack Comics* for a stay of 35 issues. Everett "Busy" Arnold was the man responsible for the Clock's appearances in the latter two titles. Arnold had been the printer for the earlier magazines and when he started his Quality line, he sought out Brenner. (He also made the smarter move of hiring Will Eisner.)

When the Clock began working in *Crack Comics*, he took on an associate named Pug Brady, who was not only tough but O'Brien's exact double. Pug eventually left and was replaced by a tough teenage girl named Butch. Soon after teaming with the feisty Butch, the Clock switched to a domino mask.

THE COMET   Although he was originally killed midway through his second year in business, he's managed to make several comebacks over the years. The Comet, created by Jack Cole, was introduced in MLJ's *Pep Comics* #1 (January 1940) and prematurely retired in #17 (July 1941). He was resurrected in the mid-1960s, the early 1980s, and yet again in the early 1990s.

The initial Comet story, written and drawn by Cole, opened exuberantly. The splash panel showed the brightly costumed hero whizzing across the sky and nearly flying off the page. Cole also provided his own blurb: "Smashing adventures of the most astonishing man on the face of the Earth." Readers learned that John Dickering, a young scientist, had discovered "a gas that is fifty times lighter than hydrogen." He found that "by injecting small doses of the gas into his bloodstream, his body becomes light enough to make leaps through the air!" Dickering further discovered "that the gas accumulates in the eyes and throws off two

The Clock, George E. Brenner, © 1940 by Comic Magazines, Inc.

powerful beams—these rays, when they cross each other, cause whatever he looks at to disintegrate completely!!!" Glass was the only thing the cross-eyed rays couldn't penetrate, so young Dickering fashioned a glass eyeshield to wear. While he was at it, he designed himself a costume as well, a red, black, and yellow outfit with stars and crescent moons all over the tunic.

The Comet was a merciless crimebuster and thought nothing of melting crooks or dropping them to their deaths from high places. Cole produced three more episodes of the saga before moving on. After his departure, the stories toned down some. Bob Wood drew the character for a spell, then Lin Streeter. In the seventeenth issue of *Pep*, the Comet was gunned down by gangsters. His brother Robert Dickering vowed to hunt down and bring to justice those responsible for his death. To do that, he became the Hangman.

The Comet made his SILVER AGE return in a Fly Girl story in *The Fly* #30 (October 1964). The magazine, after being off the stands for several months, became *Fly Man*. The Comet, along with THE SHIELD and the Black Hood, aided the titular hero in his fight against crime. Jerry Siegel did the writing, Paul Reinman the drawing. It turned out the Comet actually hadn't died in 1941, but had spent much of the intervening time on the planet Altrox. For his revived career, he wore a new costume and grew a mustache. He became part of the Mighty Crusaders and appeared in their comic book as well as in a one-shot called *Super Heroes Versus Super Villains*. That appearance, in the summer of 1966, was followed by his retirement.

In 1983, Archie included a Comet title in its Red Circle series of revivals. Editor Bill DuBay wrote the scripts and the artwork was by the team of Carmine Infantino and Alex Niño. The hero looked and sounded considerably better than he had in the 1960s. In the DuBay version, the Comet reverted to his original costume. After being shot in 1941, the Comet had been teleported to Altrox, where friends on that distant planet brought him back to life. During his long stay there, he didn't age. However, he no longer felt the enthusiasm for the superhero profession that he had in his youth. He called himself an anachronism and felt that "I was a butcher. . . . Every bit as ruthless as the savages I hunted!" This angst-ridden Comet, more depressed than the most depressed Stan Lee Marvel hero, made it through just two issues.

In 1991 DC took over the name, but abandoned most everything else for their Comet comic. Now the flying hero was a 20-year-old named Rob Connors who, because of a "bizarre accident," became "a hero who can fly and project beams of heat and tremendous energy."

COMIC CAVALCADE A companion to WORLD'S FINEST, this 96-page, 15-center featured new adventures of characters from the company's All-American division titles. The stars of *Comic Cavalcade*, which began late in 1942, were THE FLASH, WONDER WOMAN, and GREEN LANTERN. Late in 1948, the magazine changed completely, switching to funny animal fare. The changes in content are representative of some of the trends in the comic book industry in the late 1940s.

Sheldon Mayer was the editor and, in addition to the above-mentioned trio, the early issues featured Wildcat, Hop Harrigan, Sargon the Sorcerer, and Mayer's own Scribbly (see THE FUNNIES and ALL-AMERICAN COMICS.) Later additions included THE ATOM and the BLACK CANARY. The magazine also ran a series of stories concerning a character named Johnny Everyman. This was an out-and-out propaganda feature, "prepared in cooperation with the East and West Association, devoted to furthering understanding between the peoples of the world." Johnny was a handsome fellow in jodhpurs who roamed the world battling prejudice and propaganda and their advocates. "All men are created equal," he summed up at the end of one adventure. "Just give 'em a chance to prove it." The feature was drawn by John Daly and began a few months before the end of World War II.

Late in 1948, with the popularity of the superheroes dropping, the book was completely overhauled and turned into a funny animal title. From #30 onward it contained "brand new stories featuring all your old favorites." These old favorites included the Fox and the Crow, the Dodo and the Frog, and Nutsy Squirrel, all of them recruited from DC's other animal titles. *Comic Cavalcade* lasted until 1954.

COMIC MONTHLY This lonely publication was the first comic book sold on a monthly basis on newsstands. More than 10 years ahead of its time, *Comic Monthly* appeared at the end of 1921. It sold for a dime, consisted of 24 pages measuring $8^1/_2$ by 10 inches, and offered black-and-white reprints of popular newspaper strips, one title to an issue. Failing to find favor, the innovative magazine ceased after a dozen issues.

Among the comic strips reprinted, a single daily to a page, were *Polly & Her Pals*, *Barney Google*, *Toots & Casper*, *Tillie the Toiler*, and *Little Jimmy*. The magazine was published by the Embee Distributing Company. The *Em* stood for George McManus, creator of *Bringing Up Father*, which means he was an early, though virtually unsung, champion of comic books. The *bee* stood for Rudolph Block, Jr., whose father was Hearst's comics editor. The Hearst Sunday comics section was subtitled *The Comic Weekly*, a possible source of inspiration for the magazine's title. The majority of the strips were from Hearst syndicates.

Comic Monthly was seen regularly throughout 1922, but it created no imitators. The comic book industry waited until the next decade to get under way.

CONAN He first set up shop as a barbarian back in the December 1932 issue of *Weird Tales*. Conan was the creation of Robert E. Howard, a young Texan who'd begun turning out large quantities of pulp stories while still in his teens.

When he wasn't writing for the pulpwoods, he was reading them. The swords-and-sorcery facet of his work was much influenced by such authors as Talbot Mundy and Harold Lamb. He borrowed from them both, though he was never able to imitate their restraint.

"As nearly as such things can be calculated, Conan flourished about 12,000 years ago," explained L. Sprague deCamp, who revised and refurbished much of the Conan pulp material for book publication. "In this time," according to Howard, "the western parts of the main continent were occupied by the Hyborian kingdoms. . . . Conan, a gigantic adventurer from Commeria, arrived as a youth in the kingdom of Zamora. For two or three years he made his living as a thief in Zamora, Corinthia, and Nemedia. Growing tired of this starveling existence, he enlisted as a mercenary in the armies of Turan. For the next two years he traveled widely and refined his knowledge of archery and horsemanship." Conan had several odd jobs after that. He was a super-muscled, skull-splitting fellow who was fond of spending his days with lovely princesses and slave girls, or of struggling against malignant magic and sorcery. The rest of the time he got into fights.

In 1936 Howard, just 30, killed himself. His stories of Conan the Barbarian, epics of adolescent fantasies and fears, were forgotten for nearly two decades. Then gradually they began coming back into print, first as hardcovers and then, with striking covers painted by Frank Frazetta, as paperbacks.

Conan found his widest and most enthusiastic audience in the 1970s, thanks to Roy Thomas and Marvel Comics. Thomas began as a fan and by 1970 he was an editor and writer at Marvel, concentrating on superheroes. Although Thomas is often given sole credit for deciding to adapt Howard's barbarian to the comic book format, artist Gil Kane has said that he was the one who originally got Thomas and Marvel interested in experimenting with the character. At any rate, *Conan* hit the newsstands in the fall of 1970. Scripts were by Thomas and

Red Sonja, Frank Thorne, unpublished.

the art was by a young, transplanted British artist named Barry Smith. Although he initially worked in a variation of the Marvel house style, Smith soon developed his own approach. His work became more personal, more intricate, and demonstrated distinct Pre-Raphaelite touches.

Thomas's adaptions drew much praise at the time. Smith, too, attracted attention and was soon winning awards from both his peers and his fans. He left the character in 1973 and was followed by several other artists, among them John Buscema, Ernie Chan, and Gil Kane. The shaggy hero has been around in various formats ever since. Conan's early success sparked a small swords-and-sorcery boom. Marvel, for instance, tried Thongor, Kull, and Red Sonja.

Justifiably called the "She-Devil with a Sword," the comic book incarnation of Red Sonja first appeared in late 1972 in *Conan* #23. Thomas took the character from another Howard pulp tale and, changing her name slightly, let her loose in the Hyborean Age. She was the guest star in two issues of *Conan* and returned in 1974 for a single appearance in a black-and-white magazine, *The Savage Sword of Conan*. She next fought her way through two issues of *Kull and the Barbarians* in 1975, with Howard Chaykin drawing her sword-wielding escapades. Sonja then became the star of *Marvel Feature* and Frank Thorne depicted her from the second issue onward. With her bright-orange hair and her chain-mail bikini, Thorne's version of the female barbarian attracted considerable interest. Late in 1976, the she-devil got a book of her own and it continued, with a hiatus or two, until the mid-1980s.

CONGO BILL   The comic books of the 1930s and early 1940s provided employment for several fellows who were attempting to follow in the footsteps of newspaper-strip heroes like Alex Raymond's Jungle Jim and real-life celebrities like Frank "Bring 'Em Back Alive" Buck. By far the most successful of these jungle gentlemen was Congo Bill, who first appeared in DC's MORE FUN #56 (June 1940). The initial artist was George Papp.

The mustached Bill's first job consisted of guiding an archeologist-botanist who was seeking a lost city in the jungle and was also interested in the flora of the Congo region. The assignment stretched over many issues, hindered by savage tribes, a recurring purple-skinned villain known as the Skull, and an assortment of distressed young women. In the spring of 1941, Bill changed his venue and from #37 (June 1941) was to be found in ACTION COMICS. A young artist named Fred Ray took over the drawing.

Ray obviously enjoyed the feature and he put considerable effort into it. Gradually its looks changed and its stories moved away from lost cities and evil hunters to take notice of World War II. The 1942 stories are especially fine, inventively staged and filled with accurately drawn planes, weapons, and uniforms. Ray avoided heroic poses, favoring natural figures. All of this gave *Congo Bill* a sophistication that was missing from the adventures of any of the other jungle heroes.

Congo Bill, drawn by various artists— including Ed Smalle and Nick Cardy—outlived the GOLDEN AGE by several years and even got a magazine of his own for a time. Bill acquired a sidekick early in 1954 in the person of Janu the Jungle Boy. The lad was also on view in the seven issues of the *Congo Bill* comic book that appeared between 1954 and 1955. In 1959, Bill was supplanted by an ape and the title of the feature was changed to *Congorilla*. As such, it lasted until early 1960.

Cookie, Dan Gordon, unpublished, 1946.

Congo Bill, Fred Ray, unpublished, 1946.

COOKIE   The diminutive teenager first surfaced in *Topsy-Turvy Comics*, a one-shot that came out in the spring of 1945. Exactly one year later, Cookie returned in his own bimonthly, published by the American Comics Group. The prolific Richard Hughes wrote the scripts and Dan Gordon was the artist.

Cookie had the requisite supporting cast— irascible businessman father, understanding mother, beautiful blonde girlfriend named Angelpuss, slangy pal named Jitterbuck, and tall and conniving rival named Zoot. What made the feature different from most of the teenage characters then crowding the newsstands was the slapstick way it was drawn. A former animator, Gordon produced a sort of Tex Avery–*Looney Tunes* version of teen life and problems. The stories were full of pratfalls, gags involving outrageous props, lowbrow jokes, and a frenzied sort of action.

Cookie continued until 1955, although Gordon had abandoned the book sometime earlier.

—

CRIMEBUSTER   *See* Boy Comics.

CRIME DOES NOT PAY   This was a bestselling title of the GOLDEN AGE and a magazine that inspired an entire comic book genre. The first regularly issued true-crime comic, it was published by Lev Gleason and Arthur Bernhard and edited by cartoonists Charles Biro and Bob Wood. *Crime Does Not Pay* began in the spring of 1942 and stayed in business until the spring of 1955. Bernhard left fairly soon and Gleason continued alone as publisher.

When asked who had come up with the idea for the title, Bernhard replied that "Lev conceived the whole thing," turning it over to Biro to edit. The new magazine was launched in 1942 with typical Biro enthusiasm. Teaser ads in other magazines proclaimed, "IT'S COMING! The most sensational comic magazine ever created!!! The spectular masterpiece is in production NOW! Get it at your newsstand soon!" Once *Crime Does Not Pay* appeared, full-page ads for it began in the company's other titles. The copy proclaimed, "THE MOST SENSATIONAL COMIC IDEA ever is sweeping the country! Crime comics give you the REAL FACTS!! SEE for the first time how real criminals lived, stole, killed and then—" A line of copy below this particular ad, indicating they had a larger audience in mind, read, "Get 'Crime Does Not Pay'! Show it to Dad, he'll love it!"

Major influences on the genesis and evolution of *Crime Does Not Pay* were such hard-boiled periodicals as *True Detective*, *Master Detective*, and *Official Detective*. Printed on somewhat better paper than the pulp fiction magazines and illustrated with grainy photos of vicious criminals, blowzy gun molls, and bloody corpses, they offered breathless nonfiction accounts of daring bank robberies, brutal murders, and assorted crimes of passion. *Crime Does Not Pay* came closer than any comic book had before to emulating this particular blend of gritty reality, shoot-'em-up action, and titillation.

It was the contention of Gleason and his editors that the magazine was "dedicated to the eradication of crime" and for a time covers carried the slogan "a force for good in the community!" The letters page, which paid $2 for each one published, frequently featured testimonies from both teens and parents that the reading of *Crime Does Not Pay* served as a deterrent to criminal activity and delinquency.

Since *Crime Does Not Pay* replaced the superhero title *Silver Streak*, it assumed that title's numbering and the first issue was #22

(July 1942). The cover assured readers that this was "The First Magazine of Its Kind!" Inside were the true-crime cases of Louis "Lepke" Buchalter of Murder, Inc. fame; the Mad Dog Esposition Brothers; and Wild Bill Hickok. In #24, Mr. Crime was introduced, a ghostly, all-knowing wiseguy who was a cross between the nasty Mr. Coffee Nerves of the Postum ads and the sardonic hosts of radio mystery shows like *Inner Sanctum*. He hosted each issue's leadoff story and inevitably offered a pithy remark in the final panel—"The law got ALL of them! Ralph Fleagle, Royston and Absher were all hanged in Colorado State Penitentiary at Canon City! Good pupils, too, tsk, tsk!"

The magazine chronicled crooks of recent vintage, such as "Legs" Diamond, and older heavies like Billy the Kid. Most of the cases were packed with shooting, violence, and action, but little actual bloodshed was depicted. Mild sexual activity was typical, usually provided by the lady friends of the various crooks and killers.

Artwork in the early issues was by such as Creig Flessel, Harry Lucey, and Bob Montana. As the war progressed, some lesser artists worked on the magazine, but in the mid- and late 1940s George Tuska, who has been called "the premier crime comic artist," Bob Fujitani, Dan Barry, and Fred Kida were among those who improved the comic's looks. Biro limited himself to drawing most of the covers. He usually dealt in anticipation, showing the moment just before the hapless gas station attendants were buried alive, or just before the bootlegger was dropped into the lime pit.

By 1945, the combined sales of all the Gleason titles had climbed to 1.5 million and by 1947 it was over 2 million. Late in 1947, the covers of *Crime Does Not Pay* boasted "More Than 6,000,000 Readers Monthly!" Gleason and Biro were fudging here by assuming that several readers looked at each copy sold.

Crime Does Not Pay had the field pretty much to itself, despite its impressive sales, for several years. But because of the uncertain economics of the postwar period and the decline of interest in superheroes, other publishers turned to crime. Dozens of titles followed, including Gleason's *Crime and Punishment*. Much of the criticism, censorship, and boycotting that hit comic books in the early 1950s was inspired by the more flamboyant imitators of the pioneering *Crime Does Not Pay*.

GET 'CRIME DOES NOT PAY'. SHOW IT TO DAD, HE'LL LOVE IT!

Mr. Crime, © 1942 Comic House.

THE CRIMSON AVENGER   The first masked and caped crimefighter to appear in DETECTIVE COMICS, the Crimson Avenger debuted in issue #20 (October 1938). He owed a great deal to a hero of another color, namely THE GREEN HORNET. The Hornet, accompanied by his "Flight of the Bumblebee" theme, first took to the airwaves over Detroit's WXYZ and by the spring

of 1938 was being heard nationwide on the Mutual network. Whereas the Hornet was in reality Britt Reid, daring young publisher of the *Daily Sentinel*, the Crimson was Lee Travis, wealthy young publisher of the *Globe Leader*. The only person who knew the Hornet's true identity was his faithful valet, Kato, and the Crimson's secret was shared only by his Chinese servant Wing.

Like the Green Hornet, the Crimson Avenger never used a deadly weapon and preferred to put his adversaries to sleep with a blast from his gas gun. He wore a dark-blue slouch hat, a domino mask, and an Inverness-style cape of crimson hue.

The creation of artist Jim Chambers, the feature was drawn in a rough version of the basic Milton Caniff style. In his early adventures, the Crimson fought civic corruption and organized crime. Much flashier than the gumshoes and private eyes he was sharing *Detective* with, he might well have become the star of the magazine. Unfortunately for him, BATMAN showed up in #27 and the Crimson Avenger was relegated to second-banana status for the rest of his career. In fact, he dropped out of the magazine soon after his more flamboyant rival appeared and didn't turn up again for nearly a year.

He returned in #37 (March 1940). The following month, Jack Lehti, who was very much under the spell of Alex Raymond at the time, took over the drawing. By the fall of 1940, when superheroes in tights were to be found cavorting in dozens of magazines, the Crimson Avenger switched to crimson tights and tunic, yellow shorts and boots, plus a crimson cowl and cape. The gas gun became much more futuristic-looking. He added a costumed sidekick in #59 (January 1942) in the person of his very own Wing.

The Crimson Avenger also appeared in WORLD'S FINEST and *Leading Comics* and retired in 1945. DC revived him in his original costume briefly in 1988.

DAREDEVIL   The first Daredevil hit the stands in the summer of 1940 in the pages of *Silver Streak Comics*. He added a magazine of his own the following year and enjoyed a crime-fighting career that lasted throughout the 1940s. He had no superpowers, relying on his wits, his striking bilateral crimson and midnight-blue costume, and his boomerang to help him fight werewolves, ladykillers, stranglers, the enormous Asiatic villain known as THE CLAW, and even Adolf Hitler. Among those who worked on his adventures were two of the most inventive and influential artist-writers of the period, Jack Cole and Charles Biro.

Late in 1939, Arthur Bernhard, who had been involved in publishing magazines of all sorts, ventured into comics with *Silver Streak*. After a few issues he hired Jack Cole to edit. The youthful cartoonist wrote and drew the adventures of the speedy Silver Streak, cramming the pages with action, violence, monsters, pretty women, and humor.

The magazine's only other costumed hero was Daredevil, who was introduced in #6 (September 1940) in a bland six-page story drawn by Jack Binder. The next month, Cole took over the character and did something audacious by pretending he was working with a well-established hero. "DAREDEVIL BATTLES THE CLAW," announced his flamboyant cover. This was just a few months after the Human Torch (see ALL-WINNERS COMICS) and SUB-MARINER had carried on a monumental three-issue battle over in MARVEL COMICS and Cole must have assumed comic book readers were ready for another full-scale fracas. He devoted the first 16 pages of the issue to round one. It started off with an impressive splash page that mixed sex, violence, and the Yellow Peril and included a teaser disclaimer that stated, "WARNING!! You are about to read one of the most astounding tales ever portrayed in a comic magazine! If you have a weak heart, we advise you NOT to venture further!" The battle continued for four more issues and by the time it wound up, Lev Gleason had bought into the company. Cole departed and Daredevil fell into the hands of Don Rico. Gleason, however, had additional plans for the hero. In the summer of 1941, Daredevil graduated to a book of his own.

The first issue was entitled *Daredevil Battles Hitler*. Bernhard has said that the comic was an expression of his own antifascist, anti-Hitler activities. His views were shared by

Gleason. The inside back cover carried an ad for the upcoming *Daredevil Comics*: "By POPULAR DEMAND—What you've all been waiting for—the DAREDEVIL'S OWN COMIC BOOK." Bernhard and Gleason brought in Biro and Bob Wood to edit and produce the new title. Besides exploiting the combination of violence and titillation that would become a Lev Gleason hallmark, Biro added packaging tricks that eventually became industry standards. From its first issue, *Daredevil* bore an aggressive slogan—"The Greatest Name in Comics." Covers were littered with boxes of copy and multi-colored headlines that promised all sorts of delights, including money. "$100 CASH PRIZES You May WIN" was a typical Biro come-on.

Biro wrote and drew the early Daredevil yarns. He developed the habit of addressing his readers directly, often hyping the story they were about to read: "None can rival the wild fantasy that will unfold within these pages! So dim the lights and lock your doors as well, for this monster might strike at even YOU!"

In #13, Daredevil met the Little Wise Guys. The idea that a gang of feisty, two-fisted boys could be entertaining had become popular in 1937, after the Warner Brothers movie version of the hit play *Dead End*. Joe Simon and Jack Kirby had already introduced several kid gangs to comic books, so Biro wasn't covering especially new ground. Gradually the Daredevil dropped back into an avuncular role as the Wise Guys got involved with street crime, delinquency, and other sociological soap-opera subjects. It's possible that Biro intended these rather preachy tales as a counterbalance to the blood-and-guts fare he was helping concoct for Gleason's CRIME DOES NOT PAY.

At any rate, the bizarre villains and plots of Daredevil's salad years vanished and more uplifting tales took over. After playing a smaller and smaller role, he dropped out for good in the winter of 1950. The magazine, still bearing his name, continued until 1956. Biro, who'd been farming out the artwork to Carl

Hubbell, Dan Barry, and Norman Maurer, and most of the scriptwriting to Virginia Hubbell, probably didn't feel any pangs at putting the magazine out to pasture.

Daredevil, Charles Biro, © 1941 by Your Guide Publications, Inc.

DAREDEVIL (II) This Daredevil, known as the Man Without Fear, was introduced in his own magazine early in 1964. The SILVER AGE was an era of flawed heroes, and Daredevil's affliction was blindness. In real life he was attorney Matt Murdock. Because he'd lost his sight after being struck by a truck hauling radioactive materials, he acquired "incredible powers" that allowed him to navigate the city's rooftops with an uncanny sixth sense that was somewhat like radar. Daredevil headed out for his first adventures garbed in a red, yellow, and black costume that he sewed himself. By the seventh issue, his outfit was a deep red. Bill Everett illustrated Daredevil's first adventure, and Stan Lee wrote the script.

Everett was followed by Joe Orlando, Wally Wood, and John Romita. In 1966, Gene Colan became the regular illustrator of the acrobatic avenger's adventures and remained on the job until the early 1970s. In 1979, Frank Miller took over the drawing. He worked in a highly personal style that showed a variety of influences, including Will Eisner, Jim Steranko, Japanese prints, martial-arts movies, and European comic book artists such as Moebius and Guido Crepax. Miller was very much aware that page breakdowns could be used to control and manipulate time. He chopped them up horizontally and vertically, and sometimes sliced each tier into a half dozen or more frames. Readers soon took notice of Miller's novel approach and, although *Daredevil* didn't shoot straight up to the lead position on the sales charts, it was very soon in the top 20.

Late in 1980, Miller also assumed the scriptwriting. He soon introduced one of the most formidable women ever seen in comics. She was Elektra, Daredevil's most fascinating foe, and the two of them carried on a complex love–hate relationship. "Coming in at the end of a decade of wordy, introspective, unimaginative fare, Miller distinguished himself not only as a good plotter but as a dazzlingly effective storyteller," observed Will Jacobs and Gerard Jones in *The Comic Book Heroes*. A notable element of Miller's storytelling was its explicit violence. Censorship standards had relaxed considerably since the days when comic books had been tossed on bonfires by their critics, and Miller's *Daredevil* became increasingly bloody and violent.

"Elektra was truly ruthless in her assaults, with an arsenal of Oriental death-devices," commented Jacobs and Jones. "In issue 181 (April 1982) this violence reached its culmination in the grittiest scene ever presented in a mainstream comic book. In a vicious fight between Bullseye and Elektra, Bullseye not only kills his opponent but, relishing every blow, breaks her jaw, slits her throat, and thrusts a knife through her body. Costumed heroes were clearly no longer just entertainment for children."

After leaving the character in 1983, Miller returned in 1986 for a stint as writer, with Dave Mazzuchelli doing the drawing. *Daredevil*, somewhat subdued of late, continues. Elektra has returned from the dead now and then, most notably in *Elektra: Assassin* in 1986–87, with scripts by Miller and art by Bill Sienkiewicz.

DARING COMICS This was Marvel's second title. It seemed to suffer from an identity crisis and offered a different batch of characters in every issue. Not exactly a monthly, it managed to appear only eight times in its initial two years of existence. During that time, more than three dozen characters, superheroes, and otherwise came and went in its pages.

The first issue was dated January 1940. Included in that *Daring* lineup were a magician named Monako, a soldier of fortune named John Steele, a cowboy known as the Texas Kid, and a superhero called the Fiery Mask. In the second number, he was replaced by the Laughing Mask, who was joined by such newcomers as Trojak the Tigerman, the Phantom Bullet, and Zephyr Jones and his Rocket Ship. In #3 (April 1940), readers were confronted with a hero named the Purple Mask, along with the Phantom Reporter, Whirlwind Carter of the Interplanetary Secret Service, and Captain Strong.

The Fiery Mask returned in #5 when a costumed hero called the Falcon debuted. Popeye artist Bud Sagendorf contributed a humor feature about Little Hercules, a superkid. The next issue saw the advent of Marvel Boy, an early creation of the team of Joe Simon and Jack Kirby. The seventh issue didn't appear until the spring of 1941, with an entirely different cast. Leading off was the Thunderer by Carl Burgos. Also featured were the Fin by Bill Everett and Captain Daring by Simon and Kirby. In addition, Harry Sahle contributed the Silver Scorpion, a costumed lady crimebuster. This group held on for one more issue before *Daring* ended its run.

The title was changed to *Comedy Comics*,

but the Fin and the Silver Scorpion hung in among the funny stuff for one more issue. In 1944, Marvel revived *Daring*, this time featuring such established characters as the Human Torch and the SUB-MARINER. It lasted four issues.

DETECTIVE COMICS   This is the magazine that introduced Batman in the spring of 1939, and gave the DC line its name. The third of Major Nicholson's original-material comic books, *Detective* began early in 1937. Every character in it, as the title implied, was a detective of one sort or other. BATMAN, a first-rate detective himself, debuted in #27 (May 1939) and Robin joined him in #38 (April 1940). The longest-running title in comics, it is still being published and still stars Batman.

Among the other crimefighters and private eyes who've appeared in its pages over the years are Slam Bradley, Speed Saunders, Larry Steele, the CRIMSON AVENGER, Air Wave, the Boy Commandos, Robotman, Pow Wow Smith, and MARTIAN MANHUNTER.

DICK COLE   Schoolboy heroes such as Frank Merriwell had been popular in the story papers and dime novels of earlier decades and Jack Armstrong was a radio favorite in the 1930s and 1940s, but that sort of character rarely thrived in comic books. One of the few exceptions was clean-cut, blond Dick Cole, known as the Wonder Boy. Created by artist-writer Bob Davis, he first appeared in *Blue Bolt* #1 (June 1940).

Dick Cole attended prestigious Farr Military Academy. He'd spent his childhood being scientifically nurtured by kindly Professor Hiram Blair. The professor had used "rare treatments, which included everything from special vitamin serums to violet and gamma ray baths." All this, plus several extended jaunts around the world, turned Dick into a lad whose "mental and physical development was geared up to an amazing degree."

He remained a modest and self-effacing young man, despite his obvious superiority to just about everyone else in the world. When not excelling academically, athletically, and militarily at Farr, the wonder boy was performing daring deeds in the civilian world. He won the Carnegie Medal for Bravery, accomplished amazing things in Hollywood as a stuntman, subdued a horde of escaped convicts, saved a beautiful European princess from being kidnapped on the high seas, etc.

Davis's style was cartoony, diagrammatic, and full of action. His characters were forever running, jumping, and exchanging punches; a typical page resembled a storyboard for a Saturday-matinee serial. As a writer, he went in for pulp plots, full of violence and intrigue, with a few boys' book trappings like buried treasure thrown in.

Davis was killed in an auto accident in 1942 and a series of lesser artists, including Al Fagaly and Jim Wilcox, continued his feature. Dick Cole was last seen in 1949.

Dick Cole, Bob Davis, © 1941 Novelty Press, Inc.

DOC SAVAGE   Although he was a major pulp magazine hero in the 1930s and the 1940s and a success in paperback reprints from the 1960s onward, the Man of Bronze has never done especially well in comic books. Several publishers have given it a try, the first in 1940 and the most recent in 1991.

The *Doc Savage* pulp was launched by Street & Smith early in 1933 and introduced Doc and his five-man crew of gifted and colorful sidekicks. They were Renny Renwick, Long Tom Roberts, William Harper Littlejohn, Ham Brooks, and Monk Mayfair. Ham, the dapper attorney, and Monk, the tough, apelike chemical genius, were continually bickering. They were also the most popular members of Doc's crime-fighting crew. Lester Dent, using the house name Kenneth Robeson, created the series and wrote most of the novels. He mixed mystery, fantasy, and considerable humor into the monthly adventures.

Doc Savage made an inauspicious comic book debut in Street & Smith's *Shadow Comics* #1 (March 1940) (see THE SHADOW) in a dull, ill-drawn six-page story provided by Maurice Gutwirth of the Jack Binder shop. Doc was in "the heart of Africa" with only "his trusted assistant Monk" to put an end to the activities of a foreign agent who was selling guns to the natives. After two more appearances in *Shadow*, Doc was given a magazine of his own. The adventure that began in the May 1940 *Shadow* was continued in the first issue of *Doc Savage Comics*, also dated May 1940. It was a greatly condensed version of the early pulp novel *The Land of Terror*. Street & Smith was apparently aware of the competition and ads called Doc the "greatest of all Supermen." Several other characters, most of them brought over from the pulps, shared the magazine with the Man of Bronze. In his own stories, Doc Savage worked only with Monk and Ham.

In 1941, in a story written by Carl Formes and drawn by Jack Binder, Doc was abruptly converted to a costumed superhero and took to wearing a Sacred Hood that had a Sacred Ruby stuck to it. He continued in that mode until his magazine folded with the 20th issue in the summer of 1943. He then returned to backup status in *Shadow Comics*, donned a business suit, and, helped by Ham and Monk, worked as a scientific detective. Among the artists who drew his adventures were William A. Smith, Al Bare, and Bob Powell.

In 1966, after Doc had returned to public view by way of Bantam's paperback reprints of the Dent novels, Dell put out a one-shot comic book, drawn by Jack Sparling. Marvel attempted two short-lived series, one in color and the other in black and white, in the mid-1970s. Next came DC with a title that lasted from 1987 to 1990. In 1991, Millenium took over the character. All the later Docs looked like the blond storm-trooper type designed originally by artist James Bama for the paperback covers.

Doc Savage, William A. Smith, © 1942 Street & Smith Publications, Inc.

DR. FATE   He was the creation of writer Gardner Fox and artist Howard Sherman, and started out as a very mysterious and mystical character, first appearing in the spring of 1940 in MORE FUN COMICS #55. Initially, Dr. Fate was a cross between a superhero and an occult detective, a sort of costumed ghostbuster. He was soon modified into a more conventional superhero. Revived frequently in subsequent years, he's been changed and amended several times and has turned quite mystical again. The most profound modification occurred in the late 1980s, when Dr. Fate became a woman.

An early caption spoke of the original Dr. Fate, who wore a blue-and-gold costume and a metal helmet that completely covered his face, as a "man of mystery, possessor of ancient secrets." He resided "apart from mankind in his lonely tower north of ghost-ridden Salem" and called "upon secret and ancient sources for the power with which he fights unusual crimes." He described himself at this time as being "not human . . . I never was a child . . . I had no youth. . . . The elder gods created me here on Earth to fight evil sorcery!"

A dedicated reader of pulp fiction, Gardner Fox turned to *Weird Tales*, and especially to the stories of H.P. Lovecraft and his circle, for some of his inspiration. Ancient gods, evil entities, and sorcerers who practiced black magic abounded. During his first year on duty, Dr. Fate bested ancient Mayan gods, combated globemen from outer space, defeated horrors summoned from the cosmic void, visited hell, and counseled a young woman who feared she might be a wereleopard. He could also rattle off mystical incantations—"Fyoreth dignalleth!"—that rivaled the best Lovecraftian gibberish.

Fox often saw to it that, like THE SHADOW, his heroes had a trusted female companion who was in on the secret of their dual identity. A woman named Inza Cramer shared most of Fate's occult adventures and knew, eventually, whose face was behind the golden mask.

In *More Fun* #67 (May 1941), the doctor was given an origin and a civilian name. It turned out he was Kent Nelson, son of a noted archeologist. While Kent and his dad were exploring a pyramid in the Valley of Ur, "in the year 1920 or thereabouts," Kent's father was killed after the youth reanimated the ancient sorcerer Nabu, who was actually a long-ago visitor from another planet. In gratitude, Nabu offered the young fellow the opportunity to learn "the secrets of the universe." This took several years, and when Nabu felt Nelson had graduated, he bestowed upon him the Fate costume and bid him go forth.

A few issues later, the character made another step toward becoming a more conventional superhero. He showed up with a new helmet, one that allowed the lower part of his face to show. While this allowed him to smile at friend and foe alike and speak in a less muffled voice, it also robbed him of a good deal of his mystery. From then on the occult cases became few and far between. Late in 1942, as chronicled in *More Fun* #85, Dr. Fate experienced yet another change. Inza came upon Nelson surrounded by "a pile of ponderous medical books." He explained, "I'm going to become a doctor . . . a *real* doctor!" After getting through medical school in two panels, he became an intern. A caption then informed readers that "this new Doctor Fate is to have even more understanding of mankind—more dignity, more humanity!" Dr. Fate made his final house call late in 1943.

Dr. Fate, written again by Fox and drawn by Murphy Anderson, was brought back in 1965 as part of the SILVER AGE renaissance. Since then, at the hands of such writers and artists as Roy Thomas, William Messner-Loebs, and Keith Giffen, the character has undergone considerable changes. Along the way, Kent Nelson and Inza Cramer got married. A 1991 volume of *Who's Who in the DC Universe* explains some of the changes this way: "As time passed, Inza was driven mad by her life of solitude and Nelson's body began to age rapidly due to the stress of his many battles as Fate. Soon Inza died, and Nabu, expecting Nelson to die as well, transformed a young boy named Eric Strauss into an adult. He became the new Doctor Fate. . . . When Eric and Linda Strauss died in battle . . . Nabu summoned the spirits of Kent and Inza back to physical existence, giving them new bodies that were identical to their original ones. . . . Kent and Inza at long last merged to become Doctor Fate. . . . The Nelsons soon discovered that Kent could no longer join in the mystical merger for reasons that remain unknown. As a result, Inza alone now acts as Doctor Fate."

Dr. Fate was retired in 1992.

Dr. Fate, Howard Sherman, © 1940, renewed 1968 DC Comics, Inc. All rights reserved.

DR. STRANGE   Perhaps the most fortunate of magicians, he began humbly as a backup character in somebody else's comic book in the early 1960s. Gradually, though, the popularity of the Master of Mystic Arts increased, and by the late 1960s he had a title of his own. Though never as popular as the top Marvel superheroes born during the SILVER AGE, Dr. Strange has been able to keep working, with a few layoffs along the way, for the past three decades.

Dreamed up by Stan Lee, and initially drawn by Steve Ditko, the scholarly sorcerer entered comics by way of a five-page story in Marvel's STRANGE TALES #110 (July 1963). At the time, the leading character in the magazine was the new Human Torch. Lee cited as one of his sources of inspiration the radio serial *Chandu the Magician*, which first aired in the early 1930s. In that serial, American Frank Chandler learned the secrets of magic in the mysterious East. Similarly, eminent and arrogant Dr. Stephen Strange found his way to India after an accident ends his medical career. There he studied with a world-class mystic known as the Ancient One.

Back in America, Dr. Strange set up shop as a sort of consulting ghostbuster. Among his frequent early opponents were Baron Mordo, a turncoat pupil of the doctor's own old mentor, and Nightmare, a nasty straggler from the realm of dreams.

Ditko rendered the doctor's supernatural caseload in inventive ways, assimilating some of the techniques of the psychedelic posters of the 1960s. As Gerard Jones has pointed out in *The Encyclopedia of American Comics*, "Although *Dr. Strange* was never a big hit with superhero readers, it dazzled Marvel's growing number of collegiate and 'hippie' readers, including many underground cartoonists, who were convinced that Ditko and Lee were secretly sharing drug-induced hallucinations with them (a notion that no doubt would have shocked the gentlemen themselves)."

Dr. Strange's popularity continued to grow. He became the star of *Strange Tales*. Then the magazine's title was changed to *Dr. Strange* with #169 (June 1968). Except for one hiatus, that title continued until 1987. Late in 1988 came a new comic called *Dr. Strange, Sorcerer Supreme.*

Among the other artists and writers who contributed to the doctor's long, successful saga are Frank Brunner, Roy Thomas, and Jim Starlin.

DOLL MAN   *See* Feature Comics.

DONALD DUCK   A goodly portion of the success this foul-tempered fowl has enjoyed in comic books is due to one man. That man is Carl Barks, one of the few certifiable geniuses in the comics field. Although the Donald had been in funny books since 1935, it was not until Barks came into his life in 1942 that he began to blossom as a newsstand rival to the likes of SUPERMAN, BATMAN, and CAPTAIN MARVEL. Barks revitalized Donald Duck, spruced up his puckish nephews, and, for good measure, created Uncle Scrooge.

Donald Duck, with the memorable voice characterization supplied by Clarence Nash, was introduced to the world in 1934 in the Disney short *The Wise Little Hen*. Starting out in bit parts, the short-fused duck fought his way up to a starring position by 1937. He was first seen in newspaper comic sections in 1934 and was part of the lineup of *Mickey Mouse Magazine* when it started in 1935 (see MICKEY MOUSE). His first appearances in *Walt Disney's Comics & Stories*, which started in 1940, were by way of reprints of Al Taliafero's newspaper strip.

Carl Barks gained his fame by drawing ducks, but because the ducks were the property of Walt Disney, he was never allowed to sign his work. Yet, because of the quality and individuality of what he did, he gradually became one of the best-known and most admired cartoonists in the world. Born in the wilds of Oregon, Barks worked as a gag cartoonist in the late 1920s and early 1930s and then went to work for the Disney studios. Although initally hired as an in-betweener, Barks quickly displayed an inventiveness that convinced the studio that he was better suited for the story department. He remained there until the early 1940s, when he decided to quit Disney and try his hand at something else.

That something else turned out to be comic books. Before leaving Disney, Barks (along with artist Jack Hannah) had worked on a one-shot 1942 comic book titled *Donald Duck Finds Pirate Gold*, written by Bob Karp. Based on a never-produced animated cartoon, it was the first original Donald Duck comic book. Late that same year, Barks heard that Dell-Western wanted somebody to do original 10-page stories to be added to *Walt Disney's Comics and Stories*. He was hired, and his first Donald Duck original appeared in issue #31 (April 1943).

Soon after, Barks was writing as well as drawing. His most notable innovation was to broaden Donald's character. "Instead of making just a quarrelsome little guy out of him, I made him a sympathetic character," Barks recalled once. "He was sometimes a villain, and he was often a real good guy and at all times he was just a blundering person like the average human being." Donald's three nephews—Huey, Dewey, and Louie—underwent changes, too, becoming resourceful and inventive. "I broadened them like I did Donald, started out with mischievous little guys and ended up with little scientists, you might say."

Barks added full-length Donald books to his schedule in 1943. It was in the stories produced from this point onward—"The Mummy's Ring," "Frozen Gold," "Volcano Valley," etc.—that he hit his stride. With plenty of space to move around in, he created carefully plotted graphic novels. The stories were full of adventure, action, comedy, and satire. They were set in exotic locales and featured some of the best cartooning and visual storytelling ever to be found in comic books. A 1947 adventure called "Christmas on Bear Mountain" introduced Barks's major creation: Uncle Scrooge. Penurious, paranoid about protecting his vast fortune from the scheming Beagle Boys and other threats, Scrooge was nonetheless basically likable and was gruffly fond of Donald and the nephews.

Other characters that Barks brought to life included Gyron Gearloose and the supremely insincere Gladstone Gander.

Barks retired at the age of 65. Since Walt Disney's death in 1966, his contribution to the duck saga has been publicly acknowledged by comic book publishers and by the Disney organization. Barks's material has been frequently reprinted over the years. In addition, both the Gladstone line of comics and the Disney line have introduced new Donald and Uncle Scrooge stories. Most notable among the new artist-writers, and the closest in spirit to Barks, has been William Van Horn.

DON WINSLOW The stalwart Navy man, along with his pudgy sidekick Red Pennington, was first seen in a newspaper comic strip. Signed by Lt. Commander Frank V. Martinek of the Naval Reserve and produced by Carl Hammond and Leon Beroth, *Don Winslow of the Navy* began as a daily in 1934. Next the strip was reprinted, first as one of the features in POPULAR COMICS, starting in 1936, and then in *Crackajack Funnies*, starting in 1938. There were also two one-shot reprints devoted to Don and Red and their battles against such threats to the nation's security as the master spy known only as the Scorpion.

Early in 1943, Fawcett made the unusual move of issuing a monthly comic book featuring brand-new adventures of the seagoing hero drawn especially for the magazine. The Don of the comic books was a more serious fellow, and the stories concentrated mostly on wartime combat and hardware rather than the flamboyant villains of the funny papers.

Edd Ashe drew the majority of the early stories, followed by John Jordan and Carl

Pfeufer. Fawcett published its last issue in 1951 and Charlton revived the title briefly in 1955.

Don Winslow, Edd Ashe–John Jordan, © 1943 Fawcett Publications, Inc.

DOOM PATROL DC's Doom Patrol first appeared in 1963, three months before the X-MEN. Like Marvel's considerably more successful group, they are a gang of misfits presided over by a genius in a wheelchair.

The Doom Patrol first set up shop in *My Greatest Adventure* #80 (June 1963). They were recruited by a crippled, red-bearded mastermind known as the Chief. The original bunch consisted of Robot Man, a mechanical man with a human brain; Elasti-Girl, who suffered from a sort of PLASTIC MAN affliction and could grow to great height or shrink down to an extremely small size; Negative Man, who could send out a dark, negative-energy duplicate of himself for up to 60 minutes. (If his negative self didn't get back together with his positive self in an hour, he'd die.) Arnold Drake wrote the series, and it was drawn by Bruno Premiani, an Italian-born, Argentina-raised illustrator who brought an appealing realism to Drake's entertaining, though somewhat peculiar, stories. Although clearly inspired by the needling character interplay that turned Marvel's FANTASTIC FOUR into a hit, the Doom Patrol developed a special weirdness of its own by emphasizing story elements such as disembodied brains, superannuated militarists, and a whole parade of villains with physical deformities.

Because readers responded positively to the group, *My Greatest Adventure* was retitled *The Doom Patrol* with #86 and remained in business until the fall of 1968. The team returned briefly by way of reprints in 1973 and again in the early 1980s. In 1987, DC introduced a new *Doom Patrol* monthly. With the nineteenth issue, Grant Morrison became the writer and the organization entered its most bizarre phase to date.

DOUBLE COMICS   A venture of the Elliot Publishing Company of Manhattan, it offered 128 pages for just 10¢ and was the biggest bargain of the early 1940s. Publisher Albert Kanter was able to do this because he simply rebound the remaindered comics of other publishers under a new cover. The enterprising Kanter introduced *Double Comics* in 1940 and followed it the next year with *Classic Comics* (see CLASSICS ILLUSTRATED)

There were usually two or three issues of *Double* per year that packaged, as Robert Overstreet has explained, "an endless combination of pairs of remaindered unsold issues." The same cover might conceal all sorts of different couplings, a *Captain America* and a DETECTIVE COMICS, a *Mystery Men* and a *Weird Comics*, etc. The covers of the recycled comics usually featured superheroes who were to be found nowhere else. Among them were the White Flash, the Green Light, and Tornado Tim. In 1941, Elliot also put out a single issue of *Double-Up Comics*, which consisted of two rebound digest-sized comic books. The final issues of *Double* appeared in 1944.

Fawcett tried a similar venture with *Xmas Comics* in 1941, binding copies of *WHIZ*, *Master*, and *Wow*, etc., into a huge 324-page comic that retailed for 50¢. According to Overstreet, the same issues appeared in every copy and had been especially printed and set aside for that purpose. Later editions of the seasonal annual were slimmer.

DRACULA   The world's favorite vampire was introduced in Bram Stoker's novel *Dracula* in 1897. He reached the Broadway stage in 1927 and was first seen upon the silver screen, in the definitive performance of Bela Lugosi, early in 1931. The deathless count did not, however, appear in a regularly issued comic book of his own until 1972, when Marvel introduced *The Tomb of Dracula*. The artist for the entire run was Gene Colan and the writer for most of that time was Marv Wolfman.

There had been numerous comic book vampires before Dracula found regular work, especially in the heyday of horror in the early 1950s. Even the count himself had appeared sporadically. As comics historian Lou Mougin has pointed out, "Adaptions of *Dracula*, both the novel and the character, had been around for at least 20 years before Marvel's version." Avon had used the count in *Eerie* in 1953, Dell issued an adaption in its Movie Classics series in time for Halloween of 1962, and *Creepy* featured a two-part Dracula tale by Archie Goodwin and Reed Crandall in the mid-1960s. The oddest use of the character name occurred late in 1966, when Dell issued a Dracula comic book in which he appeared as a costumed superhero who vaguely resembled BATMAN. Tony Tallarico drew all three issues and also did Dell's other ill-advised superhero titles—*Frankenstein* and *Werewolf* (see FRANKENSTEIN).

The Marvel version of Dracula was set in the 1970s and dealt with a Lord of Vampires who "spreads his reign of terror across a twentieth century world." The Colan–Wolfman count was a nasty, brutal fellow with a mustache who had none of the Continental manners and sly humor of the Lugosi characterization. Among those who pursued him through the continued narrative were Rachel Van Helsing, a blonde young woman who was a descendant of Dracula's original nemesis, and Blade the Vampire Stalker, a costumed ghostbuster. The title was relatively successful and lasted for 70 issues before expiring in 1979.

Dracula®, Gene Colan. All Marvel characters and the distinctive likenesses thereof are trademarks of Marvel Entertainment Group, Inc. and are used with permission. © 1992 Marvel Entertainment Group, Inc.

THE DURANGO KID   He began his career in 1940 on the silver screen. Veteran action actor Charles Starrett portrayed the masked, black-clad avenger in a series of 60 Westerns that lasted until 1952. The profusely perspiring Smiley Burnette was his most frequent sidekick. In 1949, when many comic books were deciding to go West, Magazine Enterprises (ME) introduced a *Durango Kid* title. It ran for 41 issues and ceased in the fall of 1955.

The early issues used photo covers of Starrett in costume, black bandana masking the lower part of his face, and had an overline proclaiming him "the movies' most colorful Western star." The stories were set in the post–Civil War West, and the Kid's sidekick was a Burnette-like fellow named Muley Pike. Steve Brand was the rambling cowboy who changed into a masked avenger when trouble arose. (In the movies, the scriptwriters had never agreed as to what Steve's last name was.)

Joe Certa drew the initial stories. With the 19th issue, the dependable Fred Guardineer became the artist. One of the magazine's backup features was *Dan Brand*, about a "white Indian," which was drawn for a time by Frank Frazetta.

Durango also appeared in ME's *Best of the West* and *Great Western*.

The Durango Kid, Fred Guardineer, © 1954 by Magazine Enterprises.

THE EAGLE He first flew into view in publisher Victor Fox's *Science Comics* #1 (February 1940) and was last seen in the fourth issue of his own magazine (January 1942). Originally, a young scientist named Bill Powers came up with "specially made wings which enable him to fly" and took to flying around "at a tremendous pace" to swoop down on crooks and criminals. He wore a simple, basic hero costume that was, depending on the colorist, either red or blue.

When Powers moved over to *Weird Comics* in the autumn of 1940, he changed the look of his costume, abandoned the wings, and modified his abilities. Readers were now told that he had "discovered an anti-gravitation fluid which he spreads on his cape." He also picked up a boy companion who was known as Buddy the Daredevil Boy. Buddy initially had no costume and fought crime wearing what looked to be his underwear. Since Buddy apparently didn't spray the anti-grav solution on this outfit, he couldn't fly. The Eagle soared through the air carrying him piggyback.

Eventually, perhaps by default, the Eagle became the star of *Weird*. His costume then turned patriotic, featuring blue cowl, tunic, and tights, red shorts and boots, and a red-and-white striped cape. For good measure, there was a golden eagle on his chest. At this point the Eagle operated as a superpatriot and

The Eagle, Ramona Patenaude, © 1941 Fox Publications, Inc.

concentrated on battling Nazis who were trying to invade, sabotage, and otherwise futz up America.

A member of the Army Reserve, Powers was called to active service in the spring of 1941 and became a captain in something called the Bureau of Military Intelligence. Buddy, now a Boy Scout, was somehow allowed to tag along to various military camps. The duo's duties never prevented them from suiting up. Buddy's uniform was now a smaller replica of his guardian's. Unfortunately for a feature so patriotic, it died just as America entered World War II.

Among the artists who drew the feature were Dick Briefer, Louis Cazeneuve, Al Carreño, and Edd Ashe.

ECLIPSO Combining elements of such well-known dual identity characters as Dr. Jekyll and the Wolf Man, and also clearly inspired by THE HULK, he made his debut in DC's *House of Secrets* #61 (August 1963). Writer Bob Haney, with an assist from editor Murray Boltinoff, created *Eclipso*. Lee Elias was the initial artist, soon followed by Alex Togh and then Jack Sparling.

As an early caption explained it "the vast unknown powers of the sun and moon combined with a freakish fate to divide Dr. Bruce Gordon into two beings—one dedicated to humanity—the other to ruthless destruction!" The freakish fate befell blond, young Dr. Gordon on the aptly named Diablo Island where he'd gone to study a solar eclipse. An unfortunate encounter with a local wizard resulted in his being slashed with a mysterious black diamond as the eclipse unfolded. From then on "every time he is within the area of an eclipse, Dr. Bruce Gordon becomes the demon ECLIPSO!"

Eclipso was a bestial fellow, with one side of his face tinted blue to symbolize his double nature. He wore a purple and black costume, based on that of the local mystic back on the island. He was devoted to crime and violence, mayhem and destruction. All in all, he caused the clean-cut Dr. Gordon endless grief.

Billed as "hero and villain in one man," Eclipso hung out in *House of Secrets* until the summer of 1966 and then temporarily retired. He has returned at intervals ever since. In 1992 DC brought him back with a bang in a title of his own and in a multi-issue adventure titled *Eclipso: The Darkness Within*. This pitted Eclipso against a virtual army of superheroes and was played out in assorted titles, including some of those devoted to SUPERMAN, WONDER WOMAN and the GREEN LANTERN.

ELONGATED MAN A supersleuth whose method of operation was similar to that of PLASTIC MAN and FANTASTIC FOUR's Reed Richards, he was introduced in *Detective Comics* #327 (May 1964). Elongated Man was the creation of writer Gardner Fox and artist Carmine Infantino.

The stretchable sleuth was a redhaired fellow named Ralph Dibny who had "devoted his life to solving the world's strangest mysteries." Unlike the majority of comic book heroes, he was married. Accompanied by his wife Sue, he traveled the world and always managed, as *The Comic Book Heroes* points out, to arrive in "a new town just in time to encounter a puzzling new mystery." Although the cases of the Dibnys were light in tone, they never came near matching the later Jack Cole Plastic Man adventures for zaniness or comedy. Nor did the Elongated Man ever encounter problems of the cosmic kind that Richards and the rest of the Four routinely solved.

The malleable manhunter left *Detective* after #383 (January 1969). But he and the missus have returned to comics now and again since then. Early in 1992, for instance, DC brought forth a four-issue *Elongated Man* mini-series. Scripts were by Gerard Jones, artwork by Mike Parobeck and Ty Templeton. That time around the Dibnys were visiting Paris.

ESPIONAGE   Starring a dashing master spy known as Black X, it first appeared in *Feature Funnies* (later *Feature Comics*) in the summer of 1938. The following summer it moved over to the brand new *Smash Comics*, remaining in the magazine for a decade. *Espionage* was one of the earliest series created by Will Eisner.

It's likely that Eisner was influenced by Alfred Hitchcock's 1936 *The Secret Agent*, which was based on W. Somerset Maugham's *Ashenden*. Initially, Eisner favored mythical countries, but he made use of many images of real war. Black X was a dapper fellow with a moustache and a monocle. Sometimes aided by a turbaned associate named Batu, he fluctuated between domestic sabotage cases and missions involving intrigue in "a little seaport of the war-torn Orient" or a tussle with "a foreign pirate submarine" that was sinking American ships.

In the early issues of *Smash* the super spy was called Black Ace, but he reverted to his original alias within a few months. This version of *Espionage* was gloomier and dealt with a more violent world. In one episode Eisner commented that "once more, the blood stained fields of Europe resound with the marching of men...Cities that took centuries to build are destroyed over night ... All is sacrificed to the greatest of follies." He didn't, though, abandon the trappings of the genre. A frequent opponent, for example, was a beautiful lady spy named Madame Doom. Real countries were now named, Germany, Japan, France, and Black X operated in such cities as Washington, D.C. and Paris.

Eisner left the feature fairly soon and among the other artists who drew it were Dan Zolnerowich, Alex Kotzky, and Don Rico. After the war, X and Batu still found plenty of intrigue to occupy them in all corners of the world. *Espionage* was last seen in *Smash* #85 (October 1949).

EXCITING COMICS   The main contribution of this Pines pulphouse title was the introduction of THE BLACK TERROR, who came along in issue #9 (May 1941). The magazine started early in 1940 and made it through 69 issues before expiring in the summer of 1949. In its final years, *Exciting*, exemplifying the changes the comic book business was undergoing in the years immediately after World War II, starred a jungle girl and then a cowboy.

Before the arrival of the Black Terror, the magazine had offered readers a mix of pulp-inspired fare that included a masked crimefighter known as the Mask, a daring explorer named Ted Crane, and a planet-hopping team called the Space Rovers. During the war, the Liberator and the American Eagle, both super patriots, were added. The Terror remained the star of *Exciting* until #55 (May 1947), when Judy of the Jungle came aboard.

The redhaired jungle queen took over the cover spot for nearly the next two years, a sure sign she'd usurped the Black Terror's leading position. Very much in the SHEENA tradition, Judy's adventures unfolded in a movie matinee venue of Africa "on the fringe of the veldt near the Yazoo River." The "jungle-born daughter of an American naturalist," Judy often teamed up with handsome Pistol Roberts, a jungle ranger, to combat the evil white hunters, misguided movie makers and leopard-worshipping savages that tried to cause trouble in her patch of wilderness.

Judy was but one of the wild women added to the company's titles in the late 1940s. Princess Pantha joined the lineup of *Thrilling Comics* during this same period and Tygra took up residence in *Startling*.

Early in 1949 Judy was nudged from the top spot by a cowboy hero named Billy West. Evidently *Exciting* was hoping to cash in on yet another postwar trend. The magazine, however, ceased publication in the summer of that same year.

THE FACE   A creation of the prolific Gardner Fox, and drawn by Mart Bailey, he began his career of frightening crooks and decent folks alike in the first issue of *Big Shot Comics* (May 1940). He wasn't a superhero; all the Face had to work with was a spooky mask. It was a rubberoid thing and represented a leering, fanged creature with green skin, bright-orange hair, and blank, shadow-rimmed eyes. When popular radio commentator Tony Trent donned it, he looked like the nasty half of the Jekyll–Hyde team.

Fox described the mask as grim, fantastic, gruesome, and "the stuff of tortured nightmares." Everybody, criminals and honest citizens alike, was revolted by the looks of the Face. Typical reactions upon seeing him included "Aagh! Aagh!", "Eeeee! Eeeee!", "Gorsh—it's awful!", and "Oh, my goodness!" Trent wore a tuxedo while on the air and merely added the mask to his ensemble to turn into a crimefighter. Using fright as his main weapon—though he was also handy with a gun—he hounded the underworld.

The Face caught kidnappers, exposed political crooks, rounded up gangsters, and generally bedeviled the lawless. All of his escapades provided material for Tony Trent's broadcasts. Babs Walsh, a pretty chestnut-haired young woman who worked as his secretary, was the only one who knew Trent was leading a double life. Eventually they were married.

During World War II, Trent served as a war correspondent in the Pacific. Bailey had

The Face, Mart Bailey, unpublished.

taken over the scripting and constructed a complex serial narrative where the mask passed from hand to hand and was worn at various times by different characters. By 1946, with a couple of nostalgic exceptions, the mask was gone. The feature changed its name to *Tony Trent* and as such it continued until *Big Shot* folded in the summer of 1949.

FAMOUS FUNNIES   It was the first regularly published comic book in the standard format and the cornerstone of what was to be one of the most lucrative branches of magazine publishing. *Famous Funnies* got off to a fairly shaky start in the early 1930s and didn't get out of the red until it had been in business for more than half a year. For anyone who had a dime in the Depression year of 1934, the magazine offered dozens of strips, all of them from newspapers. The roster included *Joe Palooka, Dixie Dugan, Connie, Hairbreadth Harry, Mutt & Jeff*, and, from the third issue on, *Buck Rogers* (see MUTT & JEFF). The covers promised "100 comics and games."

The chief inventor of the four-color, modern comic book was a man named Harry I. Wildenberg. The Eastern Color Printing Company of Waterbury, Connecticut, employed him as a sales manager. Among many other jobs, Eastern Color printed the Sunday comic sections for several East Coast papers. Wildenberg, who had an advertising background, first thought of using the funnies as advertising premiums. He sold Gulf Oil on the idea of giving away a tabloid-sized book of comics at its gas stations, and that proved a successful gimmick. In contemplating extensions of comics as a premium, Wildenberg and some of his associates noticed that reduced Sunday pages they'd made as a promotion for the *Philadelphia Ledger* would fit two to a page on the standard tabloid-sized sheet of paper. After further fiddling and figuring, Wildenberg worked out a way to use Eastern's presses to print 64-page color comic books.

Wildenberg, with the help of an Eastern

salesman named M.C. Gaines, interested other advertisers in using comic books as premiums. They produced books for Procter & Gamble, Canada Dry, Kinney Shoes, Wheatena, and other companies with kid-oriented products. These giveaway editions usually had print runs ranging from 100,000 to 250,000. Wildenberg and Gaines then considered sticking a 10¢ price tag on comic books and selling them directly to children. They approached the Woolworth's chain as a possible outlet but were told that 64 pages of old comics wasn't enough value for 10¢. Eventually, in 1934, they persuaded the American News Company to distribute a monthly comic book to newsstands across the country. The new magazine was called *Famous Funnies*, a title Wildenberg had originally thought up for a soap company premium. Although the initial issue sold 90 percent of its 200,000 print run, Eastern Color lost over $4,000 on it. But by issue #12, *Famous* was starting to net $30,000 every month.

Editorial offices for the fledgling magazine were set up in Manhattan. Although Harold A. Moore, a longtime Eastern Color employee, was listed as editor, the actual editor of *Famous Funnies* throughout its entire long run was Stephen A. Douglas. Brooklyn-born Douglas was working as a professional cartoonist before he even reached his teens. He was in his late twenties when he went to work as an editor and production manager for *Famous*. During its early days, the magazine reprinted mostly Sunday pages. Besides those mentioned above, there were *Tailspin Tommy, The Bungle Family, Jane Arden* (complete with paper dolls), and *The Nebbs*.

Gradually some original filler pages began to show up. The earliest contributor was Victor E. Pazmino, who signed himself VEP. A man with an affinity for being in on the ground floor, VEP had contributed to THE FUNNIES in 1929. For *Famous* he drew a monthly page of gag cartoons and then a page about Seaweed Sam, a bubble-nosed sailor who was fond of traveling and of speaking in verse. VEP also drew nearly all the covers during the magazine's first seven years.

As it moved into its third year, *Famous Funnies* made quite a few changes in content. Several of the top Associated Press daily strips, including *Scorchy Smith*, *Dickie Dare*, and *Oaky Doaks*, were added. By the end of the 1930s, the magazine had a lineup that included, in addition to the AP strips and *Buck Rogers*, *Roy Powers*, *Eagle Scout* by Frank Godwin, *Skyroads* by Russell Keaton, and *Big Chief Wahoo* by Allen Saunders and Elmer Woggon.

After a brief fling in the early 1940s with an original superhero named Fearless Flint, *Famous* stuck pretty much with reprints. The final issue was #218 (July 1955). It was a slim 32 pages and contained no reprints save those of *Buck Rogers*. Appropriately enough, a television set figured prominently on the final cover.

Despite the fact that Eastern Color had invented the modern comic book, the company was content to concentrate on printing rather than publishing. Their Famous Funnies, Inc. subsidiary generated relatively few other titles. In the early 1940s came *Heroic* and JINGLE JANGLE and later in the decade, when teen-oriented titles were popular, the unsuccessful *Club 16* and *Jukebox*. In the early 1950s, *Personal Love* and *Movie Love* were introduced. The latter offered adaptions of current motion pictures and during its five-year run included everything from "September Affair" and "Two Weeks With Love" to "Let's Dance" and "I Love Melvin." Their final title was *Tales from the Great Book*, adapted from John Lehti's biblical newspaper Sunday page. That lasted four issues and folded six months after *Famous Funnies* itself.

Famous Funnies, Ben Thompson, © 1942 Famous Funnies, Inc.

FANTASTIC FOUR   This highly influential group was introduced in the fall of 1961. *Fantastic Four #1*, put together by editor-writer Stan Lee and artist Jack Kirby, represented the official entry of Marvel into the SILVER AGE superhero field, and the extremely popular book changed the fortunes and futures of Marvel, Lee, and Kirby.

Late in 1961, according to Lee, publisher Martin Goodman mentioned that he had noticed that one of the titles published by National Comics (DC's name at the time) seemed to be selling better than most. "It was a book called *The Justice League of America* and was composed of a team of superheroes (See THE JUSTICE LEAGUE OF AMERICA). Well, we didn't need a house to fall on us. 'If *The Justice League of America* is selling,' spake he, 'why don't we put out a comic book that features a team of superheroes?'"

Lee has said, "I would create a team of superheroes if that was what the marketplace required. But it would be a team such as comicdom had never known. For just this once, I would do the type of story I myself would enjoy reading . . . and the kind of characters I could personally relate to; they'd be flesh and blood, they'd have faults and foibles, they'd be fallible and feisty, and—most important of

Fantastic Four®, John Byrne. All Marvel characters and the distinctive likenesses thereof are trademarks of Marvel Entertainment Group, Inc. and are used with permission. © 1992 Marvel Entertainment Group, Inc.

all—inside their colorful, costumed booties they'd still *have feet of clay."*

Lee picked Kirby to work on the new project and they devised a quartet that was composed of Mr. Fantastic, Human Torch, Invisible Girl, and the Thing (see ALL WINNERS COMICS). Or, at first glance, variations on PLASTIC MAN, the original Torch, Invisible Scarlet O'Neil of the funny papers, and one more *Tales to Astonish* monster. But what excited Lee was his discovery of "the in-depth characterization that was to become a Marvel trademark." He didn't have it all worked out yet, but he suspected that superheroes struggling not only with supervillains but with the sort of personal

problems that plagued ordinary mortals ought to be interesting.

Fantastic Four #1 turned out to be the cornerstone for the entire Marvel Comics empire. Comics historian Gary M. Carter has said that it "changed the way we think of superheroes forever." The magazine had a continuing influence and, in the opinion of Gerard Jones, "nearly all modern superhero comics . . . have drawn and continue to draw upon the first 80 or so issues of *Fantastic Four* for inspiration and material."

Kirby remained with the Fantastic Four for nearly a decade, Lee a couple of years longer. Various artists and writers have worked on the feature since, including John Byrne, Arthur Adams, and Walt Simonson.

FANTOMAH   One of the most formidable ladies ever to grace the pages of a comic book, Fantomah began her career as the "Mystery Woman of the Jungle" in *Jungle Comics* #2 (February 1940).

An early caption explained some of her unsettling traits: "Fantomah, the most remarkable woman ever born, has such keen insight and so many supernatural powers, that she foresees all the events of jungle life. Through her strange wizardry, she guards the jungle's secrets and avenges the evil deeds against the jungle-born." One of her most disturbing knacks was the ability to detach her head, turn it into a skull, and cause it to go floating along after her intended victim. Seeing that glowing blonde-haired skull scowling through the foliage struck terror in many a heart. An unusually large number of crazed scientists found their way to her part of the jungle and Fantomah was kept busy outwitting the resultant super-gorillas and giant reptiles.

Another frightening aspect of the feature was the artwork of Henry Fletcher. A true primitive, he drew like a sort of deranged Grandma Moses. There's been no one like him since. Those who've never seen Fletcher's depiction of a pack of giant hypnotized phos-

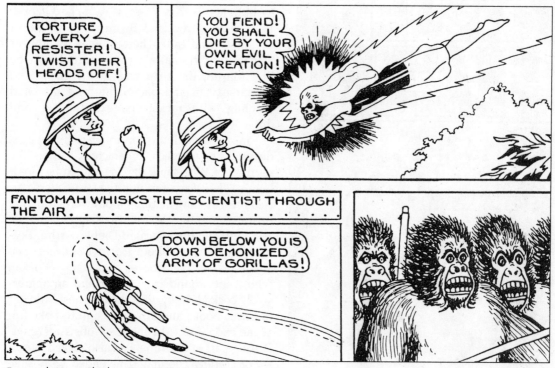

Fantomah, Henry Fletcher, © 1940 Fiction House, Inc.

phorescent reptiles eating a jungle city or his rendering of Fantomah's causing "thousands of gigantic royal panthers" to go flying through the air haven't experienced all that fantasy art has to offer.

After Fletcher departed, Fantomah soon became but a shadow of her former self. Eventually she turned into another character altogether and took to calling herself "Daughter of the Pharaohs" and hanging out in ancient Egypt. She was last seen in *Jungle* #51 (March 1944).

FAT & SLAT   *See* Minute Movies.

FEATURE COMICS   The initial title in what was to be Everett "Busy" Arnold's Quality line, it was a magazine that changed its policy and its name in midstream. Starting life in the fall of 1937 as *Feature Funnies*, it was basically a reprint title in the style of FAMOUS FUNNIES and

POPULAR COMICS. Less than two years later, when its title was switched to *Feature Comics*, several original characters were to be found in the magazine's pages.

Although the majority of the contents was reprint material—such as *Joe Palooka*, *Dixie Dugan*, *Mickey Finn*, and Ed Wheelan's *Big Top*—*Feature* did use some original stuff from the start. In the third issue, for instance, THE CLOCK began appearing. George Brenner's dapper, masked sleuth was already a comic book veteran, having appeared in such titles as FUNNY PAGES and *Funny Picture Stories*. Among the other pioneering heroes were Jim Swift, Clip Chance, and the Gallant Knight. Will Eisner, hiding behind the name Will Erwin, created *Espionage*. It starred a suave mustached and monocled chap who was known in secret agent circles as Black X. He operated out of the magazine from #13 (October 1938) through #22 (July 1939) and then jumped over to the just-starting *Smash Comics*.

Feature Comics, Al Bryant–Gill Fox, © 1943 by Comic Favorites, Inc.

to uphold the American Way." The October 1941 issue introduced Swing Sisson, one of the few bandleader heroes ever to appear in comics. Originally written and drawn by Phil Martin, the strip was in the crime and detective vein and had Swing and his band tangling with racketeers, extortionists, and dope dealers.

In between all the heroics were filler pages devoted to comedy characters. After the reprints of Wheelan's *Big Top* and Rube Goldberg's *Lala Palooza* ran out, the strips were carried on with new material. Both were drawn in turn by Johnny Devlin, Goldberg's onetime assistant, and then Bernard Dibble. Arthur Beeman drew a page about *Homer Doodle and Son* and Gill Fox contributed *Poison Ivy*. Poison, who went around in a diaper and an aggressively cocked derby, was the toughest little kid in comic books and Fox used him to poke fun at the excesses of the more serious superguys. During part of this time, Fox also served as editor of *Feature*. The magazine ended with issue #144 (May 1950).

In December 1939, *Feature* got its first superhero, and a teeny-weeny one at that. The strip was drawn by Lou Fine and written by Eisner under the name William Erwin Maxwell. Doll Man, who stood about six inches high in his stocking feet, had a successful career that stretched across nearly a decade and a half. He was in *Feature Comics* until its 139th issue (October 1949) and starred in a magazine of his own from 1941 until late in 1953. Besides the exceptional Lou Fine, Doll Man was drawn by such capable artists as Reed Crandall and John Spranger.

Among the other later additions to the lineup were a ghostbreaker named Zero, a blond jungle man called Samar, and an adventurous youth named Rusty Ryan. Rusty eventually teamed up with some of his orphan chums to form a gang of uniformed vigilantes known as the Boyville Brigadiers—"Pledged

FIREHAIR A redheaded heroine of the Old West and much admired by collectors of GOOD GIRL ART, she was first seen in Fiction House's *Rangers Comics* #21 (February 1945). Billed as a "Frontier Queen" and the "Flame Girl of the Wild West," among other things, Firehair eventually became the star of the magazine. Beginning with issue #40 (April 1948), she was featured on every cover until her departure in the spring of 1952. All scripts were attributed to the house name John Starr. The initial artist was Lee Elias, who was followed by Bob Lubbers.

Like many a character in Western novels and cowboy movies, Firehair had been raised by Indians after the death of her parents. Adopted by the Dakota tribe that took her in, she remained with them after reaching maturity. Clad in a skimpy buckskin dress, she acted as a champion of her people and helped them battle against the continuous stream of predatory white men who sought to murder, cheat, rob, and take advantage of them. Since Fiction House also published pulp magazines, they always stuck flamboyant pulpwood titles on the Girl of the Golden West's adventures, such as "The Outlaw Pack of Hangman's Mesa," "Massacre Guns at Pawnee Pass," and "Brides of the Buffalo Men."

Firehair remained in *Rangers* through issue #65 (June 1952). She was also featured in 11 issues of her own magazine between 1948 and 1952.

THE BLAZE SHOOTS UP BRILLIANTLY.. AND FROM THE BLINDING GLARE, THE FLAME APPEARS.. GRADUALLY TAKING NORMAL SHAPE..

The Flame, Lou Fine, © 1940 Fox Publications, Inc.

THE FLAME He burst forth in WONDERWORLD COMICS #3 (July 1939). The initial adventures of the yellow-clad superman were handsomely rendered by Lou Fine, but the Flame was a slow starter and took several issues to get his act together. When he first showed up, he didn't appear to have any superpowers at all—despite his name—and racketeers asked him questions like, "Who are you? What do you want?" In subsequent issues, he displayed an ability to materialize out of smoke and flame.

Well over another year went by before he really began living up to his name and revealed a hitherto-unsuspected knack for bursting into flame, burning through walls, etc. In *Wonderworld* #30 (October 1941), the Flame made another addition to his mode of operation by taking on a female companion. Known as Flame Girl, she stuck with him until the magazine folded after three more issues.

The Flame also appeared in Victor Fox's *Big 3* and in eight issues of a magazine of his own. Among the other artists who rendered his adventures were Al Carreño, Larry Antonette, and Louis Cazeneuve. The character was revived, briefly, in the mid-1950s and again in 1991.

THE FLASH Two separate and distinct superheroes, both dubbed the Fastest Man Alive, have used this name. The first Flash began in the winter of 1939 as the GOLDEN AGE was getting under way, the second appeared late in the summer of 1956 and was the herald of the SILVER AGE. Thanks to DC's liberal cosmology, each Flash is still to be found in comic books.

The original Flash debuted in *Flash Comics* #1 (January 1940), a title he shared with such characters as JOHNNY THUNDER, the Whip, and HAWKMAN. In the origin story, scripted by Gardner Fox and drawn by Harry Lampert, readers learned that college science student Jay Garrick came by his incredible speed after accidentally inhaling "the deadly fumes of the gas elements of 'heavy water.'" The first thing he did with his new swiftness was join the football team to impress his blonde girlfriend Joan Williams. Unlike less bright comic book ladies, Joan was fully aware that Garrick was also the Flash. Once he became a practicing superhero, she was not above asking him to do her a favor on occasion.

Lampert left the feature after the second issue and was replaced by Everett E. Hibbard, who did an effective job. Gradually Fox moved away from completely straight continuities and began to indulge in a certain amount of kidding and satire with the Flash. Hal Sharp ghosted some of the artwork in the early 1940s, as did the inimitable Louis Ferstadt.

The Flash, whose costume consisted of a red tunic with a lightning bolt on the front, blue tights, winged red boots, and a winged hat in the Mercury fashion, branched out and appeared in ALL STAR COMICS, *All-Flash*, and COMIC CAVALCADE. Among the others who drew him during his Golden Age go-round were Joe Kubert, Lee Elias, Alex Toth, and Carmine Infantino. The Flash left comics for the first time in 1949.

In 1956, while other editors were contemplating new genres, DC's Julius Schwartz's thoughts were turning again to superheroes. The first hero he took out of mothballs was the Flash. "Someone, I don't know who, said, 'The Flash was always one of my favorites and maybe we ought to take a crack at putting him out again.' All eyes turned to me," Schwartz once recalled. "So I said, 'OK, I'm stuck.' For some reason, I decided not to revive the original Flash, but to do a *new* Flash with the same power, super-speed. I think I wanted to do an origin, which I always found fascinating, and I didn't like the original. I worked out a story with Bob Kanigher—new costume, new secret identity, new origin. The Flash's name, Barry Allen, came from two show business personalities, Steve Allen and Barry Gray. The thing I like best about what we did is that the Flash got his inspiration of naming himself for a comic book character he read as a kid after he got doused with that lightning bolt and realized he had super-speed himself."

The revamped Fastest Man Alive was introduced in SHOWCASE #4 (September–October 1956). Carmine Infantino penciled, Joe Kubert inked. The new, improved Flash wore a bright-red costume that offered less wind resistance than that of his predecessor, mainly because he'd abandoned the tin hat with the wings on the sides. He zooms through *Showcase* #8, #13, and #14. Early in 1959, after proving he was a salable commodity, the Flash was granted a magazine of his own. Infantino remained the artist, John Broome became the scriptwriter.

The speed king got a boy sidekick in *Flash* #110 late in 1959, in the person of Wally West, aka Kid Flash. In *Flash* #123, the Golden Age Flash returned and teamed up with the newer speedster. "I had a discussion with Gardner Fox," Schwartz has said. "I said, 'Gardner, the easiest way to do it is to say you're in communication with another Earth, a parallel Earth in another dimension. Let the Flashes cross over and meet.' It was a breakthrough, to combine a Golden Age hero with a modern counterpart and have them team up." The parallel-universe gimmick not only enabled the two Flashes to work in tandem, it allowed the elder to have a career of his own once again. Over on his separate-but-equal Earth, Jay Garrick was now married to Joan Williams.

Although both Flashes have had periods of unemployment since the dawning of the Golden Age, both were working in the early 1990s.

THE FLY Never an especially impressive superhero, despite the fact that he was produced originally by the team of Joe Simon and Jack Kirby, the Fly has nonetheless recurred several times in the 30-plus years since his initial advent. He originated during the early days of the SILVER AGE, making his debut in Archie Comics' *Adventures of the Fly* in the summer of 1959. After being grounded in the mid-1960s, he rose again for a brief revival in the mid-1980s. In 1991, DC brought him back to be part of its Impact series.

According to Simon, the character began life in 1953 as Spiderman. Working with writer Jack Oleck and artist C.C. Beck, he concocted a feature about an orphan lad named Tommy Troy who turns into Spiderman by using a magic ring. Simon has admitted a similarity between their orphan and the equally alliterative Billy Batson (see CAPTAIN MARVEL). He has said that before submitting the character to the Alfred Harvey outfit, he decided to change the name to the Silver Spider. Harvey rejected it, but a few years later Simon dusted off the property, changed the character to the Fly, and sold it to the Archie people. At that point he brought in his old partner Kirby to do the drawing. Simon's account of the birth of the Fly, recounted in his 1990 autobiography, gives the impression that Kirby was not especially overwhelmed by the project.

The first issue of *The Fly*, dated August 1959, sported a Simon and Kirby cover and six inside adventures of the new character. The book was not exactly a hit, but sold well enough to persuade Archie to continue. Kirby, however, dissociated himself from the enterprise after the second issue. Simon, working with such artists as Jack Davis and Bob Powell, hung on through the fourth, when a disagreement with management caused him to depart. Most of the subsequent art was by either John Giunta or John Rosenberger. In the fifth issue, Tommy Troy grew up into an adult lawyer. In #14 (September 1961), he took on a partner named Fly Girl. The magazine stopped in the autumn of 1964 with its 30th issue.

Modifying his name, the hero returned in a *Fly Man* comic book in the spring of 1965, again partnered by Fly Girl. Jerry Siegel was providing the scripts, Paul Reinman the art. The Fly Man title, which also included guest turns by the likes of the Black Hood and THE SHIELD, made it through just nine bimonthly issues before halting in the summer of 1966. After sitting it out in limbo for close to two decades, the winged hero returned in the spring of 1983. Known once more as the Fly for this go-round, he fluttered through nine issues of his own magazine before being forced into retirement the following year. He looked considerably better during this brief reincarnation, particularly on the covers contributed by Rudy Nebres.

The Fly didn't have to wait as long for the next comeback. That took place in 1991, when DC reintroduced him as part of their Impact series. A high school boy once again in his civilian mode, his name was now Jason Troy. His source of superpower was not a ring but a fly-in-amber amulet. The creative team consisted of writer Len Strazewski and artists Mike Parobeck and Paul Fricke.

FOUR COLOR COMICS This was a blanket name used to identify the various one-shots and irregular series published by Dell from 1939 through 1962. There were 25 titles in the first run of Four Colors and over 1,300 in the second. Included under that banner were reprints of *Dick Tracy*, *Popeye*, and *Terry and the Pirates* and original-material comics ranging from characters such as Pogo and Bugs Bunny to Roy Rogers and TARZAN (See ANIMAL COMICS and LOONEY TUNES AND MERRIE MELODIES).

Dell began the initial series in 1939 with a *Dick Tracy* book. It wasn't until #19, a 1941 *Barney Google* reprint, that they actually started using the designation Four Color Comics on the books. In 1942 they began numbering all over again from 1. As Ernst and Mary Gerber point out in *The Photo-Journal Guide to Comic Books*, "The name 'Four Color' was used . . . until issue #102. However, the name [was used by fans] for the entire run."

Dell used its Four Color umbrella for a wide variety of infrequently issued titles such as *Rusty Riley*, *Uncle Wiggily*, *Henry*, *Gang Busters*, *The Brownies*, and *Wash Tubbs*. They also issued movie adaptions, from *Around the World in 80 Days* to *The Vikings*, in the Four Color line. Numerous television-show adaptions also ran, including *I Love Lucy, Leave It to*

Beaver, Sea Hunt, Wagon Train, Maverick, 77 Sunset Strip, and *The Real McCoys.* Among the artists doing the adaptions were Alex Toth and Dan Spiegle.

In addition, several titles auditioned as Four Colors before graduating to regular schedules of their own. Carl Barks's first *Donald Duck* and *Uncle Scrooge* issues appeared here, as did Jesse Marsh's first original *Tarzan* books and John Stanley's *Little Lulu* (See DONALD DUCK and LITTLE LULU). Walt Kelly contributed several titles. Besides the first *Pogo* books, he did *Easter with Mother Goose* and *Santa Claus Funnies.*

The last Four Color was #1,354, an adaption of the TV cartoon *Calvin and the Colonel* dated April 1962.

THE FOX AND THE CROW   This was a comedy team for more than a quarter of a century that first got together in a 1941 animated cartoon. Four years later, Fauntleroy Fox and Crawford Crow became the stars of DC's *Real Screen Comics.* In 1952 came a separate *The Fox and the Crow* title, which survived until 1968.

The Columbia cartoon that introduced the con man Crow and the gullible Fox was titled "The Fox and the Grapes." Released in December of 1941, it was directed by Frank Tashlin. Bob Wickersham took over the direction with the second Fox and Crow and stayed on to direct 16 more of them between 1942 and 1946. The Fox, a mild-mannered fellow, was the perennial mark of the cunning Crow. Wearing a derby, smoking a stogie, and talking with a Brooklyn accent, Crawford Crow devoted much of his energy to conning Fauntleroy Fox out of his money, his food, and just about anything else he possessed.

The animated series got off to a slow start, with one title in 1941 and one in 1942. But in 1943 Columbia turned out six Fox and Crow cartoons, followed by four in 1944.

When DC sent editor Whit Ellsworth to Hollywood to arrange for licensing animated characters, all the major funny animals, such as MICKEY MOUSE, Woody Woodpecker, and Bugs Bunny (see LOONEY TUNES AND MERRIE MELODIES), were long since spoken for. Ellsworth had to settle for the Fox and the Crow plus some of Columbia's even lesser known characters. *Real Screen Funnies,* which became *Real Screen Comics* with the second issue, first appeared in the spring of 1945. Fox and Crow were the stars, backed by Tito and his Burrito, Flippity and Flop, and Polar Playmates. The magazine was relatively successful and remained in business until 1961, having changed its name to *TV Screen Cartoons* in 1959. The team's own title lasted from 1952 to 1968 and they were also featured in COMIC CAVALCADE from 1949 to 1954. The animated movie series had ended in 1949.

The Fox and the Crow comic book stories were also a product of Hollywood, being produced by a West Coast shop managed by animator Jim Davis. The first artist was Wickersham, who was also in charge of the animated cartoons. The chief scriptwriter was Hubert Karp, another toiler in the animation field. Wickersham quit in 1948 and Davis himself took over the drawing, little suspecting how long he'd be at it. "I had no way of knowing it was going to be my bread and butter for the next 20 years," he said. Karp died in 1953 and Cecil Beard took on the writing job. Beard, who also had an animation background, enjoyed his work. "We sometimes had a rough time getting the work out," he once admitted. "We would be rolling on the floor in hysterics over some preposterous situation the characters . . . seemed to develop."

While intended for younger readers, the Fox and the Crow's adventures also attracted an older, albeit smaller, audience. Mark Evanier, television writer and comics historian, has said, "There were hundreds and hundreds of *Fox and Crow* stories done, none of them quite like any other. And, as for the quantity of laughs they wrought, well, that must number well into the billions."

FRANKENSTEIN The most famous of all the famous monsters, Dr. Victor Frankenstein's creation was introduced in Mary Shelley's novel in 1818. In this century his notoriety took a great leap forward with the release of the Universal Pictures talkie in 1931. In 1940, the Frankenstein monster lurched into comic books to make the first of many appearances.

By the time artist-writer Dick Briefer introduced the Frankenstein monster in the seventh issue of *Prize Comics* (December 1940), there had been three highly successful Frankenstein movies, each starring Boris Karloff. Briefer was obviously thinking of the actor when he created his version. Since the novel was in the public domain and Karloff wasn't, he was careful to state at the start of each comic book episode that it was "suggested by the classic of Mary Shelley." He updated the story, gave it a contemporary American setting, and showed his hulking, dead-white monster rampaging through streamlined urban settings. Within a few months he began calling the monster Frankenstein, explaining, "the name is universally accepted to be that of the ghastly creation."

A man with a strong, though slightly perverse, sense of humor, Briefer gradually tired of doing all the ghastly stuff straight. By the mid-1940s, he had converted *Frankenstein* into a comedy feature. He kidded the whole horror genre and made fun of such fads and foibles as crooners and quiz shows. The monster soon became the star of *Prize* and in 1945 began appearing in a bimonthly magazine of his own. Briefer afterwards admitted that the humorous Frankenstein was the favorite of all his comic book work. "I look back into the old comic mags of *Frankenstein*," he said, "and really marvel at most of the art and ideas and scripts that I turned out."

The humorous Frankenstein ended in the late 1940s, but the character came back in the early 1950s in a new, grim version that lasted until late in 1954.

Back in 1945, CLASSICS ILLUSTRATED had offered an adaption of the novel. Packaged by the Jerry Iger shop, it had artwork by Bob Webb. In 1964, Dell issued a one-shot *Frankenstein* in their Movie Classics series, offering the Universal Pictures version with the slogan "The Monster Is Back!!!" Two years later, in an exhibition of extremely fuzzy thinking, Dell introduced a new Frankenstein who was "the world's newest, greatest, and strangest super hero!" This unlikely combination of horror and heroics managed to struggle through only three quarterly issues. Marvel came up with its version in 1973 with *The Monster of Frankenstein*: "The most famous, most fearsome MONSTER of all!" Drawn initially by Mike Ploog and later by John Buscema and others, Marvel's monster ended in 1975 after 18 issues.

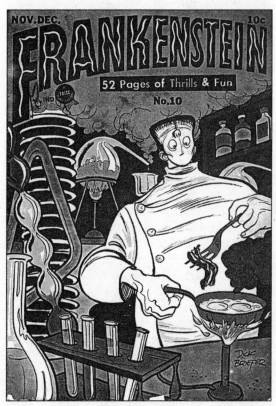

Frankenstein, Dick Briefer, © 1947 by Crestwood Publishing Co., Inc.

Scribbly, Sheldon Mayer, © 1936 by Sheldon Mayer.

THE FUNNIES   The first comic with this title was a tabloid-sized publication that flourished briefly in 1929 and 1930. In 1936, the name was reused for a conventional-format comic book. This version of *The Funnies* fared better, lasting until 1942. Then, under the modified title of *New Funnies* and offering mostly funny animal fare, the book survived into 1962.

It was George Delacorte, founder of Dell Publishing, who launched the original *The Funnies* in 1929. A weekly newsstand offering, it consisted of 24 pages in tabloid format and initially sold for 10¢. Edited by Harry Steeger, who was soon to found the Popular Publications pulp house, *The Funnies* consisted of nothing but original material. This was an innovation and, as Robert Overstreet points out, *The Funnies* was also the "first four-color newsstand publication" in the comics field.

Included in its pages were *My Big Brudder* by Tack Knight, *Deadwood Gulch* by Boody Rogers, and *Frosty Ayre* by Joe Archibald. There were also puzzles, magic tricks, and stories. The comic did not thrive, and even a price cut to 5¢ couldn't save it. The 36th and final issue appeared in mid-October of 1930.

Dell brought back *The Funnies* late in the summer of 1936, this time as a monthly 64-page comic book of the dimensions of *Famous Funnies*. It was packaged by M.C. Gaines and Sheldon Mayer and was devoted to newspaper strip reprints. The early issues drew heavily on the NEA syndicate stable, reprinting such features as *Alley Oop*, *Captain Easy*, *Boots*, *Myra North*, and *Salesman Sam*. Among the other reprints, mostly Sunday pages, were *Dan Dunn*, *Tailspin Tommy*, *Don Dixon*, *Bronc Peeler*, and *Mutt & Jeff*.

In the second issue, editor Mayer, a boy cartoonist himself, introduced *Scribbly*, a strip about a boy cartoonist. The two or three pages devoted to Scribbly were laid out like the Sunday-page reprints, each with its own logo. Mayer did this so his upstart creation could rub shoulders undetected with the real Sunday pages that were being reprinted. The Scribbly saga dealt with Scribbly Jibbet—young, diminutive, and possessed of a head of hair like an untidy haystack—and his efforts to break free the bonds put upon him by home, school, and contemporaries and enter the charmed world of newspaper cartooning. It was drawn in the youthful Mayer's scribbly, appealing cartoon style.

Gradually, other new material began slipping into the magazine. Starting with #20 (May 1938), six-page adaptions of B cowboy movies starring the likes of Tim McCoy and Jank Randall were featured. A four-page true-crime continuity called *The Crime Busters*, drawn by Alden McWilliams, started in the 21st issue. After Gaines and Mayer departed late in 1938,

The Funnies underwent further changes. With the exception of *Alley Oop* and a couple of others, the reprints were dropped. Among the new features were *Mr. District Attorney*, adapted from the popular radio show, and *John Carter of Mars*, taken from Edgar Rice Burroughs's novels about the fighting swordsman of the Barsoom (see MR. DISTRICT ATTORNEY). Burroughs's son, John Coleman Burroughs, drew most of the adventures.

Early in 1940, the magazine introduced *Rex, King of the Deep* and *Speed Martin*. With the July 1940 issue came Phantasmo, the book's first out-and-out superhero and a less-than-first-rate creation of E.C. Stoner. Issue #57 (July 1941) saw the advent of another adaption, this time of radio hero Captain Midnight. The comic book version utilized most of the radio serial trappings, including the Secret Squadron, the captain's two teenage sidekicks Chuck and Joyce, his mechanic Ichabod Mudd, and the sinister Ivan Shark and his evil daughter Fury. The feature, drawn by Dan Gormley, supplanted Phantasmo as the star.

Then, after allowing *Andy Panda* and *Felix the Cat* into its pages, the magazine made another, more drastic change. With #65 (July 1942), it became *New Funnies*. Added to the lineup were such characters as RAGGEDY ANN AND ANDY, Oswald the Rabbit, the Brownies, and Woody Woodpecker. This was by far the book's most successful phase and it reached issue #288 before ceasing early in 1962.

FUNNIES, INC.   Late in 1939, operating out of a small loft office in midtown Manhattan, a handful of artists and writers put together the first issue of MARVEL COMICS and created the foundation for today's vast Marvel empire. Using the businesslike name of Funnies, Inc., the art and editorial service went on to turn out work for several other Marvel publications as well as other assorted 1940s publishing companies.

Its founder was Lloyd Jacquet, who was neither an artist nor a writer. Once described as a man who "dressed like a head waiter and was very mannerly," Jacquet had worked with Major Nicholson on *New Fun Comics* (See MORE FUN COMICS) and then gone on to edit the Centaur line—*Funny Picture Stories, Keen Detective Funnies*, AMAZING-MAN, etc. Deciding that there was more money to be made in packaging comic books than in editing them, Jacquet set up shop as Funnies, Inc. By 1939, chiefly because of the advent of SUPERMAN the year before, the comic book business had demonstrated that big profits were to be made. More and more publishers were getting into the act, and that meant they'd need material to fill their 64-page issues. Following in the footsteps of shops started by Harry "A" Chesler and the team of Will Eisner and Jerry Iger, Funnies, Inc. intended to help fill that need.

For his initial crew, Jacquet recruited people who'd worked with him at Centaur, such as Carl Burgos and Bill Everett. Some years later, in recalling the start of the shop, Everett said, "Lloyd offered me and a fellow by the name of Max Neill a chance to go in with him and two other guys, John Mahon and Frank Torpey, on a 50–50 basis. We took a small loft office on 45th Street, and started an art service."

Unlike the competing Chesler and Eisner–Iger shops, most of the Funnies, Inc. gang didn't do their work on the premises. They just came in to drop off their work and pick up new assignments. Among those art director Everett dealt with were such artists as Bob Wood, Harry Sahle, George Mandel, Irwin Hasen, Paul Gustavson, Sam Gilman, and Bob Davis. The writers included John Compton, Ray Gill, Kermit Jaediker, and Mickey Spillane.

After the Marvel titles, the Jacquet shop's most impressive job was the two magazines they put together for Novelty Press. For this funny book division of the powerful Curtis company, which also published *The Saturday Evening Post*, Funnies, Inc. created *Target Comics* and *Blue Bolt*. It also provided artwork for *Heroic Comics*, including one of Everett's other aquatic heroes, HYDROMAN, and Tarpé Mills's Purple Zombie. *Daredevil Battles Hitler*, which became just plain *Daredevil* with the second issue, was also the handiwork of Funnies, Inc. (see DAREDEVIL). The shop packaged some of the more sedate magazines of the 1940s as well, including *Parents'* well-intentioned but dull TRUE COMICS and every school-kid's favorite crib, *Classic Comics*. (See CLASSICS ILLUSTRATED.)

As the decade progressed, Funnies, Inc. did considerable work for Fawcett Publications. The prolific Carl Pfeufer was especially active for CAPTAIN MARVEL's home company, turning out DON WINSLOW, Tom Mix, Hopalong Cassidy, and quite a few others. The Jacquet shop continued to provide work for Marvel as well, even while Jacquet himself was in the service. By the middle of the 1940s, some of the markets were less impressive—*Key Comics, Yellowjacket, Blue Circle*, and so forth. The shop stayed in business throughout the 1950s.

FUNNY PAGES The first comic book to follow Major Nicholson into the area of original material, *Funny Pages* was founded by two of his former employees and used material by several of the artists who'd contributed to MORE FUN and *New*. The premiere issue was titled *The Comics Magazine* and had a cover date of May 1936.

William Cook, a sometime cartoonist, had served briefly as managing editor for the major, and his partner, John Mahon, had been the business manager. Taking leave of Nicholson, and possibly carrying off some of the artwork from his inventory, they set up for themselves as the Comics Magazine Company, Inc. They promised readers of their new book that the features "are all original and every one of them NEW."

Like Major Nicholson's titles, *Funny Pages* consisted mostly of two-page features. Jerry

Siegel and Joe Shuster's *Dr. Occult* did business here as *Dr. Mystic* and their *Federal Men* was called *Federal Agent*. Sheldon Mayer's *The Strange Adventures of Mr. Weed* and *J. Worthington Blimp, Esq.* suffered no name changes for this guest appearance away from *New Comics*. Other artists in the early issues were Tom McNamara, Stan Randall, W.M. Allison, Ken Ernst, and Walt Kelly. From the second issue on, the magazine was running adventure stories of seven pages, an innovation for the time.

Other Cook–Mahon titles were *Funny Picture Stories* and *Detective Picture Stories*, both launched in 1936. In the spring of the following year, the partners sold out and went their separate ways.

By 1938, *Funny Pages* had changed hands for a second time and was part of Joseph

The Arrow, Paul Gustavson, © 1939 by Centaur Publications.

Hardie's Centaur line. In the 21st issue (September 1938), Paul Gustavson's the Arrow made his first appearance. A mysterious archer in red suit and cowl, he was the first costumed hero to appear in comic books after the coming of SUPERMAN. Among the other adventure features added were *Mad Ming*, starring an Oriental villain; *Mantoka*, about a shape-changing Indian, drawn by Jack Cole; and *Randall Ross, Master Sleuth*. The magazine ended with its 42nd issue, dated October 1940.

GENIUS JONES Not a serious costumed crime-fighter, he was nonetheless one of the bright spots of 1940s comic books. Created by writer Alfred Bester and artist Stan Kaye, the diminutive do-gooder—under five feet tall—made his debut in ADVENTURE COMICS #77 (August 1942). He shared the magazine with a serious bunch of heroes that included SAND-MAN, Manhunter, and Starman.

Bester, who went on to write such classic science fiction novels as *The Demolished Man* and *The Stars My Destination*, mixed satire, slapstick, mystery, and fantasy in his eight-page scripts. Kaye, a disciple of *Captain Easy*'s Roy Crane, illustrated them in an inventive, appealing fashion.

Johnny "Genius" Jones came by his nick-name because, marooned on an uncharted island while growing from boyhood to man-hood, he memorized not only the entire *Ency-clopaedia Britannica* but 700 other scholarly books as well. Roughing it on the island for over a decade also toughened Jones, turning him into a pocket-edition TARZAN.

Back in civilization and penniless, he decided to put his erudition to good use by going into business as an answer man. He fashioned a sidewalk stand—eventually motorizing it so he could travel hither and yon—and offered answers to any and all questions for a dime apiece. Some questions were easy to answer, such as who wrote the ballet *L'Oiseau de Feu* or who was the killer in a mystery novel that had the last page miss-ing, but often a question required field work. Then he donned his Genius Jones costume, consisting of tights, a cape, and a crash hel-met, all borrowed from various friends.

Once entangled with crooks and killers, Genius used his vast knowledge of everything from physics to show business to extricate himself from assorted traps and troubles. He frequently made his more serious contempo-raries look a bit dense when it came to think-ing their way out of jams. Early Bester–Kaye episodes bore such titles as "The Case of the Off-Key Crooner," "The Case of the Love-Sick Submarine," and "The Adventure of the Run-away Calculating Machine."

Bester abandoned Genius in 1944, the year he began selling scripts to *The Shadow* radio show (see THE SHADOW). Kaye continued with other, uncredited writers. The pint-sized champion of justice flourished in *Adventure* until #102 (February–March 1946) and then transferred to MORE FUN, where he remained until late 1947. Between 1943 and 1946, he also starred in the first 10 issues of *All Funny*. It seems probable that Bester was inspired in part by Lester Dent's 1937 *Genius Jones* serial in *Argosy*, which dealt with a different sort of human encyclopedia.

Genius Jones, Stan Kaye, © 1944, renewed 1972 DC Comics, Inc. All rights reserved.

GHOST RIDER Several characters have used this name over the past 40-plus years. The original Ghost Rider was a phantom cowboy and the most recent is a ghost-ridden biker.

The very first Ghost Rider began his career as a backup feature in Magazine Enterprises' *Tim Holt* #11 in 1949. In reality he was Rex Fury, a federal marshal in the Old West who dressed up in a luminous white outfit that included a glowing cape and a Stetson. Eventually he added a skull mask to his ensemble and the sight of him mounted on his glowing white stallion Spectre was often sufficient to scare even hardened owlhoots out of their wits.

Many of the tales contained supernatural elements, and ghosts, werewolves, and vampires occasionally roamed the range along with the rustlers and gunmen. During part of his run, Ghost Rider wore a cloak of darkness given to him by a "strange creature from another dimension" which enabled him "to create mystic illusions to thwart evildoers." He spoke in a flowery style and never used a contraction.

He proved popular and ME introduced a *Ghost Rider* title in 1950. Dick Ayers drew all the stories, with Frank Frazetta supplying several covers. The magazine ended in 1954 and the Western mystery man was last seen in the *Tim Holt* magazine in the summer of the following year.

Early in 1967, Marvel assimilated the character and brought out its initial version of the Ghost Rider, with Dick Ayers again as the artist. Billed as "The World's Most Mysterious Western Hero," he dressed in a glowing costume that was identical to that of his predecessor. This time around he was Carter Slade, who'd been given his phosphorescent costume by a Comanche medicine man. His horse was named Banshee. The series ended after seven issues. The character returned in 1970 and graced the first seven issues of Marvel's revived *Western Gunfighters*. During the course of this short run, Carter Slade was gunned down and his brother Lincoln Slade, also a marshal, assumed the role.

In 1973, Marvel tried something completely different and introduced a contemporary Ghost Rider who rode a motorcycle. Johnny Blaze was a clean-cut, blond young cyclist who became the unwilling host of a spirit named Zarathos. When Zarathos was in ascendency, the hapless Johnny turned into a demon biker with a blazing skull instead of a head. When in this mode, much like THE HULK, he didn't take any crap from anybody. More successful than any prior Ghost Rider, he survived for 81 issues until the spring of 1983.

The cowboy and the biker have also coexisted at times. In the mid-1970s, to avoid confusion, the Western hero appeared in a reprint series as Night Rider. Yet another Ghost Rider appeared in *Ghost Rider* #56. He was Hamilton Slade, a descendent of the Old West Riders, and, in order to save Johnny Blaze from danger, he was taken over by the spirit of the old Ghost Rider.

In 1990, writer Howard Mackie, working with artists Javier Saltares and Mark Texeira, came up with a new Ghost Rider. This time it was a clean-cut young motorcyclist named Danny Ketch who got possessed by spirits and became the biker with the blazing skull.

Ghost Rider®, Don Perlin. All Marvel characters and the distinctive likenesses thereof are trademarks of Marvel Entertainment Group, Inc. and are used with permission. © 1992 Marvel Entertainment Group, Inc.

GOLDEN AGE   This designation for the comic books of the 1930s and 1940s has been in use among fans, collectors, and dealers for several decades. The highest-priced and most sought after magazines come from this time period.

There has never been, however, universal agreement as to exactly what year the Golden Age began and when it officially ended.

According to the *Comics Buyer's Guide*, the term Golden Age "indicates the first era of comic book production—which occurred in the '30s and '40s." On the other hand, the *Overstreet Comic Book Price Guide* defines it as "the period beginning with ACTION #1 (June 1938) and ending with World War II in 1945."

GOOD GIRL ART   A phrase used by dealers and collectors and first popularized in the mail-order catalogs of the American Comic Book Company some years ago. It refers not to comics that contain drawings of good girls but rather to those that feature good drawings of pretty women.

The *Comics Buyer's Guide* defines Good Girl Art as "pinup-type pictures of leggy, busty females in 'cheesecake' poses." They add that

South Sea Girl, Matt Baker, © 1946 Universal Phoenix Features.

"some find the term offensive." Overstreet's *Comic Book Price Guide* uses the term and in its annual Market Report includes Good Girl Art as one of the comic book categories. The 1991–92 edition, for example, reported that "renewed interest was evident."

The companies that have specialized in the genre include Fiction House, Fox, and Farrell. Among the characters who owed a considerable portion of their newsstand success to the sexy way they were depicted were SHEENA and PHANTOM LADY. Matt Baker was one of the masters of the genre, as were artists Nick Cardy, Bob Lubbers, and Bill Ward. Dave Stevens, creator of the Rocketeer, pays homage to the conventions of Good Girl Art in his work.

GRAND SLAM COMICS   This was one of several Canadian titles distributed in the United States during the mid-1940s. A product of the Anglo-American Publishing Company of Toronto, *Grand Slam* starred a superhero named Commander Steel. During its heyday, Anglo-American was also selling *Three Aces* and *Freelance* on both sides of the border and publishing Canadian editions of Fawcett's *Captain Marvel*, WHIZ COMICS, and *Spy Smasher* that used all new material.

Grand Slam began late in 1941. Commander Steel, also known as the Man of Might, was usually the leading character, but several others appeared as backup during the magazine's six-year run. Among them were Dr. Destine, Red Rover, the Purple Rider, and the Crusaders. Possibly because of the affiliation with Fawcett Publications, most of the artwork in the A-A titles had the uncluttered, somewhat cartoony look of CAPTAIN MARVEL artist C.C. Beck. Ed Furness was the chief artist at Anglo-American and such American writers as Rod Reed and Otto Binder contributed some of the scripts.

Commander Steel looked somewhat like Captain Marvel, though he lacked his sense of humor. His costume consisted of blue riding

pants, boots, a wide metal belt, and a red tunic with a depiction of the scales of justice on the chest. He derived his superhero abilities from the Elixir of Power that flowed in his veins. During the war he fought chiefly against Nazis, and in the postwar period he roamed the world as an agent in the International Police Service. For a few years in the mid-1940s his magazine was sold on American newsstands. During part of that time it was merged with another A-A title and called *Grand Slam–Three Aces*.

Commander Steel, Ed Furness.

THE GREEN ARROW   Undoubtedly the most successful archer in comics, he's been letting fly with feathered shafts for more than 50 years. The Green Arrow first appeared in DC's MORE FUN COMICS #73 (November 1941) as the joint creation of editor-writer Mort Weisinger and artist George Papp. Over the years, he's fought both conventional crooks and social problems, with time out to romance the BLACK CANARY.

Although Weisinger was on record as having said that he "wasn't remotely influenced by Batman" when thinking up the Green Arrow and his boy sidekick Speedy, the feature itself actually looked and sounded like BATMAN and Robin in Robin Hood costumes, right down to the archery team's car, the Arrowmobile. Weisinger may have had other sources of inspiration than Bob Kane's dark knights. The name of his new hero seems to have been influenced by the 1940 serial *The Green Archer*. In that Columbia Pictures chapter play, the title character "mysteriously appears with his deadly bow and arrows whenever needed."

The Green Arrow—who was Oliver Queen in civilian life—and his boy-wonder accomplice went for nearly a year and a half before they got an origin. That finally happened in *More Fun* #89 (March 1943). There readers learned that young Roy Harper, who was destined to become Speedy, had been marooned in his boyhood on Lost Mesa when he and his father crashed in their helicopter. His father died, and Roy was raised by an Indian named Quoag and taught to be an expert with bow and arrow. When Queen arrived by chance on the same mesa, the two teamed up to become Green Arrow and Speedy, and proceeded to clean up a gang of crooks. An inventive team, they had an arrow for every occasion, including a drill arrow, a gas arrow, a flare arrow, a net arrow, etc. They moved over to ADVENTURE COMICS in 1946 and pursued their careers there until early in 1960. Among the other artists to draw their adventures were Bernie Klein, Cliff Young, and Jack Kirby.

In the early 1960s, Green Arrow joined the JUSTICE LEAGUE OF AMERICA and began appearing in its magazine. At the end of the decade he was redesigned by artist Neal Adams and started looking and acting, as Gerard Jones put it, "like a hip, bearded rebel." In 1970, working with editor Julius Schwartz, Adams and writer Denny O'Neil took over the *Green Lantern* title and teamed the hero with Green Arrow (see GREEN LANTERN). The magazine ushered in the era of social relevance at DC.

Among the issues that O'Neil explored in his thought stories were racism, overpopula-tion, and drug addiction. The drug abuse problem was dramatized in an unusual and unprecedented way when Speedy was revealed as a heroin addict. The relevant stories endeared the magazine to the dedicated college readers of the period and won awards for both artist and writer. Sales, however, were not much affected by the praise, and by the mid-1970s this type of crusading had pretty much ceased. Adams and O'Neil were also the ones who initiated Green Arrow's long-running romance with Black Canary.

The emerald archer got a miniseries of his own in 1983 and returned early in 1988 in a regular series written and first drawn by Mike Grell. This series bolstered his popularity.

THE GREEN HORNET   Originally a radio hero, the green-clad masked man branched out into comic books in 1940. The first *Green Hornet* magazine lasted until 1949 and the character, along with his associate Kato, has returned to the newsstands several times since.

The program originated at radio station WXYZ Detroit, created by producer George W. Trendle and writer Fran Striker, and was first heard nationwide in 1938. Although aimed at a youthful audience, the half-hour show aired in the evening and was heard three times each week for most of its run. Trendle and Striker had come up with THE LONE RANGER a few years earlier and their new hero was a contemporary version of the earlier masked man. In civilian life, the Hornet was Britt Reid, wealthy young publisher of the crusading *Daily Sentinel*. Together with Kato, who was chauffeur for both of his identities, he carried on a vigilante battle against the underworld: "He hunts the biggest of all game, public enemies who try to destroy our America!" The Hornet used a gas gun of his own invention to put lawbreakers to sleep. He traveled around the night city in a sleek, souped-up vehicle known as the Black Beauty. The show's theme song was "The Flight of the Bumblebee."

The Green Hornet was brought to comic books by the enterprising Bert Whitman, a cartoonist-writer who ran an art shop that packaged comic books. He acquired the rights from Trendle, who thought the magazine would be a good publicity gimmick and charged him no licensing fee. *Green Hornet Comics* #1 bore a December 1940 cover date and was published by a company known as Helnit. Each issue offered a half dozen or so different adventures of the masked avenger, drawn by Whitman and such shop hands as Dan Gormley and Irwin Hasen. Helnit put out six issues of the title over eight months and then gave up. At that point Whitman sold his comic books rights to Harvey Publications for $25,000. He always maintained that that was more money than anyone else ever made off the character.

Harvey changed the format, limiting the Hornet to two yarns and adding several other features, including *The Spirit of '76*, *The Zebra*, and *The Blonde Bomber* (see THE ZEBRA). As had the earlier stories, the Green Hornet adventures used all the regular characters from the radio program: Reid's pretty secretary Lenore Case, ace reporter Ed Lowry, and dense Mike Axford, who was Reid's bodyguard. Axford never tumbled to his boss's alternate identity and devoted much of his time to trying to capture the Hornet and bring him to justice. Like many another fictional vigilante, the Green Hornet was viewed as an outlaw by the police and most decent citizens.

Among the artists who drew the Hornet were Arturo Cazeneuve, Pierce Rice, Jerry Robinson, and Al Avison. The early Harvey covers were by Joe Simon and Jack Kirby. Later on, the inimitable Alex Schomburg contributed a series of his intricate panoramic covers dealing with such subjects as "Nazi's Last Stand" and "Clash with the Rampaging Japs."

The last issue was #47, dated September 1949. Harvey, always aware of the latest trends in comics publishing, had taken to calling the magazine *Green Hornet Fights Crime* back in 1946, probably in the hope that buyers would think it was a true-crime book. Later title variations included *Green Hornet*, *Racket Buster* and *Radio's Racket Buster*, *Green Hornet*.

Dell did a Hornet one-shot in 1953. After that, the character was in limbo for well over a decade. A Green Hornet television show, with Van Williams as the masked man and martial-arts expert Bruce Lee as Kato, was part of the 1966–67 season. That inspired Gold Key to produce three issues of a comic book version in 1967. Dan Spiegle was the artist.

Now Comics brought back the Hornet in a new comic book late in 1989. Later on it added a separate title devoted to the Bruce Lee version of Kato.

GREEN LANTERN   In the beginning there was just one Green Lantern, a straightforward superhero who battled villainy for the duration of the GOLDEN AGE and then retired. The SILVER AGE brought a second, and completely different, Green Lantern. The situation grew increasingly complex thereafter and at last count there were more than 3,000 Green Lanterns doing business across the universe.

The original Green Lantern was introduced in ALL-AMERICAN COMICS #16 (July 1940). There he was on the cover, as depicted by Sheldon Moldoff, in his red-and-green costume and flowing cape, charging along a girder at a tommygun-wielding thug. That was just about the only glimpse readers got of the costume that month, since the eight-page origin story inside didn't get around to showing GL dressed for crime-fighting until the final panel. The origin story told how blond engineer Alan Scott came to own a mysterious green lantern made of a strange off-planet metal. By making a ring of the metal and then putting it on and touching the lantern with it, he was converted into a superhero who could fly, be immune to bullets, and walk through walls. He had to recharge himself every 24 hours, however.

The Green Lantern was the joint invention of Mart Nodell, a young artist of modest attainments, and Bill Finger, the writer and co-creator of BATMAN. Editor Sheldon Mayer also had a hand in reshaping Nodell's original notion, which Mayer saw as an updating of the Aladdin legend, by adding superhero elements. From #26 (May 1941), the GL stories were ghosted by Irwin Hasen, who drew in a style loosely based on Milton Caniff's. In #27, Finger and Hasen introduced Doiby Dickles, the tough, overweight cabbie who became the Green Lantern's equivalent of Robin.

Finger initially concentrated on stories of urban crime, and the Green Lantern and Doiby usually tackled civic corruption and racketeering. There was mystery, fantasy, and, usually, more comedy than was to be found in the adventures of the average superman. Other writers included science fiction pros Alfred Bester and Henry Kuttner. In the mid-1940s the nasty Solomon Grundy, a villain who combined the best qualities of the FRANKENSTEIN monster and the Heap, first rose up to plague GL. Bester once admitted that he was probably the one who'd thought up Grundy. After World War II, when Alex Toth was doing much of the drawing, several more colorful villains came along, most notably the mystery woman who called herself the Harlequin.

The Green Lantern was one of the more popular of the DC characters, and he starred in 38 issues of his own magazine between 1941 and 1949. He was also one of the featured characters in the first 29 issues of COMIC CAVALCADE and appeared frequently in ALL STAR COMICS as a member-in-good-standing of the JUSTICE SOCIETY. The Green Lantern left *All-American* in the fall of 1948, after being eased out by the cowboy JOHNNY THUNDER. He made the last appearance of the first phase of his career in *All Star* #57 early in 1951.

The new Green Lantern was first seen in SHOWCASE #22 (October 1959). After auditioning again in the next two issues, he moved into his own title in the spring of 1960. "When the returns started coming in on the Flash and we saw we had a hit, the natural instinct was to do

something similar," DC editor Julius Schwartz once recalled (see THE FLASH). "That's how we decided to go ahead with Green Lantern, and I worked out the same theory of giving him a new personality, a new costume, a new everything." This time the Green Lantern was test pilot Hal Jordan, who got his ring and lantern from an alien who'd crashed on earth. The dying, red-skinned spaceman explained that he was a "space-patrolman in the super-galactic system" and that the ring, which had to be recharged at the lantern every 24 hours, gave its wearer incredible powers to be used "against forces of evil and injustice." Taking over the ring, the lantern, and the alien's uniform, Jordan became the Green Lantern. John Broome was the original scriptwriter, Gil Kane the artist.

Green Lantern, Gil Kane, © 1991 DC Comics, Inc. All rights reserved.

Gradually Schwartz and Broome embellished the background of their hero. They invented the Guardians of the Universe, an immortal bunch who had set up the Green Lantern Corps, "a group of living beings chosen from all parts of the universe to fight evil and given rings of power." Over the years, Jordan has appeared in sundry contexts. In the early 1970s he went through a relevance phase and teamed up with THE GREEN ARROW to fight social ills. Later he worked as part of the Green Lantern Corps, along with such other GLs as the black John Stewart, Guy Gardner, an alien lady named Katma Tui, a dogfaced native of the planet Bolovax Vik named Killowog and, potentially, nearly 3,600 other official Green Lanterns.

The original Lantern returned in 1963 in the *Justice League of America* and he's reappeared frequently since (see JUSTICE LEAGUE OF AMERICA). In 1991, for example, he and Doiby shared a *Green Lantern* comic book with Jordan and an assortment of other latter-day holders of the title.

HAWKMAN DC has had one hero or another flying around under this name for more than a half century. The first Hawkman was introduced late in 1939, the second early in 1961. Writer Gardner Fox created them both, and each was known as Carter Hall when not wearing his wings.

The first Carter Hall began his airborne career in *Flash Comics* #1 (cover-dated January 1940). Handsome, blond, and wealthy, Hall collected old weapons and dabbled in science. One of his recent inventions was the Ninth Metal, "which defies the pull of gravity." He also had lived before as a prince in ancient Egypt. Back there he'd lost his true love, a dark-haired lady named Shiera, when both of them were killed by a wicked priest in the Temple of Anubis. By chance, the reincarnated Hall ran into the reincarnated Shiera in the subway, and they picked up where they had left off a few thousand years earlier.

Unfortunately, their old Egyptian enemy was alive again, too, and this time around he was a crazed scientist. He had invented a huge and deadly lightning machine and was hell-bent on world domination. Kidnapping Shiera happened to be part of his plan. Vowing to rescue the young woman from his clutches, Hall dressed up in a harness of Ninth Metal and added a hawk head and wings to his ensemble, as a "grim jest, in the guise of the ancient hawkgod Anubis." Actually Anubis is a jackal-headed god, and had not Carter Hall's memory been a bit fuzzy after all those years, this entry would be about Jackalman. As Hawkman, he swooped down on the mad scientist, knocked him off with a crossbow, and saved Shiera. (It would be a running gimmick in the stories that Hawkman would use various ancient weapons from his collection to dispatch villains.)

In his early years, Hawkman specialized in odd and unusual investigations, encountering such antagonists as an off-planet giant, a talking alligator god, a golden mummy, and purple monsters who lived in New York's harbor. Among the weapons of the past used by the winged warrior were a war-ax, cestus, a quarterstaff, and a scimitar. Late in 1941, Shiera fashioned herself a costume similar to Carter's, complete with a pair of enormous wings, and began flying side by side with him as Hawkgirl. In her first costume appearance she'd called herself Hawkwoman, but that was soon changed. The team remained in *Flash Comics* until it ended in 1949. Hawkman was also a regular in ALL STAR, where he usually worked solo. He was last seen there in 1951.

Dennis Neville, sometime *Superman* ghost, was the initial artist. He was followed by such artists as Sheldon Moldoff, Joe Kubert, Chester Kozlak, and Bob Oksner.

Hawkman was one of several Golden Agers that editor Julius Schwartz revived and refurbished in the early 1960s (see GOLDEN AGE). "Hawkman had the hardest time getting off the ground," Gerard Jones pointed out in *The Encyclopedia of American Comics*. "He needed two tryouts in *The Brave and the Bold* (1961 and 1962) and then a backup series in *Mystery in Space* (1963) before finally being given his own title in 1964" (see THE BRAVE AND THE BOLD). This time around, the winged wonders, as written by Fox and drawn by Kubert, were a married couple from the planet Thanagar. "I don't know which of us came up with the name 'Thanagar,'" Schwartz has said, "but I think it's one of the best place names around. If I ever discover a planet, I'll call it Thanagar." The couple, initially named Katar Hol and Shayera, were law officers from Thanagar who pursued a shape-changing criminal to Earth. As a cover, using the more conventional names of Carter and Shiera Hall, they took over the direction of the Midway City Museum. This occupation allowed them access to the ancient weapons the original Hawks used in their work. During their last days, the original team had abandoned their hawk-head masks for more conventional cowls, but for their return Kubert brought back the earlier look.

Hawkman magazine was grounded in 1968. The winged hero was next seen in the seven-issue run of *Atom and Hawkman*. He was also a minor participant in *Justice League of America* from the mid-1960s onward where he worked without his wife. In the mid-1980s, another *Hawkman* title was tried, originally written by Tony Isabella and drawn by Richard Howell (see JUSTICE LEAGUE OF AMERICA). Hawkgirl was now known as Hawkwoman. In 1989 came *Hawkworld*, devised by artist-writer Timothy

Truman. It returned the couple, again called Katar and Shayera, back home to Thanagar for rather somber science fiction adventures.

Hawkman, Joe Kubert, © 1944, renewed 1972 DC Comics Inc. All rights reserved.

HERBIE   *See* Supersnipe.

HEROIC COMICS   This was a GOLDEN AGE magazine that went from fiction to nonfiction, abandoning superheroes and newspaper strip reprints for true stories of heroism.

It was published by the FAMOUS FUNNIES folks and began life in the summer of 1940 as *Reg'lar Fellers Heroic Comics*. The early issues featured such unconventional heroes as HYDRO-MAN, the Purple Zombie, Music Master, and Man O'Metal, along with such strips as *Flyin' Jenny*, *Don Dixon*, and, of course, Gene Byrnes's *Reg'lar Fellers*. Late in 1942 the book became just plain *Heroic Comics* and began adding assorted true-war stories. From mid-1945 onward, it was nothing but the truth.

Heroic lasted through its 97th issue (June 1955) and in the postwar years concentrated on civilian bravery as exemplified by firemen, policemen, nurses, Boy Scouts, and everyday citizens. The editor throughout was Steve A. Douglas and among the many artists he hired were Bill Everett, Tarpé Mills, H.G. Peter, Henry Kiefer, Alex Toth, Graham Ingels, and Frank Frazetta.

Music Master, Jimmy Thompson, © 1943 Famous Funnies, Inc.

HOPPY THE MARVEL BUNNY   The superpowered rabbit was introduced in Fawcett's *Funny Animals* late in 1942. Created by Chad Grothkopf, Hoppy was inspired by CAPTAIN MARVEL, wore a similarly styled red-and-gold costume and shared the magic word "SHAZAM!" with the human hero. The captain even appeared with Hoppy and the magazine's other characters on the first cover. The copy stated, "Captain Marvel welcomes the new animal heroes to funnyland."

In the early and mid-1940s, superhero fever was so contagious that—in addition to people—sundry other creatures caught it, too. The result was a super-menagerie of heroic birds and beasts. Of course, none of the critters took the notion of superheroics seriously.

Super Mouse was the earliest, debuting in *Coo Coo Comics* in the autumn of 1942, a few months before Hoppy. Marvel introduced Super Rabbit in *Comedy Comics* #14 early in 1943 and Super Duck came along in the same

year. DC's *Funny Stuff* in 1944 included McSnurtle the Turtle, a spoof of THE FLASH. Superkatt, who wasn't actually super at all, began in *Giggle Comics* at about the same time.

A small, mild-mannered rabbit in everyday life, Hoppy had but to exclaim "Shazam!" to be converted into Captain Marvel Bunny, "the fearless, flying, mightiest bunny in the world." Chad drew in an assured, animated cartoon style that mixed the whimsical with the wacky. His animals were strongly drawn and boldly inked, and his backgrounds were rich with the sort of gingerbread architecture found in the better fairy-tale illustrations. Hoppy's true love was Millie, whom he was often called upon to rescue from some sort of calamity. The stories leaned more toward fairy tales than crime-fighting and were obviously aimed at a younger audience than did the usual superhero fare.

Funny Animals lasted until the mid-1950s, published in its final days by Charlton. Hoppy hung on, but had ceased to be the Marvel Bunny. In his heyday, in the mid-1940s, he also enjoyed a title of his own.

Hoppy, Chad Grothkopf, unpublished, 1991.

HOWARD THE DUCK   Of all the ducks who have flourished in comic books, possibly the oddest was the cigar-smoking fowl named Howard. Extraterrestrial in origin but looking just like a funny animal character come to life, Howard won his own comic book in 1975, after appearing in Marvel's *Fear* and *Man-Thing*. An anomaly, *Howard the Duck* wasn't exactly a funny animal comic, nor was it a superhero title. The world in which Howard had to function was a freely rendered version of Cleveland. Confused and angry at being stranded on Earth and, as cover blurbs reminded readers, "trapped in a world he never made," Howard was as much an antihero as he was a comedy character.

Howard was talkative and cynical. Writer-creator Steve Gerber used him to comment on a wide variety of social issues. Gerber had scripted Marvel superhero titles such as *The Defenders* and Howard kidded the fairly rigid formats and formulas of the genre. Critic Dale Luciano of *The Comics Journal* has observed that Gerber's scripts had "an abrasive, zany, satirical clout without taking themselves too seriously."

Frank Brunner, the original artist, was succeeded by Gene Colan commencing with *Howard the Duck* #4. The book lasted for 31 issues and was canceled in 1979. Two additional issues that carried on the original numbering appeared in 1986 to coincide with the release of the movie *Howard the Duck*, one of the outstanding turkeys of cinema history. The sarcastic bird also appeared in the nine-issue run of a black-and-white *Howard* magazine. Gerber and Colan also turned out a cryptic and short-lived Howard newspaper strip.

THE HULK   An appealing combination of Mr. Hyde, the FRANKENSTEIN monster, the Wolf Man, and the Jolly Green Giant, he was introduced in Marvel's *The Incredible Hulk* in the spring of 1962. The cover promised "fantasy as you like it" and asked the question, "Is he MAN or MONSTER or . . . is he BOTH?" Stan Lee and Jack Kirby, who'd invented the FANTAS-TIC FOUR just six months earlier, were the creators of this "strangest man of all time!!" The Hulk got off to a slow start and was even laid off for a spell. But eventually he built an audience and he's been rampaging ever since.

Like many another superhero, the Hulk became one by accident. When mild-mannered scientist Dr. Bruce Banner rescued teenager Rick Jones from the site of a secret test of the G-bomb, Banner's frail body was "bathed in the full force of mysterious gamma rays!" In the origin story, the reluctant Banner first turns into the grim, muscle-bound Hulk at the rise of the full moon and returns to his natural self at dawn. Later he'd become the monster when ticked off. In the intro issue, the Hulk's skin was gray, but Lee decided that wouldn't do: "The color I finally opted for was a bravely bedazzling basic green." Rick Jones tagged along with Banner from issue to issue, playing a combination of Robin the Boy Wonder and Sancho Panza and trying to keep both sides of the equation under control.

The first *Hulk* magazine folded after a half dozen issues. But Hulk returned in 1965, showing up in *Tales to Astonish* in tandem, initially, with Giant-Man. The magazine became *The Incredible Hulk* in 1968 and has continued as such. Among the other artists who've drawn the emerald Jekyll–Hyde are Herb Trimpe, Steve Ditko, John Byrne, and Todd McFarlane.

HYDROMAN   Here was a fellow who was really able to look on the bright side. Had the average person, as the result of an accident, been turned into a pool of water on the lab floor, he or she might have moped or become depressed. Not so with handsome Bob Blake. When he got liquefied, it inspired him to become a crimefighter. Once his scientist friend devised a way to get him back to human form, that is. From then on, Blake, calling himself Hydroman, could turn from flesh and blood to H_2O and back again at will. His costume consisted of an airplane helmet with goggles, tights, and boots, and a transparent tunic.

Being able to puddle up whenever he wished allowed Hydroman to sneak up on his opponents in some unexpected ways. He might enter their lairs by way of the plumbing or trickle under a locked door. His special knack also enabled him to bring off some impressive escapes. He could turn to water and slip down the drain; he could even liquefy and then hide from his pursuers in the ocean. Once the crafty villains tried to slow him down by freezing him, but Hydroman used a handy miniature heater he happened to be carrying on his person and melted free of their clutches. During his earliest adventures, he fought against a gang of Oriental invaders. Caught up in the funny-book mystique, they, too, dressed in flamboyant costumes.

Hydroman flowed in HEROIC COMICS from the first issue (August 1940) through the 29th (March 1945). Bill Everett, who had an affinity for waterlogged heroes (SUB-MARINER, the Fin), was the initial artist. Mopping up after him were Ben Thompson and Henry Kiefer.

Hydroman, Bill Everett, © 1940 Famous Funnies, Inc.

IBIS In the 1940s it seemed as though almost every comic book had a magician in its lineup—mystical fellows in tuxes and capes, sporting top hats, turbans, or fezes. They waved wands, gestured hypnotically, muttered magic phrases, and worked all sorts of miracles in the service of law and order. With the possible exception of DC's ZATARA, the most successful wizard was Ibis the Invincible. A creation of C.C. Beck and Bill Parker, he set up shop in the first issue of WHIZ COMICS (February 1940) and remained with the magazine until its demise in the spring of 1953. Since his name presented a problem to his younger readers, a footnote each month explained that it was "pronounced Eye-bis."

Ibis had an origin that seems to have been inspired by the 1932 Boris Karloff movie *The Mummy*. When first seen he, too, was a mummy and reclining in a glass case in "the Egyptian wing of a famous American museum." At the stroke of midnight, he awoke and used the Ibistick, a wand described as "the most powerful weapon ever devised," to get free of his glass prison and shed his wrappings. As soon as the wand decked him out in a black business suit and a red turban, he set out to find Princess Taia

("pronounced Tie-ah"). "Ibis' first thought is of the beautiful girl from whom death separated him 4,000 years before." Find her he did and, unfazed by the long time between dates, the two teamed to "battle modern crime."

They enjoyed some pretty grim adventures over the next few years. An early caption explained, with the bleak optimism that characterized the saga, "The world is full of evil!

Ibis, Pete Constanza, © 1940 by Fawcett Publications, Inc.

But not the strongest or wickedest of enemies can prevail against Prince Ibis." Among the evils Ibis and his princess bumped into were Mayan vampire bats, sea monsters, green demons, nasty leprechauns, Death himself, satyrs, fire spirits, a wereleopard, the Flying Dutchman, the ghost of Attila the Hun, green men from another planet, the murderous mummy of Ramses (who, besides planning to loose plagues upon the world, was also collaborating with the Axis powers), and Satan. In that episode, Ibis thwarted the Prince of Darkness during one of his soul-buying shopping sprees. Satan, miffed, summoned up the spirits of such formidable folks as Nero, Brutus, and Robespierre, along with "the sweepings of the gutter!" Even so, Ibis won out. In the final panel, Taia spoke for all the magician's loyal but unsettled fans when she complained, "What a horrible adventure that was, my prince!"

Later artists on the feature included Pete Constanza, Alex Blum, Bob Hebberd, and Al Carreño. Prince Ibis also appeared in six issues of his own magazine from 1942 to 1948.

IRON MAN One of the most trouble-ridden heroes to be launched in the Silver Age, he first appeared in Marvel's *Tales of Suspense* #39 (March 1963). Another of Stan Lee's inventions, Iron Man's early adventures were written by Larry Lieber and drawn by Don Heck. Tony Stark, a multimillionaire industrialist, was the original Iron Man. Not a true superhero, he gained an incredible array of abilities by putting on "an electrically powered, transistorized/smart suit of iron armor equipped with heavy offensive weaponry."

Stark developed the suit while a prisoner of the Viet Cong. He'd fallen into their hands after stepping on a landmine, which, among other things, caused severe damage to his heart. Initially the suit of super armor kept him alive with a built-in pacemaker device. After escaping from his captors, with the help of a black chopper pilot named James Rhodes, Stark eventually returned to civilian life. He served as president and CEO of Stark Industries (now Stark International), a member in good standing of the military-industrial complex. Rhodes came to work for him, becoming his best friend.

Iron Man's favorite foe over the years was a sinister Oriental known as the Mandarin. In its early years the saga was, as *The Encyclopedia of American Comics* points out, "an odd melange of political realism, shrill anti-communist jingoism, and fanciful superheroics."

Although he eventually became less of a cold warrior, Stark's life has not been an especially happy one. Unmarried, he's suffered a series of romantic setbacks. In addition, a bullet wound to the spine left him crippled for a time and later another injury caused neural damage. For quite awhile Stark was also an alcoholic. During the periods when Stark's problems overwhelmed him, Rhodes, nicknamed Rhodey, put on the armor and served as Iron Man in his friend's place. The suit of armor has undergone many changes in both design, color scheme, and capabilities. In fact, late in 1992 Marvel issued *The Iron Man Manual* to explain all the various costume changes.

Iron Man has been a member of the Avengers and later the Avengers West Coast. Among the other frequent villains combated have been the Melter, Backlash, Arsenal, Obadiah Stane, and the Iron Monger. Numerous artists and writers have had a hand in producing his adventures, including Gene Colan, Archie Goodwin, George Tuska, David Micheline, John Romita, Jr., and Len Kaminski.

IRON VIC He enjoyed an unusual career, beginning as a superhero, switching to pro baseball, and then joining the Marines. Created by newspaper veteran Bernard Dibble, he was introduced in a 1940 United Features one-shot titled

Iron Vic. That same year he became a backup in *Tip Top Comics* and remained there until the autumn of 1944. He also appeared in three issues of his own magazine in 1947, a ballplayer again.

Dibble, who'd once played minor league ball himself, had been doing newspaper strips since the 1920s. During his career he also ghosted such features as *The Captain & The Kids* (which he took over for a time) and *Fritzi Ritz*.

In the initial *Iron Vic* issue, Dibble outlined how the unconscious Vic was found on the beach and taken to the "ramshackle old laboratory of Professor Carvel and his assistant." Injecting Vic with "a certain rare serum of mine," the professor saves his life and also converts him into a superhuman. Vic, however, is suffering from amnesia and can't recall his past life. After encountering and defeating the master criminal Dr. Spagna, Vic gets the feeling "I've played ball myself somewhere."

He tries out for a big league team called the Panthers and proves to be a whiz at the game. When he showed up in *Tip Top* #54 (October 1940), he was a ballplayer and all thoughts of superheroics were gone.

Apparently Dibble had been instructed to create a superhero. He complied briefly, but soon tired of that and turned to his real love, baseball. Vic continued to play ball, and to serve as an inspiration for kids, until late in 1942. Then he enlisted in the Marine Corps. After the war he returned briefly to the diamond.

JINGLE JANGLE COMICS   It was published by Famous Funnies, Inc. chiefly as a showcase for the talents of the inimitable George Carlson. *Jingle Jangle Comics* was edited by Stephen Douglas and intended for a young audience. It lasted from early 1942 until late 1949. Today it is collected by grown-ups who appreciate Carlson's particular blend of nonsense, burlesque, and fantasy.

Carlson (1887–1962), a cartoonist, illustrator, and puzzle maker since before World War I, had contributed to *Judge,* created numerous books of puzzles and riddles, ghosted the *Reg'lar Fellers* strip, illustrated Uncle Wiggily books, and drew the dust jacket for *Gone with the Wind.* He did his first comic book work for *Jingle Jangle Comics,* doing two features for most issues—*Jingle Jangle Tales* and *The Pie-Face Prince of Old Pretzleburg.* Carlson was fond of the *Jingle Jangle Tales* title. He had tried it earlier on an unsold children's book and on an unsold Sunday page. Obviously he had helped Douglas put *Jingle Jangle Comics* together.

Carlson had a fascination with language. He loved to come up with odd puns and to twist stock phrases into new and unexpected shapes. Among the characters who turned up in his *Jingle Jangle Tales* were the Youthful

Yodeler, who lived on a newly painted mountain and sold all kinds of weather by the yard, and the Very Horseless Jockey, who became rich from his flavored snowball business and then set out, in his steamed-up steam engine, to buy a fine mahogany horse for himself. There were also all sorts of other unusual people and props to be found in Carlson's vigorous, cluttered pages, including a freshly toasted sandwich board, a four-footed yardstick maker, and a trio of jellybeans, "all slicked up with shoe-laces neatly pressed," who went forth to seek their fortunes.

Pretzleburg, ruled over by King Hokum without much help from his pie-face offspring Prince Dimwitri, was similar in appearance and politics to the various light-opera countries to be seen in the *Tales.* The regular cast included the prince's more-or-less true love, Princess Panetella Murphy, the Raging Rajah, who was the prince's "favorite enemy," and the Wicked Green Witch. Prince Dimwitri had wide-ranging interests and adventures. In one issue, for example, he set out to win the coveted Doopsniggle Prize with his corned-beef-flavored cabbage plant and in another he took to the air in an 18-karat balloon in search of a missing bass drum.

Among the other features that inhabited

the magazine over its 42-issue run were *Hortense the Lovable Brat*, *Bingo's Frolics in Fairytale Land*, *Chauncy Chirp*, and *Aunty Spry*. Douglas recruited a variety of artists, including Jack Farr, Woody Gelman, Dave Tendlar, and Larz Bourne. Tendlar had worked as an animator from the late 1920s onward and after his *Jingle Jangle* stint also drew for Harvey humor titles. Bourne later created the *Deputy Dawg* television cartoon series for Terrytoons.

Jingle Jangle Comics, George Carlson, © 1943 by Famous Funnies, Inc.

JOHNNY THUNDER   This was a popular name for characters at DC. It had been used three times by the early 1990s, first for a burlesque superhero, then for a serious phantom cowboy, and, most recently, for a female daredevil.

The first user of the name appeared in *Flash Comics* #1 (January 1940), which was also the home of THE FLASH and HAWKMAN. As presented by writer John B. Wentworth and artist Stan Aschmeier, Johnny Thunder (called Johnny Thunderbolt in early issues) was an inept but likable young blond man who just happened to have—due to some mystical happenings in his youth—a pet thunderbolt who could perform all sorts of magic. Whenever Johnny uttered "Say you," a phonetic approximation of the word of power "Cei-u," the humanoid bolt would appear, genie-like, make a few snide remarks, and then do Johnny's bidding for exactly one hour.

Wentworth had a good deal of fun with his concept, making fun of superheroes, G-men, urban life, and assorted other targets. In the more sobersided postwar years, however, Johnny was gradually eased out of his spot by the BLACK CANARY, also a member of the JUSTICE SOCIETY, and he retired to oblivion.

The second Johnny Thunder was a Western hero who rode onto the scene in ALL-AMERICAN COMICS #100 (August 1948) a few months after the other Johnny had retired. He usurped the lead spot of the fading GREEN LANTERN. Created by writer Robert Kanigher and artist Alex Toth, he was a dual-identity character. But to become Johnny Thunder, mild-mannered blond school teacher John Tane didn't put on a mask. He simply exchanged his pin-striped dude suit for a costume of buckskins and jeans, strapped on a pair of six-guns, dyed his hair black, commenced talking in a Western drawl, and hopped into the saddle of his horse, Black Lightning.

The stories were set in a generic Old West and Johnny, son of the sheriff of Mesa City, tangled with the usual run of rustlers, owlhoots, and wildbunches. Toth's exceptional artwork was what made the feature stand out.

All-American became *All-American Western* with #103 (November 1948), switching to all-cowboy fare and keeping Johnny Thunder as the star. In the spring of 1952, when the magazine became *All-American Men of War*, Johnny moved into *All-Star Western*. He continued there until the title ended in 1961. Kanigher remained the scriptwriter, but Gil Kane eventually took over as artist. Near the end of the run Johnny encountered a recurrent white-clad outlaw queen known as Madame .44.

In 1985, DC introduced a lady private eye named Jonni Thunder. She starred in a four-book miniseries and was seen no more.

Powerhouse Pepper™, Basil Wolverton. All Marvel characters and the distinctive likenesses thereof are trademarks of Marvel Entertainment Group, Inc. and are used with permission. © 1992 Marvel Entertainment Group, Inc.

All Star Comics, E.E. Hibbard, © 1941, renewed 1969 DC Comics, Inc. All rights reserved.

JOKER COMICS This was one of the earliest comic books devoted entirely to funny stuff and it introduced Basil Wolverton's peerless Powerhouse Pepper to the world. In its eight years of existence, it also showcased the work of other major graphic humorists such as Al Jaffee and Harvey Kurtzman. *Joker* was a Marvel title. The first issue had a cover date of April 1942.

In addition to Wolverton's hairless super-

hero, there was Jaffee's screwball police procedural, *Squat Car Squad*. In the vein of Bill Holman's newspaper-page *Smokey Stover*, the feature offered not only crime and detection but appearances by the artist himself, publisher Martin Goodman, and others of the convivial staff. *Snoopy and Dr. Nutzy* was a detective burlesque and *Rolly & Solly* kidded the Army. Both changed artists regularly.

Among the other features were *Eustis Hayseed*, *E. Radicate De Bugs*, *Tommy Gunz*, and *Dippy Diplomat*. TESSIE THE TYPIST commenced in the second issue, initially offering a series of one-page office gags. Tessie the Typist was a pretty blonde, and soon she was being featured on each of the covers.

Harvey Kurtzman, who'd drawn mostly superheroes thus far in his comic book career, started doing a strange, funny, and somewhat surrealistic filler page entitled *Hey Look* in the spring of 1946. The future inventor of MAD was the only new zany added to the staff.

In the postwar years, pretty girl characters

began to dominate the lineup. In addition to Tessie were Millie the Model, Nellie the Nurse, Hedy of Hollywood, Patty Pinup, and Daisy. The humor in the stories about these assorted young women wasn't screwball or slapstick but closer to what would now be labeled sitcom. A true loon like Powerhouse Pepper was increasingly out of place in such surroundings and after issue #31, in the spring of 1948, he was seen no more. *Joker*, with the funny ladies in charge, continued until the summer of 1950. As an omen of what was going to happen to many comic books in the early years of the upcoming decade, *Joker Comics* became *Adventures in Terror* with its 43rd issue. Among the early "tales of strange suspense" that it offered were "The Thing in the Cave," "The Torture Room," and "Spawn of the Vampire."

JOURNEY INTO MYSTERY   It began life in 1952 as another of Marvel's horror titles. Two years later, during increased public criticism of gruesome comics, *Journey into Mystery* was toned down and began dealing in fantasy and science fiction. This was followed by a period when giant monsters were given star billing. Then in 1961, as the revival of interest in superheroes grew, the magazine introduced THOR.

The first 18 issues offered tales of terror, complete with zombies, vampires, werewolves, and ghouls. The covers were suitably horrific, frequently depicting ambulatory skeletons and walking corpses. Things quieted down during the magazine's fantasy phase. In the late 1950s, Jack Kirby, aided by editor-scripter Stan Lee, began drawing stories that showcased huge monstrous creatures who were obviously trying to outshine Godzilla. Kirby, who maintained that his creatures were never meant to be repellent, called his monsters "lovable." They included entities named Gruto, the Glob, and Xemnu. Steve Ditko contributed a variety of short fantasy and science fiction tales during this period.

Lee, working with Kirby, came up with the Mighty Thor and used *Journey into Mystery* #83 (August 1961) to introduce him. The magazine retained its title until early in 1966 and then became *Thor*.

Among the many artists who contributed were Bill Everett, Bernard Krigstein, Joe Maneely, and Russ Heath.

JUSTICE LEAGUE OF AMERICA   Part of the SILVER AGE revival at DC, the JLA made hero teams popular again and inspired Marvel to come up with the FANTASTIC FOUR. After resurrecting THE FLASH and GREEN LANTERN, editor Julius Schwartz next recaptured a whole team of superheroes from the past. Taking the JUSTICE SOCIETY from the defunct ALL STAR COMICS, he rechristened it the Justice League. The membership roster now had the names of the Flash, Green Lantern, AQUAMAN, WONDER WOMAN, and MARTIAN MANHUNTER on it. Gardner Fox, the scribe for the original gang, was brought back to write the book-length adventures of the new one. The team was introduced in THE BRAVE AND THE BOLD #28 (March 1960). Mike Sekowsky, a disciple of Alex Toth, was the initial artist.

"It was a thrilling moment for DC's older fans," *The Comic Book Heroes* observed. "And there were signs—letters from grateful adults scattered throughout the country—that the number of fans was steadily growing. With his intelligent sense of fun, Schwartz was beginning to reach an audience who would normally have put comic books behind them."

After three tryout issues, the JLA was promoted to its own magazine in the autumn of 1960. It continued through #261 before shutting down in the spring of 1987. A new comic book, titled simply *Justice League*, started up the following month. For a time it was called *Justice League International* and in the spring of 1989 a separate magazine, *Justice League Europe*, was launched.

Like any organization, the JLA has experienced personnel changes in the three-plus decades that it's been involved in crime-fighting and crisis control. Such characters as BAT-MAN, GREEN ARROW, Mr. Miracle, BLUE BEETLE, the Red Tornado, BLACK CANARY, Captain Atom, Rocket Red, Firestorm, SUPERMAN, CAPTAIN MAR-VEL, Elongated Man, Vixen, Booster Gold, and Guy Gardner have all carried membership cards.

THE JUSTICE SOCIETY OF AMERICA   Before this group was organized late in 1940, there had never been a superhero team. Formed in DC's ALL STAR COMICS #3, the Justice Society of America was the joint creation of editor Sheldon Mayer and writer Gardner Fox. The crime fighting, spy-smashing organization was in continuous operation until early in 1951 and has reappeared several times since. Among the founding members were the FLASH, the GREEN LANTERN, HAWKMAN, the SPECTRE, and DR. FATE.

Begun as a quarterly, *All Star* brought together characters from other DC titles. The bright-yellow cover of the first issue, which showed panels ripped from four of the strips, was designed by Mayer, who also drew the logo. The first meeting of the JSA was held in #3 (Winter 1940) and in #4, which was the first

bimonthly issue, there was a theme running through all the stories. The heroes teamed up in each issue to defend America against spies, travel to the planets, feed the starving of Europe, and defeat such villains as the Brain Wave, the Psycho-Pirate, and Solomon Grundy. Fox wrote all the novel-length adventures through #34 (April–May 1947). At first the characters' regular artists drew the individual chapters.

Over the years, the makeup of the Justice Society fluctuated and among those who sat around the conference table were JOHNNY THUN-DER, WONDER WOMAN, THE ATOM, STARMAN, SAND-MAN, Wildcat, and the BLACK CANARY. The later writers were Robert Kanigher and John Broome. The final issue of *All Star* was #57 and bore a cover date of February–March 1951.

The JSA came out of retirement in the SIL-VER AGE and, thanks to the DC notion that the GA characters and the SA characters existed in parallel worlds known as Earth-Two and Earth-One, they were able now and then to coexist with the newer JUSTICE LEAGUE and to appear in the latter group's magazine. They have also appeared elsewhere, and some of them made up the All Star Squadron.

KATY KEENE "America's Pin-Up Queen" began modestly in 1945 as part of somebody else's comic book. She gradually built up a following among the virtually untapped girl audience and by the mid-1950s was appearing in three separate titles of her own. Katy Keene retired in 1961, but returned in 1983 and remained on the scene until 1990.

Bill Woggon, who had assisted his brother Elmer on the *Big Chief Wahoo* newspaper strip, created Katy. She made her debut as a backup feature in *Wilbur* #5 (1945), which was published by the Archie folks. Her appeal soon became apparent and she was added to the lineups of *Laugh*, *Pep*, and *Suzie*. In 1949, she graduated to a magazine of her own. The book appeared just once that year, once in 1950 and twice in 1951. *Katy Keene* became a quarterly in 1952 and went bimonthly a year later. In 1955, two more titles appeared, *Katy Keene Fashion Book Magazine* and a 25¢ comic called *Katy Keene Pin-Up Parade*.

Although the largest part of her audience was composed of teens and preteens, Katy wasn't a teenager. She was a full-grown young woman who worked first as a model and later as a Hollywood starlet. Apparently just about every girl in America goes through a phase where she wants to be a model or a fashion designer. Katy, whose life was taken up mostly with modeling, posing, and dating, appealed to an audience that had been unmoved by superheroes or funny animals. Added reader involvement was ensured by Katy's mischievous little sister, Sis, a pigtailed troublemaker who acted as Katy's accomplice, conscience, and cheerleader. Katy's boyfriends included boxer K.O. Kelly, millionaire playboy Rudy Von Ronson, and movie idol Erroll Swoon.

Woggon encouraged reader participation, an especially important element in Katy's success. Readers were invited to send in designs for Katy's outfits, which were rendered by the artist and other staffers. Each contributor was credited by name and hometown. As cartoonist and longtime Katy Keene fan Trina Robbins has pointed out, "Each episode featured countless costume changes, with every outfit designed by a different reader."

Woggon, who drew in a simple and direct cartoon sytle, once said that he was influenced by comic strips like *Fritzi Ritz*, *Brenda Starr*, and *Tillie the Toiler*, each of which occasionally included paper dolls and gave credit to readers who submitted fashion designs. The work of George Petty, the airbrush artist who painted pinups for *Esquire,* was another influence. "The Petty Girl was indeed my favorite," Woggon admitted, "and inspired me to create . . . Katy Keene."

Woggon employed several assistants over the years, including Hazel Marten, Cassie Bill, Floyd Norman, Bob MacLeon, Tom Cooke, and Bill Ziegeler. The chief revival artist was John Lucas.

KA-ZAR Two separate Marvel heroes have played TARZAN under this name. The first, after a brief stint as a pulp fiction hero in the mid-1930s, became a comic book jungle man in 1939 when he debuted in the first issue of MARVEL COMICS. The second wildman to do business as Ka-Zar was a product of the SILVER AGE and flourished from the mid-1960s to the mid-1980s.

The original Ka-Zar was the first comic book imitator of Tarzan. The blond jungle lord had started imitating Edgar Rice Burroughs's hero a few years earlier in the pages of a pulp magazine. There were three issues of the *Ka-Zar* pulpwood, starting with the October 1936 number: "Through the menacing brooding jungle stalked the mighty white youth Ka-Zar, discovering, fighting, conquering beasts, savages and white men who came to kill and steal the golden treasures from the primeval heart of the Congo."

The first adventure in *Marvel* repeated the origin story first told in the pulp by a writer signing himself Bob Byrd. Little David Rand's parents crashed with him in the fierce African jungle. His mother died and David and his somewhat crazed dad lived on in the wilds to become a sort of father-and-son Tarzan team. They made friends with the animals and David—after learning lion lingo—became especially close to a mighty lion named Zar.

After his father was murdered by an evil renegade emerald hunter, David more or less moved in with his lion chum and took to calling himself Ka-Zar, which means "brother of the lion." In his earliest adventures Ka-Zar was a teenager, but by the fourth issue of *Marvel Comics* he was full-grown.

Ka-Zar, billed as the "guardian of the wild Belgian Congo animals," spent a good deal of his time shooing unscrupulous white hunters out of the jungle. He seems to have gotten along fairly well with the black residents of his world and usually reserved his ire and violence for encroachers. Eventually he became more involved in current events and was "successful in destroying Nazi and Fascist fortresses in the jungle." Because he was an Englishman, he felt justified in going to war against the Axis powers earlier than many American heroes did.

Ka-Zar's jungle was a somewhat spartan place, and few if any women found their way into his domain. He took his leave after *Marvel* #27 (January 1942). The artist throughout was Ben Thompson. A gag cartoonist at heart, Thompson did most of his research into African life and lore by studying old Burne Hogarth Sunday *Tarzan* pages.

The new improved Ka-Zar, reinvented by Stan Lee, first popped up as a guest in *X-Men* #10 in 1965 (see X-MEN). This time around, the Lord of the Jungle was actually a British lord named Kevin Plunder. He had grown up in a tropical kingdom known as the Savage Land that was said to lie "buried far beneath the frozen wastes of Antarctica." Like the earlier holder of the title, this Ka-Zar had blond shaggy hair and wore nothing more than a knife and an animal-skin loincloth. Unlike his predecessor, he spoke like the Johnny Weismuller–movie Tarzan.

After many guest shots and team-ups, including appearances in *Daredevil, Spider-Man,* and *The Hulk,* over the next few years, Ka-Zar drew a permanent berth in *Astonishing Tales* (see DAREDEVIL, SPIDER-MAN, THE HULK). He

Ka-Zar™, Ben Thompson. All Marvel characters and the distinctive likenesses thereof are trademarks of Marvel Entertainment Group, Inc. and are used with permission. © 1992 Marvel Entertainment Group, Inc.

appeared in the first 20 issues, beginning in 1970. Lee and Jack Kirby did the initial stories, followed by Gerry Conway and CONAN artist Barry Smith.

The jungle man moved into a comic titled *Ka-Zar* in 1974, where he first met up with the feisty Shanna O'Hara, a SHEENA lookalike who operated as Shanna the She-Devil. Their initially antagonistic relationship blossomed into a romance and eventually they were married. Ka-Zar was benched in 1977, but returned, along with his leopard-skin-wearing mate, in 1981. *Ka-Zar the Savage* lasted until the summer of 1984. In addition to an occasional domestic scrap, his life was further complicated by his evil brother Parnival, who sullied the family name by doing vile deeds as a villain known as the Plunderer.

KID COLT He was representative of the dozens of cowboy heroes who crowded the newsstands in the decade or so after the end of World War II. Kid Colt was introduced by Marvel in the summer of 1948, but unlike most of his colleagues, he didn't hang up his spurs for several decades.

The Kid was a lanky blond hombre who wore a red shirt, jeans, a rawhide vest, and a black Stetson. He carried two Colt .45s in his gun belt. Like many another Western hero, he was considered an outlaw but was actually a champion of justice. As one grizzled sheriff explained it, "The Kid's an outlaw only 'cause some bushwhacker killed his dad! He lit out after the killer an' settled the score! Since then he's been ridin' alone! Some call him an outlaw, but many's the time he's been a lawman's friend!"

Misunderstood throughout his career, Kid Colt roamed the West, "hunted, driven, living like a wolf." He was a relatively popular character and his magazine reached #229 before he was put out to pasture in 1979. The first four issues were titled *Kid Colt, Hero of the West.* The name was then changed to the more appropriate *Kid Colt, Outlaw.* Among the many artists who drew the wandering owlhoot were Syd Shores, Joe Kubert, Dick Ayers, and Gene Colan.

The rise of television and the popularity of cowboy shows acted as one of the inspirations for the wave of Western comic books in the 1950s. Marvel was especially fond of cowboys with the word *kid* in their names and during that decade it devoted titles to the Texas Kid, the Two-Gun Kid, the Rawhide Kid, the Outlaw Kid, the Arizona Kid, the Apache Kid, the Western Kid, the Kid from Texas, and the Kid from Dodge City.

LADY LUCK The best-known and most success-ful masked woman in GOLDEN AGE comics was Lady Luck. She was created by Will Eisner and drawn initially by Chuck Mazuojian, and she made her debut in the first issue of the weekly *Spirit* newspaper insert in June of 1940. In 1943, *Smash Comics* began reprinting her four-page adventures. She was last seen in five issues of her own magazine, which folded in the summer of 1950.

As a caption explained, "Two lives are led by Brenda Banks, society girl. . . . One as an idle heiress . . . the other as the elusive enemy of crime know as Lady Luck."

To convert to her alter ego, blonde Brenda slipped into a simple green frock with a sham-rock at the throat, a short green cape, and a wide-brimmed, flat-crowned green hat. For a mask she used a transparent green veil over the lower part of her face. Though not much of a disguise, it served to fool friend and foe alike. During World War II, the deb detective specialized in swatting spies and saboteurs, both German and Japanese.

Nick Cardy was the second artist and dur-ing his stint the feature lightened up some. During his stay, Brenda hired a large Latino chauffeur named Peecolo. He knew the secret of her double life and often assisted her on

cases. When Cardy was drafted in 1942, Eisner brought in Klaus Nordling to draw and write *Lady Luck*. Nordling converted the feature into

Lady Luck, Klaus Nordling, © Will Eisner.

a screwball mystery–comedy, a mixture of crime-fighting and satire. His major new character was the dithery little Count DiChange, who was as trouble-prone as Lois Lane.

Nordling stayed with the character for four years, turning out more than 200 four-page adventures before stepping aside. He was replaced by Fred Schwab. When Brenda got her own magazine, Nordling returned as the official artist.

LITTLE LULU She was created by cartoonist Marge Henderson Buell for a series of gag panels that began in *The Saturday Evening Post* in 1935, but it's as a comic book character that Little Lulu is most fondly remembered. The smart little girl with the corkscrew curls, bright-red dress, and tiny red hat made her comic book debut in Dell's Four Color #74 in 1947. The long-running comic, although officially titled *Marge's Little Lulu*, was actually masterminded by artist-writer John Stanley.

What Stanley provided, after having written and drawn the first couple of issues of *Little Lulu*, were rough storyboards for artist Irving Tripp to follow. "To say that Stanley 'wrote' *Little Lulu* is actually a little deceptive," comics historian Mike Barrier has stated, "since he was responsible for more than the plots and the dialogue. He sketched each story in rough form, so that he controlled the staging within each panel and the appearance and attitudes of the characters." Stanley's pages would be enlarged, inked by Tripp (with occasional assists from Gordon Rose and others), and lettered.

Stanley inherited Lulu's boyfriend/antagonist Tubby from the original gag cartoons—wherein the fat boy was named Joe—but he invented most of the other characters, including truant officer Mr. McNabbem, Wilbur Van Snobbe, Witch Hazel and Little Itch, and the bullying West Side Boys. As Barrier has pointed out, Stanley's conception of Lulu is quite different from the bratty kid of the *Post*

era. Eventually, "Lulu . . . became a 'good little girl' who outsmarted the boys instead of triumphing through sheer brass, as she had in the past. Many of the stories built around the rivalry theme are ingenious and funny, and the best of them spiral upward until the boys become the victims of comic catastrophe."

Little Lulu's adventures were clever and low-key. These attributes, coupled with Stanley's simple storytelling style, entertained a generation of kids and inspired many of them to remain fans into their adult lives.

Stanley worked on *Little Lulu* until 1961. In all, he was responsible for about 150 issues. The comic book continued without him, until 1984 although many post-Stanley issues merely reprint his earlier stories.

THE LONE RANGER A multimedia cowboy and certainly one of the best-known masked men of the 20th century, he first rode out of the West in 1933. That was by way of the *Lone Ranger* radio show, originating over station WXYZ in Detroit. The deep-voiced do-gooder, his great horse Silver, and his faithful Indian companion Tonto soon captured the hearts and imaginations of millions of kids across the country. By the mid-1930s, the show was heard nationwide over the Mutual Broadcasting System, sponsored by, among others, more than a dozen regional bread companies. The masked man conquered other media and pulp magazines, movie serials, Big Little Books (BLB), and a comic strip followed. The Lone Ranger made his first comic book appearance in 1939.

A variation on many earlier masked avengers of pulps, dime novels, and movies, the Lone Ranger was cobbled together by a group that included station owner George W. Trendle, station dramatic director James Jewell, and scriptwriter Fran Striker. Striker also had a hand in the newspaper strip launched by King Features Syndicate late in 1938. The first comic book was a premium, an original one-shot drawn by BLB artist Henry Vallely and given

Lone Rider, Jack Kirby, 1939.

While no masked cowboy came near rivaling the Lone Ranger in comic books, several gave it a try. Some, like the Masked Ranger in MORE FUN and the Phantom Rider in *Star Comics*, actually beat him to the newsstand. Among the other GOLDEN AGE competitors were the Masked Raider in MARVEL COMICS, Nevada Jones in ZIP COMICS, and the Vigilante in ACTION COMICS. FAMOUS FUNNIES had begun reprinting a newspaper strip entitled *The Lone Rider* in #62 (September 1939) under the title *Lightnin' and the Lone Rider*. It had been syndicated by Robert Farrell's low-budget Associated Features Syndicate for a short time and was drawn by a young cartoonist who signed himself Lance Kirby. That was the first time Jacob Kurtzberg had used the Kirby last name, and before he had decided to take Jack as a first name. When *Famous* ran out of reprints, Kirby was hired to draw a few extra installments.

away by an ice cream cone company. The David McKay Company issued a reprint comic of the strip in 1939, too. The masked man's strip was included in the lineup of McKay's *King Comics* and *Magic Comics* as well.

In the mid-1940s, Dell began using an occasional Lone Ranger reprint issue as part of its Four Color series. In 1948, it started a regular bimonthly title. After the 37th issue in the summer of 1951, Dell stopped reprinting the Charles Flanders newspaper strips and switched to original material. Tom Gill and his staff did the drawing, which was even tamer than that of Flanders. Among the writers was Paul S. Newman, also a scripter on the strip. During the 1950s, when the masked man was a television favorite, Dell also published a comic book devoted to his horse Silver and one devoted to Tonto. The final Lone Ranger comic book was issued in 1962.

LOONEY TUNES AND MERRIE MELODIES A profitable and long-running funny animal title, it launched such noted Warner Brothers animated cartoon characters as Bugs Bunny, Porky Pig, and Elmer Fudd in comic books. The first issue of *Looney Tunes and Merrie Melodies* appeared late in 1941 and the 246th, and final, one of the first series in the summer of 1962. It was revived as simply *Looney Tunes* in 1975 and continued until 1984. Dell published the first run and Whitman Publishing packaged the book, chiefly from its Southern California offices. The second series was put out by Whitman alone under its Gold Key colophon. Among the artists contributing to the early issues were Walt Kelly, Roger Armstrong, and Chase Craig.

In the beginning, the stories were turned out on both coasts. Based in Los Angeles were Craig, who also served as editor, Armstrong, and contributors such as Win Smith. Kelly, who'd returned East after toiling in the Disney studios, was in New York, as was newspaper veteran George Storm, who did considerable

Pat, Patsy, and Pete, Walt Kelly, © 1943 by R.S. Callender.

work for the magazine during its first year.

Porky Pig, known for his stutter and the fact that he never wore pants, had first appeared on the screen in 1935. In the comic book, accompanied by his girlfriend Petunia, he was the featured star for the first few issues before being nudged out of the limelight by Bugs Bunny. Both Craig and Armstrong drew his action-packed adventures.

The outgoing Bugs was introduced in a 1938 Warner cartoon. The first Bugs Bunny stories in *Looney Tunes* were drawn by Win Smith, who a decade earlier had worked briefly on the *Mickey Mouse* newspaper strip (see MICKEY MOUSE). Storm drew Bugs for the next few issues after that.

The magazine also offered separate stories about Elmer Fudd and the mouse Sniffles, partnered here with a blonde little girl named Mary Jane. Kelly's first strip was *Kandi the Cave Kid* and it was credited, as were all the other features in each issue, to Leon Schlesinger, the non-drawing producer of the movie cartoons. *Looney Tunes* also gave space to an alternating variety of other characters, such as Chester Turtle, Ringy Roonga, and Charlie Carrot, one of the few vegetables ever to star in a comic book

of his own. Charlie's ladyfriend was a tomato.

Pat, Patsy, and Pete, about two kids and a talking penguin, was not a Warner property, but it ran in the magazine for several years. Smith started it, then Storm took over. Kelly drew six extremely slapstick episodes in 1943.

Porky Pig branched out into a book of his own in 1942 and his regular series lasted until 1984. Bugs Bunny also first appeared on his own in 1942 and his regular series folded in 1984, too. DC brought him back in 1990 in a miniseries.

LUKE CAGE, POWER MAN   Marvel's increased social awareness in the early 1970s, coupled with a desire to find new ways to boost sales, led the company to introduce black characters. The first black superhero was a tough urban mercenary named Luke Cage. He debuted in his own title, *Hero for Hire* #1 (June 1972). Archie Goodwin scripted, with art provided by penciler George Tuska and inker Billy Graham.

The new hero was introduced as an unjustly convicted prisoner named Lucas. As the result of an experiment by the prison doctor, which went seriously awry, Lucas was converted into a superman. He now possessed, as the *Marvel Universe* handbook explained it, "superhuman strength, very dense muscle and bone tissue, and steel-hard skin. . . . Power Man can punch through several feet of most modern, conventional building materials." Thus equipped, he broke out of prison and headed for New York to find the man who'd framed him.

Dressed up in yellow boots, black tights, open-fronted yellow shirt, and metal headband, looking like a cross between a superhero and a Belafonte-type folk singer, he set himself up as Luke Cage, Hero for Hire, doing business as a wall-smashing, head-breaking private investigator. After about a year and a half, Cage began calling himself Power Man and started behaving in a less gritty and more conventionally superheroic manner.

In the spring of 1978, Marvel teamed Cage with Iron Fist, a martial-arts superhero created in 1974 by Roy Thomas and Gil Kane. The result was *Power Man and Iron Fist*, a title that continued until 1986. Cage returned again in 1992.

Among the other African-American heroes who came into being in the 1970s were Marvel's Black Panther and DC's Black Lightning.

MAD Artist-editor Harvey Kurtzman's major contribution to American culture, it was introduced as a four-color comic book in the fall of 1952. Published by EC's William Gaines and created and edited by Kurtzman, *Mad* was converted to a black-and-white magazine in 1955 and as such continues to this day. Kurtzman departed soon after the change to black and white and was replaced by Al Feldstein as editor.

Lone Stranger, Jack Davis, © William Gaines.

Mad has remained steadfastly adolescent and irreverent for generations, never tiring of taking satirical potshots at such sitting ducks as movies, television, and advertising. In addition to Kurtzman, the magazine brought fame to such artists as Jack Davis, Don Martin, Allan Jaffee, Mort Drucker, and Sergio Aragones. Its mascot Alfred E. Neuman became a national celebrity. Over the years, *Mad* inspired dozens of imitations, including *Panic*, *Sick*, *Crazy*, *Cracked*, *Madhouse*, PLOP!, *Not Brand Ecch*, and *Humbug*.

MAGNUS This rebellious resident of the year 4000 A.D. was introduced in Gold Key's *Magnus, Robot Fighter* early in 1963. He continued his robot-bashing for the next 14 years, through 46 issues. Russ Manning was the original artist and writer. Magnus returned in the 1990s by way of two of Valiant Comics titles.

The stories were set in North Am, "the incredible city that covers every habitable area of the North American continent." Robots, originally built to serve humans, had gradually become "the masters of men." Magnus was a sort of futuristic TARZAN, raised in isolation by a benevolent robot and "trained to rely on my brain, rather than on tools." For good measure his mentor, the kindly, gold-plated 1A, also taught him a super-karate that enabled him to smash metal with just the chop of his bare hand. Returned to North Am, he set out at once to disable as many tyrannical robots as he could. Teamed with the lovely blonde Leeja Clane, Magnus found a wide assortment of mechanical men to disable over the years.

In the early 1990s, Jim Shooter's Valiant line licensed the character and featured him in a series of new adventures, drawn by Bob Layton, and in a second title reprinted Manning's earlier work.

MANHUNTER   *See* Martian Manhunter.

THE MAN IN BLACK   He was one of the earliest hosts in comic books and paved the way for such later presenters of weird tales as the Old Witch and the Crypt-Keeper (see TALES FROM THE CRYPT). The Man in Black, written and drawn by Bob Powell, first appeared in the mid-1940s and got a book of his own in the mid-1950s.

The feature was strongly influenced by some of the dramatic radio shows of the period. The very successful *Inner Sanctum* had a sardonic host called Raymond to introduce each week's grim tale. On *The Whistler* and THE MYSTERIOUS TRAVELER, the title characters served as hosts and narrators of the weekly stories of murder, larceny, adultery, and plans gone awry. And on *Suspense* during several seasons before the advert of Powell's character, the host was actually known as the Man in Black.

Powell's Man in Black first appeared in Harvey Publications' *Front Page*, a one-shot, which, despite its name, went in for weird tales. The following year he showed up in another one-shot, *Strange Story*. In 1946 and

1947 he appeared in four issues of THE GREEN HORNET and one of *All New*. As might be expected, the character dressed in black, somewhat in the DRACULA manner, complete with cape. His hair was combed to suggest horns and his face was always in deep shadow. He introduced himself as Mr. Twilight and in his earliest appearances he would usually apologize for keeping his face hidden. "It's quite necessary as one look at my face is fatal!" he explained. "You see . . . I'm . . . DEATH!!"

In the early stories, he was often intent on collecting a soul and was sometimes an actual participant in the story he was telling. In the later stories he passed himself off merely as Fate and was a more simple narrator, commenting on the strange workings of destiny. The stories varied, involving everything from gloomy castles to Japanese secret agents to gremlins. Powell illustrated them in the realistic, slightly cartoony style he would later use on THE SHADOW.

A decade passed before the Man in Black was seen again, this time in his own magazine. Between the fall of 1957 and the spring of 1958, Harvey published four issues of *Man in Black*. In 1965 came *Thrill-o-Rama*, showcasing *The Man in Black Called FATE*. It was the fate of this comic to last just three issues. Powell's character was not quite done for, though. Alfred Harvey printed two issues of a *Man in Black* reprint in 1990 and 1991.

MARTIAN MANHUNTER   A superhero who came along between the GOLDEN and SILVER AGES, J'Onn J'Onzz was introduced in DETECTIVE COMICS late in 1955. He was never a major attraction, but the Martian Manhunter was still plying his trade almost 40 years later.

J'Onzz was first seen in *Detective* #225 (November 1955) in a six-page story that explained that he'd been transported from Mars as the result of an experiment conducted by Professor Mark Erdel. Unfortunately for the big, green-skinned alien, the professor's contraption couldn't send him home and Erdel further complicated the situation by dying of a heart attack. J'Onzz, realizing he was stranded, assumed human shape and coloration and changed his name to John Jones. He then—rather easily for someone who'd only been on Earth for a day—got a job as a plainclothes police detective. As a cop, the manhunter made use of an assortment of abilities not available to the average law enforcer. In a piece in *The Amazing World of DC Comics*, Mark Gruenwald pointed out that these capabilities varied and multiplied from issue to issue and "in #226 he displayed psychokinesis and precognition . . . in #227 he could read minds . . . in #228 he was shown to be able to 'see through solids' . . . #230 introduced super-hearing."

The initial artist on the feature was Joe Certa, who was also working on the *Joe Palooka* newspaper strip at the time. Many of the Manhunter characters have the same strong-jawed, wide-shouldered look to be found in the boxing saga.

John Jones departed *Detective* in #326 (September 1963) and seemed to have died, but the Martian Manhunter, went on without his alter ego. He showed up in various DC titles, including *House of Mystery*, ADVENTURE, and WORLD'S FINEST. He also showed up in THE BRAVE AND THE BOLD #50 (October–November 1963) in a team-up with THE GREEN ARROW. This was the issue that launched the team concept to that title. He'd also been a now-and-again member of the JUSTICE LEAGUE OF AMERICA since its founding in 1960 and continuing into the 1990s.

DC had been partial to the Manhunter name long before J'Onzz came along. Ed Moore began doing *Manhunter* for *Adventure Comics* late in 1940, which featured a plainclothes crimefighter named Paul Kirk. Early in 1942, Joe Simon and Jack Kirby converted Kirk into a crimson-costumed hero who lasted for two years. Even after the advent of the Martian Manhunter, Paul Kirk came back to fight crime

as just plain Manhunter. Written by Archie Goodwin and drawn by Walt Simonson, his adventures appeared in *Detective Comics* in the 1970s.

MARVEL COMICS   It began late in 1939 and was officially known as *Marvel Mystery Comics* from the second issue on. This was the magazine that introduced such characters as the Human Torch, the Angel, and SUB-MARINER to newsstand audiences and served as the foundation of today's Marvel Comics empire (see ALL WINNERS COMICS). In its original form, the book lasted until the spring of 1949.

Publisher Martin Goodman went into the comic book business in the summer of 1939. Until then, he'd been publishing a string of pulp fiction magazines under various company names. He did cowboy pulps as well as such titles as *Dynamic Science Stories*, *Uncanny Tales*, and *Marvel Science Stories*. When he was approached by the FUNNIES, INC. shop, Goodman was persuaded that the time was right to branch out into comic books. The result was *Marvel*. Goodman called his company Timely Publications for this go-round.

The Human Torch, the Angel, and Sub-Mariner proved a durable trio. During *Marvel Comics'* early years other characters came and went, including the Masked Raider, a low-budget LONE RANGER; Electro, a giant red robot; Terry Vance, a schoolboy sleuth and the first character Bob Oksner ever drew; the Vision, a green, mystical fellow dreamed up by Joe Simon and Jack Kirby; the Patriot, yet another red, white, and blue-costumed hero; and KA-ZAR, a blond TARZAN borrowed from an earlier Goodman pulp.

Eventually most of the backup characters were let go. The Torch and Sub-Mariner remained, joined in 1946 by CAPTAIN AMERICA. *Marvel* had introduced MISS AMERICA late in 1943 and she stayed on until the end of 1947. In the postwar years Marvel added several new women, including the BLONDE PHANTOM, Sun Girl, and Sub-Mariner's underwater associate Namora.

The magazine sputtered out with its 92nd issue (June 1949). From #93 (August 1949) it was called *Marvel Tales* and offered horror stories with such titles as "The Ghoul Strikes," "A Witch Is Among Us," and "The Thing in the Sewer."

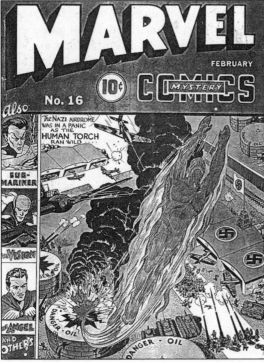

Marvel Comics®, Alex Schomburg. All Marvel characters and the distinctive likenesses thereof are trademarks of Marvel Entertainment Group, Inc. and are used with permission. © 1992 Marvel Entertainment Group, Inc.

MARY MARVEL Fawcett was the earliest publisher to realize that it could get more mileage, and revenue, out of a successful superhero by creating a family of related characters. Mary Marvel was sister to both CAPTAIN MARVEL and Billy Batson, and she followed the advent of CAPTAIN MARVEL, JR. by exactly a year. She was introduced in *Captain Marvel Adventures* #18

(December 1942) and then became the star of *Wow Comics* with #9 (January 1943). She was the first teen superheroine, and her stay in comics lasted until late 1953.

When Mary Batson was introduced, it was explained that she and her brother had been separated as babies. After being reunited, Mary discovered that Billy's magic word "SHAZAM!" also worked for her. Though still a teenager, as Mary Marvel she had all of the powers of Captain Marvel and wore a skirted version of his red-and-gold costume with the lightning bolt on the front. She appeared in *Wow* until the autumn of 1947, in 25 issues of her own title from 1945 to 1948 and in *The Marvel Family* until late in 1953.

Most of the adventures of Mary Marvel were written by the prolific Otto Binder. Marc Swayze was the original illustrator, then Jack Binder, with considerable early help from his shop, became the regular artist.

The Mary Marvel stories were never very serious, although they involved her with spies, criminal masterminds, and assorted crooks. During Mary's *Wow* adventures, two other Marvel Family members were born. In #18 (October 1943), a middle-aged gentleman introduced himself as her long-lost Uncle Dudley from California. Mary told him she didn't recall having an uncle, but he assured her, "Everybody has an unknown uncle from California." He was, of course, a fraud, a con man in the W.C. Fields vein who'd managed to get a look at Mary's diary and discovered her secret. He tried to con Mary further by claiming he could turn into Uncle Marvel by saying "Shazam!" He actually brought off a spurious change by shucking his suit to reveal a rumpled, homemade Marvel outfit underneath.

Uncle Dudley hoped to get rich by setting up Shazam, Inc. Mary soon tumbled to him, but found him "a dear old man and really kind-hearted." They teamed up on several occasions.

An actual relative of Uncle Marvel's showed up in 1945, one Freckles Dudley, a teenage girl about the same age as Mary. She took to donning a costume and calling herself Freckles Marvel, but never claimed to have superpowers.

Fawcett obviously hoped that Mary Marvel would lure more girls into becoming regular comic book buyers. In 1945 *Wow* introduced a Mary Marvel Club "just for girls!" Dues were 10¢. There were also several ads for a line of girls' clothes and accessories bearing the Mary Marvel label. These were being offered through the mail, but the ads maintained they were also available "in leading stores everywhere."

Mary Marvel returned to comics as an occasional backup in the mid-1970s, when DC brought back her brother in *Shazam!* She also made cameo appearances in the 1987 *Shazam!* miniseries.

Master Comics, Mac Raboy, © 1941 by Fawcett Publications, Inc.

Mary Marvel, Marc Swayze, © 1942 by Fawcett Publications, Inc.

MASTER COMICS   This was another comic book that began life in a tabloid-sized format. Master Comics came along early in 1940 and was Fawcett's second title. The first, WHIZ COMICS, introduced CAPTAIN MARVEL and Spy Smasher, but *Master* didn't have a single winner in its initial lineup. In the seventh issue, Bulletman

joined the cast and in the 11th the star-spangled Minute Man. It wasn't until #23 (February 1942), however, that the magazine acquired its most successful hero in the person of the blue-clad CAPTAIN MARVEL, JR.

The first three tab issues offered 48 pages and sold for 15¢. After that the page count was dropped to 32 and the price to a dime. The resident superhero was a prosaic blond fellow known as Master Man, the "World's Greatest Hero." Backing him up were such characters as a masked avenger operating as the Devil's Dagger, a seagoing hero named Shipwreck Roberts, and the magician El Carim, "whose name read backwards spells miracle."

With issue #7 (October 1940), *Master* assumed normal 64-page comic book size and merged with two of Fawcett's even more unsuccessful titles, *Slam-Bang Comics* and *Nickel Comics*, which was the original home of Bulletman. The first artist on Captain Marvel, Jr. was Mac Raboy. His covers from late 1941 through mid-1944 were quite impressive in the boldness of their design and the quality of their artwork.

Among the characters added later were Hopalong Cassidy, NYOKA, and RADAR. The magazine ended with its 133rd issue in the early spring of 1953.

MICKEY MOUSE Walt Disney's renowned rodent debuted in 1928 in the pioneering sound cartoon *Steamboat Willie*. He first appeared in a newspaper strip early in 1930 and reached the newsstands in the summer of 1935 in *Mickey Mouse Magazine*.

The magazine was issued by K.K. Publications, a partnership between the Whitman Publishing Company and Disney's Kay Kamen. A former department store executive and advertising man in Kansas City, Kamen had been hired by the studio in 1932 to set up a merchandising department and handle the licensing of the Disney cartoon animals. Kamen worked out of offices in New York.

MMM was not a true comic book. Slightly larger in dimensions, it was printed on heavier stock and consisted of just 32 pages. In the early issues, young readers got just 4 pages of comics. The rest of the magazine contained stories about Mickey, fairy tales (sometimes from writers such as A.A. Milne), poems, puzzles, a joke page—*Wise Quacks* edited by DONALD DUCK—and sundry features and fillers. Editor Oskar Lebeck contributed an assortment of original strips and stories, most notably a feature about Peter the Farm Detective. By 1940, five pages of Disney reprints, including the *Mickey Mouse* daily newspaper strip and, usually, a *Donald Duck* Sunday, were included.

Walt Disney's Comics & Stories replaced Mickey's mag in the fall of 1940, with Dell now joining in the act. At first the new book was made up almost entirely of newspaper reprints—Floyd Gottfredson's splendid mock-adventure *Mickey* dailies, Al Taliafero's funny gag-a-day *Donald* strips, and various Sundays including the *Silly Symphonies* pages. Beginning in 1943, the leadoff story in the magazine became an original Donald Duck adventure. The artist and writer was the gifted Carl Barks. Eventually the Gottfredson reprints were replaced by new Mickey continuities. By the mid-1950s Paul Murry, former animator and gag cartoonist, was drawing the new Mickey Mouse tales. These were humorous adventures, usually continued from issue to issue, which gave Murry the chance to draw the mouse and his sidekick Goofy in a variety of settings, from the steamy jungles to frozen Arctic wastes to haunted castles. Murry developed an appealing and recognizable Mickey of his own, one that was not the mouse of the movies or even of the newspaper strip. He stayed with the character until the publisher, Whitman-Western, closed up shop in 1984.

In 1941, Mickey began appearing in a title of his own that lasted until 1984. In 1986, both *Mickey Mouse* and *WDC&S* were revived by Gladstone, and in 1990 Disney took over publication.

MILITARY COMICS Introduced in the summer of 1941 just a few months before America entered World War II, it showcased an assortment of unorthodox military heroes and dealt with combat in various locales around the world. Will Eisner was the original editor, and the undisputed star of *Military* was his creation, BLACKHAWK.

After the war, the title was changed to *Modern Comics*, but Blackhawk remained the leading character and appeared on every cover. *Modern* ceased publication with #102 (October 1950).

Among the other militant characters who frequented the magazine during its lifetime were the Death Patrol, the Blue Tracer, the Sniper, and Pvt. Dogtag. Bill Ward's sexy blonde TORCHY became a somewhat-unexpected addition in 1946. Artists for the magazine included Bob Powell, Klaus Nordling, Jack Cole, Reed Crandall, Dave Berg, and Alex Kotzky.

Private Dogtag, Bart Tumey, © 1943 by Comic Magazines.

MINUTE MOVIES   This feature was originally a popular newspaper strip in the 1920s and 1930s that was revived by its creator, Ed Wheelan, for *Flash Comics*. It began in issue #12 (December 1940), replacing an earlier Wheelan effort, and lasted until late in 1944.

Wheelan, who drew in the same appealing "big-foot" style he'd been using for several decades, offered his readers six- and eight-page spoofs of every sort of motion picture. Typical of the titles of his monthly productions were *Manhattan Madman*, *The Hazards of Hazel*, *Murder Mix-Up*, and *Intrigue*, a historical melodrama set in the little French coastal town of Trigue. Each movie starred the Wheelan stable of actors—dashing blond Dick Dare, demure blonde Hazel Dearie, and sinister Ralph McSneer. Each and every Minute Movie was directed by Art Hokum.

Two of the comedy players, Archibald Clubb and Fuller Phun, now and then appeared as Fat & Slat in short comedy fillers. After *Minute Movies* folded, Wheelan used the team in a *Fat & Slat* comic book. It was one of the first EC titles. The last issue appeared in 1948.

MISS AMERICA   A youthful heroine in the MARY MARVEL mode, she was introduced as a backup feature in MARVEL COMICS #49 (November 1943). She wore a sedate crimson costume with a star-spangled shield emblazoned on the chest, a crimson beanie, and a blue cape and specialized in combating crooks, spies, and saboteurs on the home front. Among her powers were the ability to fly and a sixth sense that warned her of impending trouble. Otto Binder, the author of the Mary Marvel scripts, wrote many of the early stories and the artwork was by various members of the Marvel bullpen.

After World War II, Madeline Joyce, who was actually Miss America, went to work for a counterspy organization in Washington, where she spent most of her time chasing former Nazis who were trying for comebacks. The stories also emphasized Madeline's regular wardrobe—an indication that Marvel was probably aiming at a female audience.

Miss America got a title of her own in 1944, but it was soon converted into a combination comic book and slick magazine that was similar to Parents' *Calling All Girls*. She was dropped from the lineup after a few issues, but *Miss America Magazine* continued without her and lasted until 1958.

MR. DISTRICT ATTORNEY The two-fisted D.A. was originally a radio hero first heard over the airwaves in 1939. The show was from the stable of Philips H. Lord, who was also responsible for *Gang Busters*. Mr. District Attorney's adventures became part of Dell's THE FUNNIES in the summer of 1939. In late 1947, DC introduced him in a comic book, and there he brought criminals to justice for over a decade, outlasting the radio show and the subsequent television series.

Inspired by the career of New York District Attorney Thomas E. Dewey, the program detailed the efforts of the unnamed D.A. to smash rackets and jail gangsters. He was aided by a loyal secretary named Miss Miller and a tough sidekick named Harrington. Harrington called him "Chief," but the sidekick's exact official status was never made clear. All three central characters appeared in the comic book version, but the two males took care of all the action. Mr. D.A. was drawn as a handsome young man, Harrington as a cigar-chomping roughneck in a derby. The descriptive phrases of the radio show opening were sometimes used in a leadoff caption—"Champion of the people . . . defender of truth . . . guardian of our fundamental rights of life, liberty, and the pursuit of happiness."

Each episode ran six pages and many of the stories were continued from issue to issue. Mr. District Attorney went after the usual racketeers, plus an occasional saboteur. The feature ran from #35 (Septemeber 1939) through #64 (May 1942). Several artists drew it, including Maurice Kashuba and Jim Chambers.

DC introduced a *Mr. District Attorney* comic book late in 1947, about a month after starting a title based on Lord's *Gang Busters*. This D.A. was a more mature fellow, showing a touch of gray at the temples. Harrington was younger, redheaded, and wore a fedora instead of a derby. His exact job was still not clearly defined. Miss Miller took a more active part in these postwar adventures, which involved racketeers, highjackers, con men, and assorted urban crooks. The DC book ended late in 1958 with the 67th issue. Among the artists were Charles Paris, longtime BATMAN inker, and Howard Purcell.

MORE FUN COMICS Under its original title of *New Fun*, this was the first regularly issued comic book of the 1930s made up of original material. It was founded by the enterprising Major Malcolm Wheeler-Nicholson and became the cornerstone of the DC empire. During its heyday, *More Fun* introduced such characters as THE SPECTRE, DR. FATE, THE GREEN ARROW, and SUPERBOY.

The first issue of *New Fun* bore the cover date February 1935. Billed as the Big Comic Book and "the New Magazine You've Been Waiting For," it was tabloid-sized. It had a full-color cover, but the 32 interior pages were black and white. All the new strips were laid out like Sunday funnies and none, with a single exception, got more than one page. The package was eclectic. In addition to humor and adventure comics, there was a two-page Western yarn, a sports page, radio news, movie news, instructions for building a model airplane, and a popular-science page.

Among the to-be-continued features were *Sandra of the Secret Service, Cap'n Erik, Buckskin Jim*, and *Jack Andrews, All-American Boy*. Gag cartoonist Lawrence Lariar contributed *Barry O'Neill*, a serious adventure page that pitted pipe-smoking Barry against the insidious Oriental villain Fang Gow. Henry Kiefer, a European-trained artist who became one of the most successful comic book hacks, drew *Wing Brady*, about a Foreign Legionnaire who was also an aviator. Jack Warren was on hand with a cowboy humor page starring Loco Luke, and Tom McNamara provided a kid page. Artist Clemens Gretter, collaborating with writer Ken Fitch, drew *Don Drake on the Planet Saro* and *2033/Super Police*, the earliest science fiction features created for comic books.

Because of the shaky state of the major's

finances, he often didn't get around to paying his artists the modest fees—usually $5 per page—he'd promised. This resulted in both ill will and staff changes. Lariar left and was eventually replaced by Leo O'Mealia. Other artists and writers also were persuaded to come into the fold. Vincent Sullivan began doing a cartoony kid adventure strip titled *Spike Spalding* and Whit Ellsworth contributed an Orphan Annie simulacrum called *Little Linda*. Contributions began coming in over the transom as well. From out in Cleveland, Jerry Siegel and Joe Shuster submitted *Doctor Occult*, about a ghost detective who "has sworn to combat supernatural evil in the world." They used the pen names of Legar and Reuths.

The sixth issue of the magazine was dated October 1935 and the next January 1936. That tardy seventh issue bore the name *More Fun*. Under its new title, the magazine format began shrinking and by the ninth issue it was the same size as FAMOUS FUNNIES and the other new comics showing up on the newsstands. The major and his new editors Sullivan and Ellsworth kept adding color pages, and the magazine was looking more presentable—and much less like a compilation of rejected newspaper Sundays—as it entered its second year.

Features continued to come and go, as did artists. O'Mealia introduced *Bob Merritt and His Flying Pals*, and Siegel and Shuster introduced a new cops-and-robbers strip titled *Radio Squad*. Creig Flessel, fresh from the pulps, joined on in the 12th issue to draw *Pep Morgan*, about an all-around college jock. Flessel also began doing many of the covers. As 1937 ended, six- and eight-page stories were the rule.

Early in 1938, Major Nicholson ceased to be a publisher, and *More Fun* and the other titles he'd started passed into other hands. That was the year of SUPERMAN, but the magazine paid him no mind for quite a while, content to keep going along with cowboys, cops, and adventurers. Then in issue #52 (February 1940) the Spectre was introduced, written by Jerry

Siegel and drawn by Bernard Bailey. A few months later in #55 (May 1940), *More Fun* added another weird hero in the person of Dr. Fate. He was the creation of Gardner Fox and was drawn in a stylized, spooky style by Howard Sherman. A month after the doctor appeared, a more down-to-earth hero, CONGO BILL, joined on. Johnny Quick, King of Speed, zipped onto the scene in #71 (September 1941). He got his swiftness by reciting the formula 3X2(9YZ)4A, a bit trickier to toss off than "SHAZAM!" Mort Meskin drew the feature in its handsomest days.

AQUAMAN and Green Arrow came aboard in #73. The aquatic hero was the invention of Mort Weisinger and artist Paul Norris. Weisinger also cooked up the adventures of Green Arrow and his boy sidekick Speedy. Because they were more likable than the ghostly Spectre and the mystical Dr. Fate, Green Arrow and Speedy soon became the stars of the magazine. They got most of the covers plus 13 pages right at the front of the book. Not until #101, early in 1945, did another new costumed hero show up, the small but formidable Superboy.

In that same year, aware of the declining interest in costumed heroes, DC began to convert *More Fun* to a humor book. By issue #108 (March 1946), the conversion was complete and only such characters as GENIUS JONES, Dover and Clover, and McNamara's Gas House Gang were to be found in its pages. *Jimminy and his Magic Book* was added early in 1947. A fantasy drawn in a style inspired by that of Walt Kelly, *Jimminy* remained the leadoff feature through the magazine's final issue, #127 (November–December 1947).

MUTT & JEFF   The mismatched pair began appearing in comic books in 1910, several decades before a single superhero flew onto the scene. Bud Fisher's *Mutt & Jeff* continued to be featured in various comic book formats between 1913 and 1929. In the 1930s, when modern comic books began, the team was part of the lineup of the first regularly issued newsstand title, FAMOUS FUNNIES. They later showed up in POPULAR COMICS, ALL-AMERICAN COMICS, and a title of their own.

Fisher's feature, initially starring only Mutt, began as a newspaper daily in 1907. It eventually turned into a gag strip, built around the conflicts between the tall, chinless Mutt, who was quick-tempered, henpecked, and dedicated to a lifelong quest for easy money, and the short, dapper Jeff, who was the traditional wise fool.

In 1910, Ball Publications issued *Mutt & Jeff Cartoons*, a 50¢ book that reprinted one strip per page. Ball followed it with four more over the next half dozen years. In 1916, the firm of Cupples & Leon took over, beginning a series of square, 48-page books that sold for 25¢. When *Famous Funnies* got going in the early 1930s, reprints of *Mutt & Jeff* Sunday pages were included. M.C. Gaines included reprints in *All-American*, which he put together for DC in 1939. That same year he introduced a *Mutt & Jeff* reprint title. It began as an annual and, finally, in 1943 became a bimonthly. The covers were drawn by Sheldon Mayer.

Dell took the title over in 1958. In 1960, Harvey became the publisher and stayed with the magazine until its end in 1965. Original material was used in later issues.

THE MYSTERIOUS TRAVELER Yet another spooky host for a series of weird tales, he held forth in Charlton's *Tales of the Mysterious Traveler*. The magazine was based on a defunct radio show and lasted from the summer of 1956 to the spring of 1959. It ended, appropriately enough, after its 13th issue. A great many of the short yarns spun by the phantom commuter were illustrated by Steve Ditko.

The Mysterious Traveler, a sustaining, unsponsored program, was heard over the Mutual network from 1943 to 1952. Inspired by such earlier creepy shows as *Inner Sanctum* and

The Whistler, it offered a weekly succession of unsettling tales narrated by the mysterious host. "This is the Mysterious Traveler, inviting you to join me on another journey into the strange and terrifying," said actor Maurice Tarplin at the start of each show, giving the impression he'd just sat down beside you on your evening-commute train. "I hope you enjoy the trip, that it will thrill you a little and chill you a little." As the train sound effects faded, the strange story would begin.

Charlton carried this over into the comic book. Ditko, who provided the majority of the artwork from the second issue onward, drew the Traveler as a lean, grim-faced man in voluminous overcoat, scarf, and snap-brim hat. His layouts were imaginative, drawn in his best Joe Kubert–inspired style, with the narrator looming ominously between the panels. Among the other artists who contributed to the title were Dick Giordano and Matt Baker.

MYSTERY IN SPACE This was one of the many science fiction comic books to come along in the 1950s. DC's *Mystery in Space* began in 1951 and lasted until the mid-1960s. It was edited by Julius Schwartz and was the long-time home of the interplanetary hero Adam Strange.

The first issue, which offered 48 pages for a dime, bore an April–May 1951 cover date. *Mystery in Space* began as a comic book equivalent of the science fiction pulps of the 1940s. In fact, the early issues contained stories scripted by pulpwood veterans Edmond Hamilton and Manly Wade Wellman. The emphasis was on variety and there was only one recurring series, a space opera starring the Knights of the Galaxy. Schwartz's regular writers included Gardner Fox and John Broome. Much of the artwork was provided by Carmine Infantino, Murphy Anderson, and Gil Kane.

Gradually other series were introduced, including one dealing with Interplanetary Insurance, Inc. and another devoted to the Space Cabbie. Finally in #53 (August 1959)

came Adam Strange. The red-suited planet-hopper had been introduced in SHOWCASE late in the previous year. Strange was an Earth man, an archaeologist by trade, who chanced to be struck by a ray known as the Zeta-Beam: "Instantly he is teleported across 25 trillion miles of space to the planet Rann of the star-sun Alpha Centauri." Once on Rann, he found love in the person of Alanna, lovely daughter of a noted scientist, and became involved with battling assorted tyrants and ne'er-do-wells. The only snag was that the Zeta-Beam effects would wear off eventually and Strange would go zooming back home. Fortunately, new beams hit Earth now and then and, once he'd figured out the schedule, he became a space commuter.

Gardner Fox wrote the series, very much under the influence of Edgar Rice Burroughs's John Carter of Mars novels. Infantino and Anderson provided the drawing. As Will Jacobs and Gerard Jones point out in *The Comic Book Heroes*, Adam Strange was a man who enjoyed some highly unusual life experiences. "No sooner would he materialize on Rann than he would find himself facing a man-eating vacuum cleaner, a giant sentient atom, a huge magnifying glass that floated in the sky and burned the cities below with sunlight, or even a giant duplicate of himself. Soon even Adam was wondering wryly why some impossible menace always seemed to strike Rann when he arrived."

Adam Strange remained in the magazine until the mid-1960s and *Mystery in Space* folded a few issues later. The title, using reprints, was briefly revived in 1981.

NEW TEEN TITANS   *See* Teen Titans.

NICK FURY   He was a Marvel comic book hero with two separate and distinct identities—a hard-bitten World War II soldier and a high-tech superspy. As Sgt. Fury, he led his Howling Commandos in innumerable battles against the Nazis throughout the 1960s and 1970s and as Nick Fury he's carried on espionage missions as an agent of SHIELD since the late 1960s. Stan Lee and Jack Kirby formed the original writer–artist team on both incarnations.

The first issue of *Sgt. Fury and His Howling Commandos* had a cover date of May 1963 and introduced Nick Fury, who was, as Lee has described him, "a hard-as-nails, two-fisted, tough-talking, fast-moving, cigar-chomping, lusty, gutsy, brawling leader of men, albeit with a soft, easy-touch heart—which hardly ever showed." On the cover of #1, the sergeant was urging his men, "Keep movin', you kunkheads! Nobody lives forever! So get the lead out and follow me! We got us a WAR to win!" With his crew of misfits, Fury fought World War II until the early 1980s. Kirby had drawn his share of gangs and teams over the years, from the Boy Commandos to the FANTASTIC FOUR, and he han-dled this bunch with ease and enthusiasm.

The Howlers included Reb Ralston, Dum Dum Dugan, Pinky Pinkerton, Dino Manelli and Gabriel Jones, a black jazz musician. Like the earlier Sgt. Rock's Easy Co. over at DC, the Howling Commandos was an anachronisti-cally integrated group.

In 1965, Fury began leading his double life. According to Lee, he was inspired by numer-ous fan letters asking about what the sergeant had done after the war. "I was intrigued by the idea of having two magazines featuring Nick Fury," he once explained, "one dealing with his exploits during World War II and the other bringing him up to the present—but doing what?"

The answer came from television, where *The Man from UNCLE* had begun the previous autumn. Lee invented the secret intelligence agency known as SHIELD: Supreme Head-quarters International Espionage Law-Enforce-ment Division. "We were going to out-Bond Bond," he said, "and out-UNCLE UNCLE." The new Nick Fury feature was introduced in STRANGE TALES #135 and blurbed as "The Great-est Action-Thriller of All Time!" Middle-aged now and wearing a black patch over his left eye, Fury was initiated into SHIELD and began his seemingly endless battle against an evil organization known as Hydra, which was bent on encircling the Earth.

Jim Steranko played an important part in the rise of Nick Fury. Late in 1966 he joined Marvel and started working as Kirby's inker on the feature. A few issues later, he took over writing and drawing the crusty superspy's escapades. Fans and readers were impressed, and by the spring of 1968 Nick had a magazine of his own.

An artist with wide-ranging and eclectic interests, Steranko created a personal and compelling collage for Nick Fury. "Everything from films, from radio, pulps, business, everything I could possibly apply from my background, including the magic I've done, the gigs I've played—everything goes into every comic story," he once explained. "Nick Fury became Steranko." Steranko used a whole bag of graphic tricks to catch and hold the reader's attention. He mixed the Marvel style, as then personified by Kirby, with the techniques of Will Eisner and Bernard Krigstein and added the flash of op-art posters. Steranko didn't stay with Nick Fury long, but he left his mark on him.

The sergeant ended his military career in the early 1980s, but has continued, with some time off, as a secret agent. The most recent *Nick Fury* series began in the summer of 1989. Leaner, and possibly meaner, Fury is still a state-of-the-art superspy. He still wears the eye patch, chomps on a cigar, and drops his Gs. SHIELD, however, now stands for Strategic Hazard Intervention, Espionage and Logistics Directorate, "the world's top multinational intelligence agency." Nick Fury is its leader.

NYOKA She was a successful jungle girl in a movie serial before she appeared in comic books. Republic Pictures released the 15-chapter *Perils of Nyoka* in 1942 and that same year Fawcett issued a one-shot comic based on it. In 1944, she became a backup feature in MASTER

Nyoka, Harry Anderson, © 1946 by Fawcett Publications, Inc.

COMICS and in 1945 a regular *Nyoka* comic book began appearing. The intrepid heroine was last seen on the newsstand in 1957.

The genesis of the character is somewhat confusing. Republic's 1941 serial *Jungle Girl* starred Frances Gifford as a woman named Nyoka Meredith. The title cards and the publicity credited *Jungle Girl* to Edgar Rice Burroughs. TARZAN's creator had indeed once written a novel of that title and the studio had paid him for the movie serial rights, but the book took place in an entirely different jungle and there was nobody named Nyoka in it. She was entirely the invention of the scriptwriters.

When it came time for a sequel, Republic decided not to pay Burroughs any further money, according to Jack Mathis in *Valley of the Cliffhangers*. So the heroine of the second chapter play, portrayed by Kay Aldridge this time, was named Nyoka Gordon. She's the one Fawcett used in its comic book. Unfortunately, Fawcett titled the magazine *Jungle Girl*, thereby adding to the confusion. Artist Harry Anderson provided the artwork.

The Nyoka of the republic serial was not a jungle girl in the SHEENA sense. She didn't dress in a leopard-skin costume, nor did she swing from tree limbs and vines. She was a courageous young woman who, along with her father and her boyfriend, encountered numerous perils and pitfalls while exploring a very Hollywood sort of wilderness.

The Nyoka who started appearing in *Master* led a similar life and usually wore a blouse, shorts, moccasins, and a gun belt. The title of the feature offered a combination of both serials—*Nyoka the Jungle Girl*.

Drawn by Jack Sparling, the first story extended, serial fashion, over nine issues and involved Nyoka with a mysterious Death Rug. As in the movies, each installment ended with a cliffhanger and a teaser: "Has the bloody curse of the Death Rug struck again? Will it finally doom poor Nyoka, now that the two men she loves best are powerless to help her?" The serials continued in *Master* until the penultimate issue in 1953.

Fawcett's *Nyoka the Jungle Girl* magazine started up in the winter of 1945 and lasted until 1953, when the company abandoned comics. Charlton took up the jungle girl in 1955 and hung on until 1957. Harry Anderson was the artist on the early Fawcett issues.

PADLOCK HOMES He was the preeminent burlesquer of Sherlock Holmes. This creation of Ed Wheelan was first seen in *Champ Comics* in the spring of 1942 and moved over to *Speed Comics* in 1943.

Besides being a spoof of Sir Arthur Conan Doyle's celebrated sleuth, *Padlock Homes* was also a parody of detective melodramas in general, movie serials, and just about anything else that caught Wheelan's fancy. Homes, who came equipped with a deerstalker cap and meerschaum pipe, was aided by Dr. Watzis in his ceaseless struggle to nab the Professor, described as a chap with a "nasty knack for wrongdoing." The Professor was aided by a quartet of masked henchmen known as the Fiendish Four.

The mock adventure serial had always been one of Wheelan's strong suits, and he obviously enjoyed turning out the Homes saga, which lasted until the spring of 1945. He was especially deft with the synopses that led off each chapter: "That night Padlock Homes and his American assistant, Nick O'Tyme, entered the Club Fiasco disguised as a couple of other fellows. During the evening the Professor sneezed off his toupee and trick moustache and was immediately recognized by the great detective . . ." and "The great detective, Padlock Homes, disguised as a large rock, has captured his archenemy, the Professor, but . . ."

THE GREAT DETECTIVE

Padlock Homes, Ed Wheelan, © 1943 Family Comics, Inc.

PEN MILLER In the days when superheroes dominated the newsstands, it was the rare 1940s comic book artist who could be very autobiographical in his work. An exception was Klaus Nordling, who was able to put a good deal of himself into this feature because it was not about a costumed crimefighter but a cartoonist. Blond, pipe-smoking Pen Miller differed from his blond pipe-smoking creator in that he was a detective as well as an artist. He was also a mite taller.

Pen first set up his drawing boards in *National Comics* #1 (July 1940). Will Eisner was the editor of the magazine, whose star was that quintessential superpatriot Uncle Sam. Pen Miller was introduced as a "famous comic magazine cartoonist" and "an amateur detective of wide reputation." He was apparently doing well in both vocation and avocation, since he lived in a handsome apartment and had an Oriental valet named Niki to look after him. His initial case involved solving the murder of a corpse left in Pen's own bedroom. Since Pen "revolves his plots around criminal cases he has solved," getting tangled with real-life crimes such as this one cheered him up. He found mystery and crime everywhere, even while vacationing, and never ran out of inspiration. He remained on the *National* staff through #22 (April 1942), then jumped to *Crack Comics* with issue #23 (May 1942).

The cartoonist-detective stayed on the job until early in 1949 and then retired. In his later adventures, he graduated to being a newspaper cartoonist, doing a true-crime strip that he used to chronicle his cases and to needle crooks and crime bosses who were still at large. Nordling, who also wrote the feature, was never completely serious about either detection or cartooning.

PENNILESS PALMER Comic books in the 1930s and 1940s had room not only for serious private detectives but also for investigators who took a humorous approach to law and order. The longest-running and most successful of these lightweight sleuths was Penniless Palmer, a luckless private eye who began his career in DC's *Star Spangled Comics* #6 (March 1942) and remained in business for a half dozen years. Penniless was short, curly-haired, and optimistic: "a million dollar detective who never has a cent to his name." His secretary was Bunny South, a pretty blonde whose rich father helped finance the detective agency, and his assistant was a large, amiable hulk named Oxie. Unlike most of his comic colleagues, Penniless was a clever and competent investigator who solved every mystery he tackled. His major problem was holding on to his fees; he was prone to donate them to charity or use them to pay off his overdue bills. Most of his cases, which unfolded in six and eight pages, were fairly well-constructed and even made use of clues and deduction.

His cases were often unusual, involving Penniless and associates with such problems as a drunken parrot, a haunted cuckoo clock, a cat with laryngitis, a gang of dancing mice, and hoodlums who were buying up all the nickels in town by paying a quarter for three of them.

The feature was created by an artist named R.L. Ross, who drew in a fairly realistic cartoon style. He did but three episodes before vanishing forever. Among the other interesting artists who depicted Penniless's caseload were newspaper strip veterans George Storm and Paul Fung. Penniless was also a regular in DC's humor title *All Funny*.

PHANTOM LADY She was a sex object throughout the major phase of her career and earned a place in comic book history not because of her capabilities as a crimefighter but because of her provocative appearance during the period when the venturesome publisher Victor Fox was printing her adventures. The Phantom Lady, in a more demure incarnation, first appeared in 1941. Her heyday with Fox was from 1947 to 1949 and she has returned, in various stages of undress, several times since.

A product of the Eisner–Iger shop, the Phantom Lady feature first appeared in Quality's *Police Comics* #1 (August 1941) and originally was drawn by Arthur Peddy. She was a backup character in the magazine, which starred the Firebrand, PLASTIC MAN, and, a bit later, THE SPIRIT. In everyday life she was Sandra Knight, the debutante daughter of a United States senator. The dark-haired Sandra's first costume was made up of a one-piece yellow swimsuit, yellow boots, and a green cape. Although she battled crime and espionage in and around Washington, D.C., without benefit of a mask or even a change of hairdo, no one ever recognized her as the well-known deb. She had no special powers, and her only weapon was a blackout flashlight that surrounded her opponents in darkness.

When artist–writer Frank Borth took over in 1943, he gave Phantom Lady a fuller figure, a costume with cleavage, and a domino mask. She left *Police* after the 23rd issue (October 1943).

Fox began publishing a *Phantom Lady* comic book in the summer of 1947 and also used her in *All Top Comics*. The material was provided by Jerry Iger, who'd been running a shop of his own since parting with Eisner several years earlier. Apparently he never gave up on a character. Matt Baker, one of the leading exponents of GOOD GIRL ART, drew the feature. "The revived Phantom Lady wore an even skimpier costume and had a noticeably larger bosom," pointed out *The Encyclopedia of American Comics*. "She had also developed a marked fondness for being tied up and chained, and she frequently appeared in these states, especially on covers." The title ended early in 1949 and was replaced on the Fox roster by a romance comic titled *My Love Secret*.

Though gone, Phantom Lady was far from forgotten. In his *Seduction of the Innocent* (1954), Dr. Fredric Wertham reprinted Baker's cover for #17 and captioned it, "Sexual stimulation by combining 'headlights' with the sadist's

dream of tying up a woman." Late that same year, Robert Farrell, another satisfied Iger customer, published a *Phantom Lady* title. This time the lady crimefighter appeared in a less-revealing costume and battled with Communists. The book lasted just four issues. Baker also worked on this version.

DC, which licensed many of the Quality characters, notably BLACKHAWK and Plastic Man, brought back a more sedate Phantom Lady to serve as part of the Freedom Fighters group in the mid-1970s. Americomics, paying homage to the Matt Baker version, has kept an alternate Phantom Lady going.

Phantom Lady, Matt Baker, © 1947 Fox Features Syndicate.

PICTURE NEWS This was an unusual experiment that attempted to present current events, interviews, and feature articles in a comic book format. *Picture News* was edited by veteran newspaper editor Emile Gauvreau. Its first issue bore a cover date of January 1946. The magazine was not a success and expired the following year after just 10 issues.

It was published by Connecticut newspaper publisher Leigh Danenberg. John Lehti, just out of the service, was art director. In touting the magazine in his editorial messages, Gauvreau, who'd served as editor of the *New York Graphic* and the *New York Mirror*, told readers to get into the habit of reading the magazine. "You'll like it for its honest message of what's going on in our age, and also for its wonderful entertainment." A typical issue of *Picture News* included a profile of Cardinal Spellman, a piece on the Baby Boom, a bio of ballplayer Hank Greenberg, an essay on the atom bomb, and a think piece on returning veterans and their problems. It was probably the only comic book ever to do a story about George Bernard Shaw. In addition to the serious fare, there was a page of humorous comment on the news of the day by long-time newspaper strip artist Milt Gross.

Lehti, who'd drawn such heroes as the CRIMSON AVENGER for DC, provided some of the art himself. Also on his team were Nat Edson, Emil Gershwin, and Harry Anderson. Although the artwork was attractive and effective, the content was usually rather bland and polite. With the ninth issue, Lloyd Jacquet's FUNNIES, INC. shop was brought in to liven things up. In the 10th, and final, issue a heroic boy reporter named Dick Quick was added, but even the addition of fiction didn't help.

Picture News, Jack Lehti, © by 299 Lafayette Street Corporation.

PICTURE STORIES FROM THE BIBLE Publisher M.C. Gaines, one of the pioneers of the business, believed that comic books could be used to educate as well as entertain. *Picture Stories from the Bible*, introduced in 1942, represented his first major attempt to broaden the horizons of the medium. It was a considerable departure from *Flash Comics*, ALL STAR COMICS, *Sensation Comics*, and other Gaines titles.

Gaines first tried *Picture Stories from the Bible* as an 8-page Sunday newspaper insert, similar in format to the weekly SPIRIT booklets. It started appearing in a limited number of comic sections in April of 1942 and wasn't successful. The first issue of the 64-page comic book, published under the DC colophon, hit the stands in October and made use of the newspaper material. It offered adaptions of the Old Testament stories of Noah, Joseph, Moses, and Jonah, among others.

Gaines ran ads in the other titles he packaged for DC. "Here are the exciting and daring stories of the Old Testament heroes in the same color continuity you like to read," explained the copy. For those who couldn't find the new magazine on the stands, there was a coupon. In the magazine itself Gaines stated, "In this and succeeding issues, we are offering the great Stories from the Bible, done for the first time in the popular color continuity technique. We believe—and we hope—they will make boys and girls read the Bible itself." To vet each issue, an advisory council had been gathered together. It included a rabbi, a priest, and Dr. Norman Vincent Peale.

The scripts were by Montgomery Mulford, who'd previously written *The Blue Beetle*, and the artwork was by a relative newcomer named Don Cameron. He drew in a simple style that avoided action and violence. Gaines and his staff covered the Old Testament in four issues, the last of which appeared in the summer of 1943. Next came three issues devoted to the New Testament, appearing annually from 1944 to 1946. Cameron still provided the interior art, but the covers for 1944 and 1945 were drawn by Everett E. Hibbard, who was also doing THE FLASH at the time. Because of wartime paper restrictions, the New Testament issues were cut to 48 pages. Gaines offered special quantity prices to Sunday schools and churches.

Although some of his colleagues, including his editor Sheldon Mayer, didn't think much of his turning the Bible into a series of comic books, *Picture Stories* sold millions of copies. After parting with DC, Gaines founded Educational Comics and published *Picture Stories from American History*, *Picture Stories from Science*, and *Picture Stories from World History*. He'd also contemplated a comic book devoted to mythology but never got around to publishing it.

PLANET COMICS The first comic book devoted exclusively to science fiction began late in 1939. It was published by Fiction House, the outfit that also was responsible for the *Planet Stories* pulp magazine, and offered not only space opera but, eventually, a great deal of what came to be called GOOD GIRL ART. A line on the cover promised "weird adventures on other worlds" and *Planet Comics* certainly provided those right up to its final issue in 1953.

Almost from the start, the editors of the magazine were aiming at an audience of adolescent boys, so each cover featured an attractive young woman not overly burdened by clothes. The youths who favored *Planet* were science fiction buffs as well, meaning each cover also depicted alien creatures and spacemen wielding sizzling ray guns and atomic swords, plus plenty of rocket ships and futuristic architecture. The covers also used considerable printed copy to lure the customer inside. "FLINT BAKER Battles The Nightmare Monsters of Space's Forbidden Isle in 'Winged Man-Eaters of the Exile Star,'" one cover blurb promised. Another cried out, "The Earthman Battles The Invading Hairy Hordes of Mars, God of War, to Save 'The Warrior Maid of Mercury.'" And so it went from issue to issue, with boldface type announcing encounters with the Lizard Tyrant of the Lost World, the Green Legions of Xalan, and the Behemoths of the Purple Void.

In addition to such science fiction concepts as space travel and interplanetary warfare, the magazine relied on heroes and heroines, recurring characters who'd compel readers to keep coming back for more. The intended star of the first issue was Flint Baker, a handsome, dark-haired fellow who could be seen on the cover, perched on the wing of his crimson spaceship battling one-eyed, green monsters on Mars. Backup characters included Spurt Hammond, Captain Nelson Cole of the Solar Force, Auro, Lord of Jupiter, and the Red Comet, a sort of galactic superhero.

Characters came and went, including Planet Payson, Tiger Hart, and Amazona, the first woman to have a feature of her own. In the fourth issue Gale Allen arrived. She commanded a battalion of rocket-piloting women, known first as the Girl Patrol and then as the Girl Squadron. In her early adventures, Gale was rather demurely attired in tunic, riding britches, and boots. Gradually, however, she

Mars, Joe Doolin, © 1944 by Love Romances Publishing Company, Inc.

and him in "the once-beautiful city of Miami," and another in the remains of Hollywood. The planet was in such sorry shape because it had been brutally invaded by "the slaughter-mad warriors of Volta." The ugly, green Voltans were unabashedly rotten, behaving in even worse fashion than the Nazis they were based on.

The covers, scripts, and artwork in the early issues were provided by the shop run by Will Eisner and Jerry Iger. When Eisner and Iger split up, Iger's new shop provided most of the material. Nick Cardy, John Celardo, Lee Elias, Artie Saaf, Leonard Starr, Bob Lubbers, and Murphy Anderson were contributors at one time or other. *The Lost World* was drawn at various times by Cardy, Graham Ingels, George Evans, and Lily Renee. The chief cover artist was Joe Doolin. From 1943 through 1951, he produced over three dozen flamboyant variations on the basic themes. The second most prolific cover artist was Dan Zolnerowich, who drew all but one of the covers from January of 1941 through July of 1943.

began shedding clothes. Eventually the regulation Girl Squadron uniform consisted of metal bra, shorts, and gun belt.

As the 1940s progressed, the art and editorial content of *Planet* placed increasing emphasis on the female form, and new lady stars were added. Mysta of the Moon, dubbed a "queen of science," debuted in issue #36 and Futura followed in #43. *The Lost World* started in the November 1942 issue. Although it featured a nearly naked blonde named Lyssa, the star was a husky chap known as Hunt Bowman. For the most part the stories were set in what was then the future, namely the 1970s. Bowman, who was an excellent archer, roamed a future Earth that lay in ruins. One episode would find Lyssa

PLASTIC MAN Not all the superheroes of the 1940s were completely serious about their trade. Notable among those who were less than reverent about the business of crime-fighting was Plastic Man. Created by Jack Cole, he made his modest debut in the first issue of *Police Comics* (August 1941).

Cole's narratives mixed fantasy, cops and robbers, violence, and humor. His drawing style, a blend of the straight illustrational approach with the exaggerations of animated cartoons, was ideally suited to depicting Plastic Man's bouncy gangbusting adventures. He wrote his own blurb for the initial yarn, proclaiming, "From time to time the comic world welcomes a new sensation! Such is PLASTIC MAN!!! The most fantastic man alive! Vermin of the underworld shudder at the mention of his name! And yet he was once one of them!"

Like other Cole characters, Plas was a reformed criminal. Eel O'Brien by name, "the toughest gangster afoot . . . wanted by the police in eight states." While involved in a safe-cracking caper at a chemical works, Eel was drenched in acid. Left to fend for himself by his gang, he wandered out of the city, "through swamps, then up a mountain side." He passed out and awakened later to find he'd been taken in and cared for by a kindly monk who ran a peaceful mountain retreat. The monk's faith in him caused Eel to reform on the spot. Shortly after that, he realized the acid bath had given him the ability to stretch his body into all sorts of shapes. "What a powerful weapon this would be . . . AGAINST CRIME! I've been FOR it long enough! Here's my chance to atone for all the evil I've done!!"

In Plastic Man's early months on duty, he had some rather unusual adventures. He broke up a narcotics ring that was smuggling dope across the Canadian border inside coffined corpses, tangled for two issues with a gang of lesbian racketeers—"women of abnormal physical development bent on a city-wide protection shakedown"—destroyed a pair of evil-doing disembodied hands, outwitted a rather prosaic gang of jewel thieves, and then defeated a mad scientist who was causing death and devastation with a giant eight ball in which he traveled across the countryside. With issue #9 (May 1942), Plastic Man moved up to the front of the book and became the star of *Police*.

Part of the fun of the feature were the disguises and shape changes Plas undertook in his pursuit of crooks and scoundrels. During his first few months, he transformed himself into, among other things, a giant flying squirrel, a quivering junkie, a rather plump matron, a fire-hose, and a glamour girl. He also stretched, shrank, bounced, rolled like a hoop, and squeezed through keyholes. All the while he was spying on crookdom as Eel O'Brien. In his

red costume and dark glasses, Plas worked for the police force, but the cops' standing order to arrest O'Brien was a source of frustration to his stretchy second identity. Cole never did figure out a way to resolve this dilemma and in the second year he simply dropped the dual-identity idea.

In *Police* #13 (November 1942), Plastic Man got a sidekick. Woozy Winks looked something like the then-popular movie comedian Lou Costello. As a result of saving a wizard's life, Woozy was granted invulnerability and found that nothing, from a bop on the head to a dive off a high cliff, could harm him. After using his gift to commit a few crimes Woozy, too, reformed and joined up with Plas. From this point on, the stories took on more humor and Plastic Man stopped working for the police and became an FBI agent.

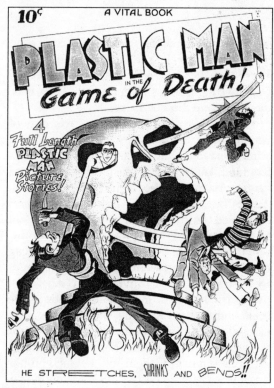

Plastic Man, Jack Cole, © 1943 by Vital Publications, Inc.

In 1943, the first complete *Plastic Man* comic book appeared. It was followed by a second a year later and, finally, in 1946 the title began a regular schedule. Because of the increasing demands for material, other artists began drawing the bouncing hero. Bart Tumey was the first, followed by Alex Kotzky and John Spranger.

Plastic Man was bounced from *Police* after #102 (October 1950). The magazine itself continued for three more years, presenting crime and private-eye material. The *Plastic Man* comic book limped along until 1956, although Cole had given up the character to become a very successful gag cartoonist for *Playboy*. DC licensed the character and has made several attempts, using assorted teams of artists and writers, to revive Plas. None has been successful, chiefly because Cole was really the only one who knew how to do him just right.

PLOP! This comic book, which surfaced in 1973, was DC's belated attempt to imitate MAD, as well as *Humbug* and TALES FROM THE CRYPT. Despite contributions from several *Mad* artists, the 25¢ hybrid did not thrive.

The first issue of *Plop!* had a cover date of September–October 1973. Joe Orlando, a *Mad* alum, served as editor and the contributors included Wally Wood, Basil Wolverton, and Sergio Aragones, also from *Mad*. Wolverton concentrated on covers. The magazine also employed artists not known for their light touch, notably Berni Wrightson and Alex Toth.

The contents mixed satirical pieces, gag cartoons, and short weird tales. The hosts from DC's straight horror comics—Cain, Abel, and Eve—also appeared in *Plop!* to introduce the issue and conduct the letter's column. A typical issue would offer an eight-page humor story by Aragones, seven or eight pages of gag cartoons—most of them of a black-humor

sort—and a couple of short, rather grim horror yarns drawn by the likes of Mike Sekowsky and Wrightson.

Apparently there was not a large audience for this particular blend of material and *Plop!* flopped. It ended with its 24th issue in the late fall of 1976.

POCKET COMICS The first digest-sized comic book, it was introduced by Alfred Harvey in the summer of 1941. Measuring $5^1/_4$ by $7^1/_4$ inches, *Pocket* offered 96 pages of full-color comics and sold for 10¢. Included in the lineup of costumed characters were Red Blazer, Spirit of '76, the Phantom Sphinx, THE ZEBRA, and THE BLACK CAT.

The magazine collapsed after just four diminutive issues. While a few of the characters survived, only the Black Cat went on to become a full-fledged star. She appeared in *Speed Comics* and in a book of her own.

Harvey also tried three digest-format issues of *Speed* before realizing that the world wasn't yet ready for comic books of unorthodox size.

POGO *See* Animal Comics.

POPULAR COMICS The first imitator of the ground-breaking FAMOUS FUNNIES was published by Dell and packaged for them by M.C. Gaines and Sheldon Mayer. The initial issue of *Popular Comics* had a cover date of February 1936 and included on its roll of newspaper strip reprints were *Dick Tracy, Terry and the Pirates, Little Orphan Annie, Tailspin Tommy,* and *Mutt & Jeff.*

Mayer and Gaines left the magazine late in 1938 and by that time it was running fewer reprints and more original material. There

Popular Comics, Jim Chambers, © 1940 by R.S. Callender.

were, for instance, six-page comic book adaptions of cowboy movies with such hard-riding stars as Gene Autry and Tex Ritter. When Oskar Lebeck took over as editor, more new features were added, including *The Masked Pilot*, *Gang Busters*, and *The Hurricane Kids*. *Martan the Marvel Man*, a science fiction effort about invading aliens, debuted in #46 (December 1939). *The Voice*, about a detective who became invisible by donning a specially treated cellophane suit, came next. Next was *Professor Supermind and Son*, which dealt with a scientist who turned his offspring into a flying superhero. Though rather bland in content, it was nicely drawn by veteran pulp illustrator Ralph Carlson.

As the 1940s progressed, the magazine gradually reverted to its reprint policy. By #90 (August 1943), only *Gang Busters* survived, sharing the pages with *Smilin' Jack*, *Toots and Casper*, *The Gumps*, and *Terry*. By the time it ceased publication in the summer of 1948, *Popular* was a slim bimonthly.

RADAR He was a comic book hero of the World War II period created expressly for propaganda purposes. Radar appeared regularly in Fawcett's MASTER COMICS, starting with #50 (May 1944), and the Office of War Information (OWI) in Washington, DC, supervised his adventures. The fact that the OWI was using the character as a propaganda conduit was never mentioned in the magazine.

Created by editor Will Lieberson and drawn by Al Carreño, Radar was introduced in *Captain Marvel Adventures* #35 the same month he took up residence in *Master*. Radar, whose real name was Pep Pepper, worked for an international police organization. His first jobs involved thwarting Nazi efforts at subversion and espionage. Radar wore a white trench coat, green suit, and tan fedora. He could read minds, pick up messages from his bosses by way of telepathy, and see through obstacles with his radar vision. After the war ended in 1945, he continued in business for another year and a half. His peacetime enemies are "the men who threaten to destroy peace, and plunge the nations again into the turmoil of fascism and war."

Lieberson met OWI officials during a visit to Washington. "The committee included Clifton Fadiman, Rex Stout, and Paul Gallico. Their job was to turn out propaganda that the younger readers would really pay attention to," he once said in an interview. Lieberson persuaded them that the best way to do this would "be in the form of comic book stories which the kids would never suspect were outright propaganda." Lieberson came up with the basic idea for *Radar* and the committee members supplied ideas and story lines for the first stories. Never an especially popular character despite his good intentions, Radar was last seen in *Master* #87 (January 1948).

Radar, Al Carreño, © 1945 by Fawcett Publications, Inc.

RAGGEDY ANN AND ANDY   This feature, based on the illustrated books by artist-writer Johnny Gruelle, first appeared in comic books in 1942. The world's favorite rag dolls were introduced almost simultaneously in Dell's *New Funnies* and in a Four Color one-shot. They remained in comics until 1973.

Starting in #65, they shared *New Funnies* with such characters as Andy Panda, Oswald the Rabbit, and Felix the Cat. The first comic devoted entirely to the adventures of the gentle, kindhearted pair was #5 in Dell's Four Color series. This was followed by three annual one-shots, and in 1946 a regular *Raggedy Ann and Andy* monthly began. As in Gruelle's popular storybooks, the two functioned in a world in which dolls, humans, animals, and assorted fantasy characters coexisted. In addition to Ann and Andy, the comic book stories regularly used such members of the Gruelle stock company as Grinny Bear, Beloved Belindy, Snoopwiggy, Sunny Bunny, the Loonies, the Camel with the Wrinkled Knees, and Marcella, the golden-haired little girl who owned the dolls.

Gruelle, who died in 1938, had nothing to do with the comic book appearances of his characters. The chief artist was Walter Kerr, a children's book illustrator since the early part of the century and an artist for the Hearst papers in the 1920s. He drew the stories in a distinctive style that owed little to that of the dolls' creator. Among the writers was John Stanley.

The monthly was edited by Oskar Lebeck and usually opened with a 14-page Kerr story about the Raggedys. Other features in the magazine included *Billy and Bonny Bee*, first drawn by Frank Thomas, *Animal Mother Goose* by Walt Kelly, *The Brownies*, often drawn by Kelly, and *The Hair-Raising Adventures of Peterkin Pottle* by Stanley, which starred a bespectacled, daydreaming junior Walter Mitty.

When the monthly shut down in 1949, Raggedy Ann and Andy returned to one-shots. From 1971 to 1973 they appeared in a six-issue series for Gold Key.

REAL AMERICAN #1   One of the few openly liberal crimefighters of his day and just about the only native American, he was first seen in *Daredevil* #2 (August 1941). After earning a law degree at a Midwestern university, Jeff Dixon returned to the reservation when he learned that his father, Chief White Falcon, had been framed for murder. Rather than relying on his legal training to save his dad from the clutches of the corrupt town officials, Dixon decided to resort to vigilante justice. He decked himself out in a feathered headdress, war paint, and a skull mask and went after the real killer. He rode a gray stallion who also sported a skull mask and he also called himself the Bronze Terror.

His goals were explicit, as a typical introductory caption explained: "Jeff Dixon, full-blooded Indian and prominent lawyer, becomes the Bronze Terror in order to save his people from the wicked, cruel, and corrupt vermin who are oppressing them."

The vermin the Bronze Terror specialized in exterminating were almost always crooked civic officials and government employees, the sort who accused Indians of un-American activities and then put them to work on road gangs, or who mismanaged natural resources. Since this wasn't the sort of thing most costumed heroes went in for, the Bronze Terror never really caught on. He hung up his skull

Real American #1, Dick Briefer, © 1941 by Your Guide Publications, Inc.

and feathers after *Daredevil* #11 (June 1942).

His creator, Dick Briefer, fared better with some of his other features, most notably his version of FRANKENSTEIN.

RED DRAGON   While most comic book magicians dressed in tuxes and top hats or turbans, this redheaded mystic wore only shorts and sandals. Later he got rid of the footgear and added an Oriental-style vest. He first appeared in the sixth issue (March 1943) of Street &

Red Dragon, John Meditz, © 1943 by Street & Smith Publications, Inc.

Smith's *Red Dragon Comics* and later became a regular in *Super-Magician.*

American Bob Reed was raised in China. After his parents were killed by the Japanese, he became the Red Dragon, using the "ancient magic-lore" he'd been studying to fight the invaders. He was aided by his young Chinese sidekick Ching Foo and by his dragon lizard Komodo. The Red Dragon could perform a wide range of impressive magic and he could fly, levitate, teleport, change size and shape, and generally confound his enemies. He accomplished all this by speaking the words of power "Po she lo."

After *Super-Magician* ceased in 1947, he appeared in a magazine of his own again. Therein, the Japanese having been long since defeated, he and his crew visited the worlds of Gulliver, Alice, and the Arabian Nights. He was last seen in the summer of 1948.

A gifted artist named John Meditz, who enjoyed a short-lived career in the 1940s, drew many of the Red Dragon's adventures. Among the others who illuminated his magical encounters were Al Bare, Joe Maneely, and the exceptional pulp magazine illustrator Edd Cartier.

RED SONJA   *See* Conan.

RICHIE RICH   This phenomenal little fellow has appeared in more separate titles than just about any other character in comic books. Since Richie Rich first appeared in 1960, he's starred in more than three dozen different magazines. The books were published by Harvey Comics and never gave artist or writer credits.

Richie, the Richest Kid in the World, usually appeared in five-page humorous adventures. The stories ranged from simple sitcom to mystery, science fiction, and mild horror and involved a crew of regulars that included Cadbury the Perfect Butler, Irona the robot maid, Richie's pudgy parents, his girlfriend Gloria, Reggie Van Dough, his nasty little cousin, and Dollar, his dog.

Richie proved popular and his titles began to proliferate. For many years they were issued at the rate of two and three a week. The first was *Richie Rich*. Among the many others were *Richie Rich Millions*, *Richie Rich Diamonds*, *Richie Rich Vault of Mystery*, *Richie Rich Success*, and *Richie Rich Bank Book*. The Poor Little Rich Boy remained in business until 1982. In 1986, on a considerably more limited basis, he returned to comics again.

Artist Ernie Colon worked on *Richie Rich* for a quarter of a century, and Warren Kremer was another longtime contributor. Lennie Herman was a frequent scriptwriter.

ROBOTMAN The top mechanical man of the GOLDEN AGE, he first appeared in DC's *Star Spangled Comics* #7 (June 1942). Jerry Siegel, much influenced by pulp science fiction robotics, created the character. Paul Cassidy and other members of the SUPERMAN shop handled the early artwork.

Robotman was a late-season replacement. *Star Spangled* had begun several months earlier with a lineup headed by Siegel's Star-Spangled Kid, as drawn by Howard Sherman. Neither the red, white, and blue hero nor Armstrong of the Army and Captain X of the Royal Air Force evidenced any newsstand magic, and with the 7th issue the magazine was revamped. Simon and Kirby's Newsboy Legion took over the lead spot and Robotman joined the backup ranks.

According to the origin story, Robotman had been a regular human being, "rich, young Professor Robert Crane." While working on a new robot with his assistant in his "palatial laboratory-residence," he was fatally shot by burglars. His quick-thinking associate removed his brain and plopped it into the skull of the robot. Thus was born Robotman, who at first looked quite a bit like the Tin Woodman of Oz. In order to function in a world that believed him dead, Crane adopted the alias Paul Dennis and

Robotman, Jimmy Thompson, © 1946, renewed 1974 DC Comics, Inc. All rights reserved.

fashioned synthetic skin to wear over his metallic face and hands. He then began a dual-identity life, passing as a human until it was time to fight crime as Robotman.

The character's finest hour came in the autumn of 1943, when Jimmy Thompson took over the feature. A newspaper veteran, Thompson achieved just the right mix of the humorous and the straight in his drawing, a blend that suited the not-quite-serious exploits of the metallic sleuth. In *Star Spangled* #29, Thompson introduced Robbie the Robot-dog. Built by Robotman, the mechanical sleuth hound was initially a polite and sedate creature. But after a hiatus of a few issues, Robbie came back in a slightly altered form. Besides having acquired a shaggy-dog suit to wear as a disguise over his metal body on certain occasions, he had a new personality. Feisty and vain, he now read Sherlock Holmes and assured his metal master he was a crack investigator himself. Once Thompson had his basic team, he went on to produce a long string of attractive-looking, entertaining yarns. He drew the character throughout its run in *Star Spangled*, which ended in #82 (July 1948), and stuck with Robotman when he moved into DETECTIVE COMICS as of #138 (August 1948).

Thompson left the job in 1949. Among the later artists was Joe Certa. Otto Binder, who'd written about a robot named Adam Link in the *Amazing Stories* pulp in the late 1930s, contributed scripts in the late 1940s. Robotman ended the first phase of his career at the end of 1953. In 1963, an entirely different Robotman became a member in good standing of the DOOM PATROL.

ROY ROGERS COMICS   The King of the Cowboys made his comic book debut as part of Dell's Four Color series in 1944. After 13 scattered issues, the Republic Pictures star graduated to a regular title of his own. *Roy Rogers Comics* flourished for 145 issues, from 1948 to 1961.

The comic book adventures of Roy Rogers were similar to his movies. They were folksy, wholesome, and loaded with riding and shooting. There wasn't much singing, though. Albert Micale was one of the earliest artists and among the later ones were Alex Toth, Jesse Marsh, and Russ Manning. The magazine's title was changed to *Roy Rogers and Trigger* in 1955. Roy's horse was featured in a series of his own that ran to 17 issues between 1951 and 1955. Dale Evans, the cowboy's frequent co-star and his wife in real life, also starred in a comic book.

The popularity of cowboys on television in the 1950s inspired numerous comic book titles showcasing Western actors, living and dead. They included Gene Autry, Johnny Mack Brown, Rocky Lane, Rod Cameron, Tim Holt, John Wayne, Buck Jones, and Tom Mix.

SAD SACK He was a very unusual character to become a comic book favorite of children. Sad Sack began as the focal character in a raunchy pantomime strip aimed at servicemen during World War II. George Baker, a soldier himself, created Sad Sack for the service weekly *Yank*, taking the name from the Army slang phrase "a sad sack of shit." After the war, a toned-down, civilian Sad Sack became the star of a newspaper strip and in 1949 Harvey introduced the hapless loser in a comic book.

Eventually the Sack of the comic books started talking, and in the spring of 1951 he returned to the Army. Baker drew the covers but had nothing to do with the stories. In 1953 Fred Rhoads, a former Marine who'd drawn for *Leatherneck* magazine and who'd assisted on *Snuffy Smith* and *Beetle Bailey*, became the artist on the *Sad Sack* title. Rhoads also wrote the stories, which proved to have a tremendous appeal to preteen and early teenage boys. He created dozens of new characters and during his stay with the feature drew nearly 10,000 pages of material. One of the backup artists was Joe Dennett, a sometime assistant on the *Mutt & Jeff* strip (see MUTT & JEFF).

The character kept branching out into new titles. At the high point, there were more than a dozen. "You'll like every Sad Sack comic," Harvey ads assured young readers. "You'll want to OWN every one of them!" Among the magazines were *Sad Sack's Army Life*, *Sad Sack's Funny Friends*, *Sad Sack U.S.A.*, *Sad Sack Laugh Special*, and *Sad Sad Sack*. For a time there was even a *Sad Sack and the Navy*. The longtime, long-suffering GI vanished from the stands in the early 1980s.

SAM HILL Billed as "America's hard-boiled, wise-cracking sleuth," he appeared in seven issues of his own magazine in 1950 and 1951. What he was, actually, was a very close imitation of the radio version of Dashiell Hammett's Sam Spade.

The Adventures of Sam Spade, Detective had taken to the air in 1946, with Howard Duff starring. This Spade was considerably different from the movie Spade portrayed by Humphrey Bogart in the 1941 version of *The Maltese Falcon*. He was hard-boiled, to be sure, but much more given to wisecracks. The weekly episodes usually mixed whimsy with violence to create a hybrid that might be called screwball noir. Spade narrated his own cases, dictating his reports to his secretary Effie. Every case was referred to as a caper and the shows boasted such titles as "The Dry Martini Caper," "The Farmer's Daughter Caper," and "The Fairly Bright Caper." Howard Duff eventually turned the Spade role over to Steve Dunne, and *Sam Spade* ended its run on the airwaves in 1951. Hill was a handsome, dark-haired fellow with a dead-white forelock. His secretary was named Roxy. The case histories he dictated to her had titles like "The Lethal Lobster Caper," "The Carnival Killing Caper," and "The Crying Corpse Caper." There was some violence and some sex, but nothing as strong as what could be found in the average true-crime comic book of the period. Hill tried to act as tough and clever as his radio idol, but he never quite managed to bring it off.

Harry Lucey did an admirable job of illustrating the capers and Archie Comics, hiding behind the name Close-Up, Inc., published the magazine.

THE SANDMAN   DC has been especially fond of this name and by the early 1990s four different characters had operated as the Sandman. The first was a costumed crimefighter who appeared in 1939 and the most recent is a supernatural entity who was introduced in 1989. In between came two superheroes.

The original Sandman, the joint effort of writer Gardner Fox and artist Bert Christman, began in ADVENTURE COMICS #40 (July 1939). In everyday life, this modern Robin Hood was Wesley Dodds, a millionaire playboy who was also a brilliant inventor and CEO of the Dodds-Bessing Steel Corporation. When night fell, he put on a green business suit, fedora, gas mask, and purple cape to become the Sandman. Like his namesake, he brought sleep—chiefly to crooks, gangsters, and evildoers—using a special gas gun of his own invention. Although he was dedicated to bringing "justice in a world of injustice," he was often misunderstood and was "wanted by police forces on two conti-

nents." Fox got his ideas from such pulp fiction heroes as THE SHADOW, the Spider, and the Phantom Detective. He was also influenced by THE GREEN HORNET, the popular radio avenger who used a gas gun to subdue his foes and who was also considered a criminal by the law. Dodd's constant companion was Dian Belmont, the only person who knew his secret identity. She was not only an expert safecracker but the daughter of the district attorney.

For the next two years, the Sandman operated in a pulp-hero manner, dealing in cases that mixed mystery and fantasy. In addition to his duties in *Adventure*, he found time to serve on the JUSTICE SOCIETY over in ALL STAR COMICS. After Christman, Ogden Whitney, Creig Flessel, and Chad Grothkopf drew his adventures. In the fall of 1941, Chad and editor Whit Ellsworth decided to update the character, and in *Adventure* #69 Sandman appeared in yellow tunic and tights and purple trunks, cowl, and cape. He traded in his gas gun for a wirepoon gun, which was good for everything from felling giant bees to scaling skyscrapers. Sandman also gained a boy companion known as Sandy the Golden Lad. Paul Norris carried on with the artwork for two issues before Joe Simon and Jack Kirby took charge of the feature.

Using the storytelling techniques they'd developed on CAPTAIN AMERICA, the team revitalized Sandman. They began to build some of the stories around dreams, nightmares, and other aspects of the realm of sleep. The old Sandman had been pushed out of the star spot by later heroes such as Hour-Man and Starman, but with the advent of the Simon–Kirby team the new Sandman moved into the leading spot. And from #74 (May 1942) on, Sandman and Sandy appeared, with one exception, on the next two dozen-plus covers. Other artists on the feature were Cliff Young and Phil Bard. Sandman and Sandy called it a night after #102 early in 1946.

The old original Sandman, complete with gas mask, returned now and again during the

SILVER AGE, showing up in some issues of JUS-
TICE LEAGUE OF AMERICA for JLA and Justice
Society team-ups. The original Sandy popped
up on occasion, sometimes as a member of the
All-Star Squadron. Late in 1974 Simon and
Kirby, long parted, joined forces again to invent
a brand-new Sandman for DC. This one was
Dr. Garrett Sanford, who operated as a costumed superhero over in the Dream Dimension, "a palen of existence on which what people see in dreams actually exists." This Sandman made it through six issues of his own
magazine. In the late 1980s, a fellow named
Hector Sanders Hall, who'd been doing business as the Silver Scarab, assumed the Sandman role and filled in for Dr. Sanford.

Finally, in 1989 a British creative team consisting of writer Neil Gaiman and artists Sam
Kieth and Mike Dringenberg came up with yet
another Sandman. This one is actually Mor-
pheus and hangs out in the Dreamworld,
where many strange and unusual things occur.

SCRIBBLY   *See* The Funnies and All-American
Comics.

SEÑORITA RIO The "bewitching American
secret agent" was first seen in *Fight Comics* #19
(June 1942). Fiction House, the fountainhead of
GOOD GIRL ART, published the title and each
issue was chock full of sexy ladies in various
stages of undress. The señorita, "America's
lovely daring spy ace," managed to hold her
own against all the competition. In her initial
adventure she appeared in a skintight scarlet
evening gown, a bathing suit, and her underwear. Unhampered by all the costume changes,
she thwarted a Nazi spy ring based in Brazil
with ease in just eight pages. Readers learned
in this pilot episode that she was actually starlet Rita Farrar, "who soared to fame with the
opening of her new picture, 'Lady, Dance No
More,'" and that she faked her suicide in Rio
de Janeiro in order to go underground and

Señorita Rio, Nick Cardy, © 1943 by Fight Stories, Inc.

become an American spy. She was motivated
by patriotism and by the fact that her fiancé
was killed at Pearl Harbor.

In subsequent adventures, Señorita Rio
tackled Nazi-paid guerrillas who were sabo-
taging the Brazilian rubber crop, destroyed a
secret Nazi airfield, and took care of sundry
other spies and scoundrels. She was a crack
shot and also good in hand-to-hand combat
against both men and women. Her daredevil

escapades were hardly hampered by the fact that the scriptwriters were laboring under the impression that the language spoken in Brazil was Spanish and not Portuguese. The correct spelling of her name, by the way, should have been Senhorita Rio.

The first artist on the feature was Nick Cardy, who'd just graduated from *Lady Luck* (see LADY LUCK). He did an excellent job, devoting as much care to the backgrounds and props as he gave to the lady spy's figure. Artie Saaf followed him and then Lily Renee. The señorita was last seen in *Fight* #71 (November 1950).

SGT. FURY AND HIS HOWLING COMMANDOS *See* Nick Fury.

SGT. ROCK   DC's bestselling soldier first went into battle in *Our Army at War* #81, which bore a cover date of April 1959. Writer Robert Kanigher created the character. Joe Kubert was the artist from the sergeant's third appearance onward.

The stories were set during World War II and Sgt. Frank Rock was topkick of a platoon called Easy Co., also known as "the Combat Happy Joes of Easy." He and his men did the majority of their fighting in the European Theater of Operations. Kanigher's idea of combat owed as much to movies and John Wayne as it did to research, and Rock's gang had the same colorful mix of men as might've been found in an MGM epic of a decade or so earlier. Among the personnel were Wildman, Bulldozer, Ice Cream Soldier, Little Sure Shot, Troubador, and Jackie Johnson, a black. Kanigher fudged on Johnson, giving Rock the only integrated platoon in World War II.

The adventures were gritty, grim, sentimental, and full of technicolor heroics. The sergeant narrated most of his battle reports himself: "Here's a war story that'll tear at your heart . . . or my name ain't Sgt. Rock!" Kubert did a commendable job of illustrating the Easy tales. Russ Heath also drew the feature.

The sergeant's name eventually began appearing on the covers in larger and larger letters. Finally, with #302 (March 1977), the magazine was retitled simply *Sgt. Rock*. It held on longer than any other war comic, expiring at last in the summer of 1988. It was followed later in the year by a series of reprints called *Sgt. Rock Special*.

THE SHADOW   This multimedia hero first appeared in comic books early in 1940. By that time he had long been a success in both his own pulp fiction magazine and on his own radio show. In the same year that the comic book was launched, Columbia Pictures issued a 15-chapter movie serial and the Ledger Syndicate offered a daily newspaper strip. All these Shadows were supposed to be the same fellow, but there were considerable differences between the versions. The most important difference had to do with invisibility.

The first issue of Street & Smith's Shadow pulp had a cover date of April 1931 and was intended to be a quarterly. But the mysterious nemesis of crime, as created by young Walter B. Gibson under the pen name Maxwell Grant, proved to be an immediate hit. The new magazine soon became a monthly. The Shadow of the pulps wasn't an easy man to get to know. In the first novels, in fact, even Gibson didn't seem quite sure who he really was. The Shadow never appeared before the reader undisguised and often he lurked in the background, more like the sinister villain of a movie serial than a crime-fighting hero. The novels, especially those of the early 1930s, were usually about the people he worked on and through, the crooks he destroyed and the agents he manipulated. Gibson was turning out mystery thrillers, not fantasies. His Shadow was a grim avenger out to destroy crooks and evildoers and live up to his reputation as gangdom's foe. He didn't exhibit the slightest tendency to become invisible.

The Shadow used a large and diversified staff. "He works a lone hand," explained a blurb, "yet he has able aides in Harry Vincent, a presentable young man who can make himself at home anywhere; Burbank, who serves as communications contact for all the agents; Clyde Burke, reporter on the *Classic*; Cliff Marsland, who served a term in prison for a crime he did not commit and whose innocence was known only to The Shadow. . . . Mann, the calm-looking broker, is another link in The Shadow's small but compact army of crimebusters." He also relied on a cab driver named Moe Shrevnitz. The professional end of crimebusting was represented by Commissioner Weston and Joe Cardona, ace detective from New York headquarters.

Among the Shadow's many aliases were those of millionaire playboy Lamont Cranston, Fritz the police-station janitor, and Kent Allard, daredevil aviator.

A somewhat different Shadow came to radio in the fall of 1937. He was Lamont Cranston in real life and was not only the foe of gangsters but of mad scientists, ghouls, vampires, and assorted other creepy opponents. This Shadow had the ability to become invisible at will. Eventually it was revealed that, many years before, he'd picked up the knack of clouding men's minds so they could not see him. The new Cranston had a lovely companion named Margo Lane who shared the knowledge that he was in reality the mysterious Shadow. Margo never learned from experience, and she would continually walk into old dark houses alone or put her faith in obviously crazed friends.

With the exception of Moe Shrevnitz, none of the Shadow's pulp crew made it onto the radio. On the other hand, Margo, whom Gibson never much cared for, was added the the pulpwood novels. Orson Welles was the original radio Shadow; Agnes Moorehead played the first Margo.

The earliest comic book Shadow was a variation on the pulp character and had abso-

lutely no talent for invisibility. By 1941, however, he was turning invisible with ease. To indicate that he was unseen by those around him, the comic book pages printed his figure in blue ink, apparently unaware that seeing an invisible man spoiled the fun somewhat. Among the artists to draw the feature were Vernon Greene, Jon L. Blummer, Al Bare, Charles Coll, and Bob Powell.

According to Shadow authority Will Murray, Gibson "wrote all the Shadow's comics adventures from 1940 to 1946. . . . Gibson enjoyed writing the comic, but he didn't take it seriously. To him the real Shadow appeared in the pulp title." Gibson turned in many an incoherent yarn. He tried to adapt his full-length pulp novels to 12- and 14-page stories and also indulged his habit of building plots around magic tricks and mathematical puzzles. Gibson realized, according to Murray, that "it was easier to resurrect old pulp villains and write new stories around them, so a host of deceased Shadow adversaries took on full-color life. These included his greatest foe, Shiwan Khan, the descendant of Genghis Khan . . . and Gibson's most bizarre pulp villain, Monstradomus . . . who controlled a variety of prehistoric and mythological creatures."

Shadow Comics ended in the summer of 1949 with its 101st issue. The character was next seen in the summer of 1964 in Archie Comics' *The Shadow*. In this ill-advised outing, with scripts by Jerry Siegel and artwork by Paul Reinman, he was a costumed superhero whose recurrent nemesis was Shiwan Khan. The magazine folded after eight issues.

DC took up the Shadow in 1973, bringing back the hawk-nosed, cloaked avenger of the Gibson pulps. Gangdom's foe, this version blazed away with his automatic and hadn't the slightest notion of how to cloud men's minds so that they couldn't see him. Denny O'Neil was the writer. The artists included Mike Kaluta and Frank Robbins. DC's first try ended in 1975 after just a dozen issues. It brought him back in a miniseries in 1986 and in a regular series the next year that lasted until 1989. In the 1990s came *The Shadow Strikes*, a monthly written by Gerard Jones and drawn by such as Dan Spiegle and Eduardo Barreto. This was yet again the pulpwood Shadow, with Margo along, and the stories were set several decades in the past. It folded in 1992.

SHAZAM The most powerful magic word in comics, it converted teenage radio newscaster Billy Batson into the World's Mightiest Mortal, CAPTAIN MARVEL.

The word was an acronym that stood for Solomon, Hercules, Atlas, Zeus, Achilles, and Mercury. By saying it aloud, Billy took on the abilities of this group of gods and heroes—wisdom, strength, stamina, power, courage, and speed. The transition from youth to superhero was always accompanied by an impressive boom of thunder and a flash of lightning. The captain also wore a zigzag of yellow lightning emblazoned across the chest of his crimson tunic.

Shazam was also the name of the ancient wizard who had bestowed superpowers on Billy. In 1973, when Captain Marvel returned to comics after a hiatus of nearly two decades, his magazine was entitled *Shazam!* That was because Marvel Comics had introduced an entirely different Captain Marvel of its own and trademarked the name.

Mary Batson, Billy's sister, became MARY MARVEL by shouting, "Shazam!" She, however, used a feminine version of the magic word. In her version the letters stood for Selena, Hippolyta, Ariadne, Zephyrus, Aurora, and Minerva.

SHEENA She was the Queen of the Jungle and an inspiration to dozens of jungle girls who followed her. Sheena, a product of the Eisner–Iger shop, originally appeared in an overseas tabloid called *Wags*. In 1938, Iger persuaded pulp publisher Fiction House to reprint much of the *Wags* material in a tab-sized comic book titled *Jumbo Comics*. At first the blonde jungle girl was not the star of the outsized magazine, but shared it with an assortment of other characters. By the magazine's second year, after it had shrunk to standard size and she had adopted her leopard-skin costume, Sheena was the leading lady of *Jumbo*. From the 18th issue (August 1940) on, no other character ever appeared on a cover.

Although her monthly adventures bore impressively awesome titles such as "Beasts of the Devil Queen," "Sabre-Tooth Terror," "Land of the Stalking Dead," and "Victims of the Super-Ape," they were standard pulp and B-movie jungle fare. One issue it was cruel slave traders, the next it was Nazi invaders intent on damming up all the streams in the part of the jungle she ruled over. What gave Sheena the edge over TARZAN, KA-ZAR, and the other jungle do-gooders of the early 1940s was the fact that she was quite a bit more interesting to look at—especially to the adolescent schoolboys and horny GIs who made up a large portion of her reading public during the World War II years. Not that Sheena was simply another sparsely clad pinup. She was a very tough lady, capable of tackling gorillas, crocodiles, lions, and even warthogs. She was especially good with a knife and while dispatching an animal foe she would exclaim lines like, "My knife is swifter than your claws, killer!"

Aside from apes, lions, and elephants, the regular cast was small. The only other full-time character was Sheena's gentleman explorer friend, a handsome chap named Bob Reynolds who wore jodhpurs and had the thankless task of playing second fiddle to the jungle queen. When nothing else was going on, Sheena could always get an adventure going by rescuing the hapless Bob from some peril he'd stumbled into. Numerous blacks appeared in the feature, but they were either docile tribesmen who considered her the ruler of their wilderness domain or hostile savages bent on some bloody scheme.

Sheena appeared in the entire 167-issue run of *Jumbo* as well as 18 issues of her own title before retiring in 1953. She appeared in a 1955 syndicated television show and a 1984 flop movie.

The comic book scripts were contributed by a variety of writers and always attributed to the nonexistent W. Morgan Thomas. Mort Meskin was the first artist, followed by Bob Powell and Bob Webb. Eisner, Dan Zolnerowich, Artie Saaf, and Nick Cardy were among the artists who drew her titillating magazine covers.

Sheena, Artie Saaf, © 1943 by Real Adventures Pub. Co., Inc.

THE SHIELD   The earliest superpatriot in comic books was introduced in *Pep Comics* #1 (January 1940). While never as popular as CAPTAIN AMERICA, the Shield has had a career that has extended, with several fallow periods, over a half century.

Until the Shield came along, no superhero had ever donned a costume based on the American flag. He established the fashion for red, white, and blue ensembles that was followed by Minute Man, Captain Flag, and Captain America, to name but a few. Irv Novick was the artist, Harry Shorten the writer. Also known as the G-Man Extraordinary, the Shield was in everyday life redheaded Joe Higgins, who worked as an FBI agent. The only person who knew of his alternate identity was J. Edgar Hoover, who appeared in early episodes to send the Shield out on his spy-smashing missions.

Readers were told that Higgins's superpowers came from his uniform. "This uniform, of his own secret construction, not only is bullet and flame-proof but gives him power to perform extraordinary feats of physical daring and courage," explained a caption. "Wearing his shield, he has the speed of a bullet and the strength of a Hercules. With these powerful forces, he shields the U.S. Government from all enemies. The four white stars on the field of blue signify to what he has devoted his life—truth, justice, patriotism, and courage."

The Shield got a boy sidekick in *Pep* #11 (January 1941), a redheaded lad named Dusty the Boy Detective. The new team devoted the next several months to combating a master criminal and super-saboteur known as the Vulture. With the coming of World War II, the exploits of the Shield and Dusty grew bloodier and more violent. The Axis villains they confronted were a bloodthirsty lot that included the Strangler, the Fang, and the Hun. While all this was going on, Novick was also adding quite a few GOOD GIRL ART touches, such as upthrust bosoms, bondage, and stocking tops. The Shield, upstaged by ARCHIE in the postwar years, hung on until *Pep* #65 (January 1948). From 1940 to 1944 he had also appeared in a quarterly called *Shield–Wizard Comics*.

After being benched for over a decade, the

Shield was reactivated in the spring of 1959 to participate in the SILVER AGE revival movement. Although his costume was similar to his earlier one, he was an entirely different person. This new Shield was in reality Pvt. Lancelot Strong and the premise of his new magazine, that of an Army private who doubled as a star-spangled superhero, was quite close to that of Captain America, undoubtedly because Archie Comics had hired Joe Simon and Jack Kirby to refurbish the character. The new comic was called *The Double Life of Private Strong*.

The new, improved Shield comic book looked as though it had been turned out in haste, and the hero had little of the appeal of Simon and Kirby's earlier superpatriot, Captain America. He wasn't even able to equal the success of their short-lived cold warrior, Fighting American. Simon maintained that *Private Strong* was canceled after two issues "not because of poor sales but because DC Comics threatened a lawsuit" because of similarities to SUPERMAN. Despite the threat of legal action, the Shield did risk two more appearances the following year, as a guest in two issues of *The Fly* (see THE FLY).

In the mid-1960s, the Shield was back again, appearing as part of the Mighty Crusaders hero group and as a solo act in *Fly Man*, *Mighty Crusaders*, and *Mighty Comics*. As comics historian Lou Mougin pointed out, "Shield of the Sixties was Bill Higgins, son of the original 1940s Shield; his pop had been turned into an iron statue by a fiend called the Eraser, whom Shield, Jr. promptly wiped out in his first solo adventure." That time around, the Shield was drawn by Paul Reinman, with scripts by Jerry Siegel. By the fall of 1967 he was back in retirement.

The star-spangled hero accomplished a rather interesting return in the 1980s. In 1983, Archie Comics brought back Pvt. Strong and passed him off as the Shield in three issues of his own magazine. The following year saw four issues of *The Original Shield*, starring the other Shield.

Undaunted by his poor track record, DC brought out a Shield title in 1991. In this incarnation, which borrowed from all the earlier versions, he was a soldier named Joe Higgins.

THE SHINING KNIGHT   *See* Adventure Comics.

SHOWCASE   This was the magazine that played a major role in launching and sustaining the SILVER AGE of comic books. Edited by Julius Schwartz, DC's *Showcase* began in 1956 as a place to try out various features.

Its first three numbers auditioned such nonwinners as *Fire Fighters* and *The Frogmen*. Things changed with #4 (October 1956), which introduced the new FLASH. Comics historian Gary M. Carter described this issue as the catalyst for the Silver Age and added that "collectors view it as one of the two most valuable and sought after" magazines from that period.

Showcase #6 launched the CHALLENGERS OF THE UNKNOWN, #22 featured the new, improved GREEN LANTERN, and #34 (October 1961) offered an updated version of THE ATOM.

Among the other characters showcased in the magazine were the Sea Devils, Rip Hunter—Time Master, AQUAMAN, THE SPECTRE, and the Metal Men. The final issue appeared in 1978.

SILVER AGE   This is a term that denotes a period beginning in the mid-1950s when superheroes made a successful comeback in comic books.

It's generally agreed that the Silver Age began with the publication of DC's *Showcase* #4 (October 1956), which introduced the new, improved FLASH. Other early milestones included the advent of DC's new GREEN LANTERN and its introduction of the JUSTICE LEAGUE OF AMERICA in 1960. Marvel got into the act in 1961 with the FANTASTIC FOUR.

According to Robert M. Overstreet, the Silver Age officially ended in 1969.

THE SILVER SURFER The most mystical and philosophical of the Marvel superheroes was a silver-colored, bald-headed alien who looked somewhat like a giant hood ornament and zoomed around the galaxies on his atomic surfboard. Also known as the Sentinel of the Spaceways, he was yet another creation of the team of editor-writer Stan Lee and artist Jack Kirby and was first seen in *Fantastic Four* #48 (March 1956) (see FANTASTIC FOUR). He moved into a magazine of his own in the summer of 1968.

When the Surfer first surfaced, he was serving as the herald for the villanous Galactus, "a powerful . . . godlike giant who roamed the galaxies" doing bad deeds, but he was soon converted to a good guy. Lee has said that "the more I studied him, the more I got into his thoughts and his dialogue, the more I saw him as someone who would graphically represent all the best, the most unselfish, qualities of intelligent life."

After being "besieged and bombarded by impassioned requests to give The Silver Surfer his own magazine," Marvel introduced the book in 1968. Stan Lee continued as writer and John Buscema, the house's leading emulator of Kirby, was the artist.

In the origin story, which took up 38 pages, readers learned that the Surfer had once been a bald-headed, but pink-fleshed, resident of the planet Zenn-La. Through a complex chain of events, Norrin Radd came face to face with Galactus, who decided to make him his herald. Part of the initiation process involved encasing Radd's body "in a life-preserving silvery substance of my own creation." Galactus also provided the newly minted Surfer with "an indestructible flying board . . . yours to command . . . with but a single thought!" Due to a policy conflict that arose during Galactus's initial confrontation with the Fantastic Four, the Surfer was dismissed and dumped on Earth. Being chrome-plated seemed to add to Radd's introspective bent and he was now frequently given to flying around on his board, hands locked behind his back, pondering such imponderables as, "How much longer am I destined to endure a fate I cannot even comprehend?" and "Time is long and fate is fickle." Like many of Lee's most serious characters, the Surfer never used a contraction in speech or thought.

The Silver Surfer's first magazine continued until the autumn of 1970, and he has also dropped in on the FF over the years. In 1987 Marvel brought him back in his own title again, with Marshall Rogers as the first artist. And in 1988 Lee and Jean Giraud (aka Moebius) collaborated on a miniseries/graphic novel.

Silver Surfer®, Jean Giraud (Moebius). All Marvel characters and the distinctive likenesses thereof are trademarks of Marvel Entertainment Group, Inc. and are used with permission. © 1992 Marvel Entertainment Group, Inc.

SLAM BRADLEY He was one of the earliest private investigators to operate in comic books and was billed as an "ace freelance sleuth, fighter and adventurer." His first case, which involved him in mystery and murder in the bowels of Chinatown, was chronicled in DETECTIVE COMICS #1 (March 1937). He was the creation of Jerry Siegel and Joe Shuster.

As his name hints, Slam was a rough-and-tumble operative who used his fists more often than he used a magnifying glass. He owed as much to Roy Crane's freewheeling soldier of fortune, Captain Easy, as he did to the private eyes of pulps and the movies. And just as Easy had the diminutive Wash Tubbs as a sidekick, Slam had Shorty Morgan. They teamed up, after considerable show of reluctance on Slam's part, during the first case.

Slam and Shorty investigated crimes and misdemeanors in Hollywood, on Broadway, in Mexico, and in the frozen North. Siegel and Shuster, being longtime science fiction buffs, eventually involved their detective team in rocket ships, magic, and even time travel. It was in this feature that they began experimenting with the use of full-page splash panels. This was a novelty in the 1930s, when most comic book pages were laid out as sedately as those of newspaper Sundays.

After SUPERMAN became a success, Shuster turned over the drawing of *Slam Bradley* to assistants. Next came Mart Bailey, and with *Detective* #40 (June 1940) Howard Sherman began a long association with the feature. He had an attractive style that blended elements of cartoon and illustration. Slam and Shorty occupied eight pages at the back of the book, handling murders, kidnappings, and assorted rackets with ease and humor. Shorty, who'd grown a bit taller by this time, was feisty and cynical and not always anxious to rush into danger. Slam remained as belligerent as ever.

By the mid-1940s, when artists such as John Daly and Martin Naydel were rendering the strip, the caseload was made up mostly of whimsical and slapstick crimes. Sherman returned in the postwar years and remained with the duo until they solved their final case in *Detective* #152 (October 1949).

DC has revived Slam now and then, such as in *Detective Comics* #500 (March 1981). According to a recent DC *Who's Who*, Slam is still active as a private eye in Gotham City, but poor Shorty is dead.

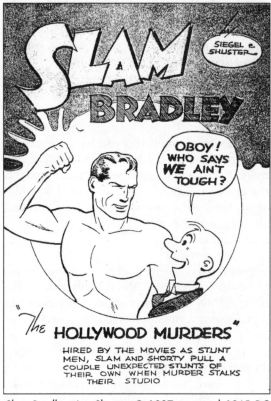

Slam Bradley, Joe Shuster, © 1937, renewed 1965 DC Comics, Inc. All rights reserved.

SPARKY WATTS He was the first character to spoof SUPERMAN. Sparky began his rather unusual career in the spring of 1940 as the star of Boody Rogers's daily newspaper strip. The strips were reprinted in *Big Shot Comics* beginning in 1941, and late in 1943 the magazine began running original *Sparky Watts* stories. When Rogers got out of the Army in the mid-1940s, he returned to drawing his mock superhero. Sparky remained in comic books until 1949, and in addition to *Big Shot* he appeared in 10 issues of his own magazine.

When first encountered, blond, bespectacled Sparky was working his way through college by selling magazine subscriptions. Exposure to a cosmic-ray machine converted him into the strongest man on Earth. During his newspaper-strip career, he sabotaged Nazi submarines by tying knots in their periscopes, singlehandedly laid an oil pipeline from Texas to New York, discovered that the only way he could shave his super beard was with a blowtorch, shrank down to the size of a speck when his cosmic ray charge wore off, played professional baseball (he first had to overcome a tendency to throw the ball so high it came down with ice on it), and joined the Air Corps and then had trouble explaining why he didn't need a plane.

The regulars in *Sparky Watts* included Doc Static, inventor of the cosmic-ray machine that transformed Sparky (the machine looked suspiciously like an old box camera with a big lightbulb screwed on top); Slap Happy, an ex-pug whose feet had become immense after an accidental cosmic-ray treatment; and Yoo Hoo, a Chinese war orphan who came to share the ménage. There were also assorted pretty women for Sparky to have trouble with.

Sparky Watts, Boody Rogers, © 1947 by Columbia Comic Corporation.

Almost all of them fell in love with him, but due to his super strength he couldn't risk kissing one without fear of breaking her jaw.

Besides concerning himself with the social life of the superhero, Rogers was one of the few who gave serious thought to the theory of flight. Most supermen seemed to fly by magic and clearly behaved in ways that were impossible under the known laws of physics—unless they used the Sparky Watts method, which was to flap your arms like a bird's wings. Unlike all the other superheroes, Sparky never took off his mild-mannered glasses when he was doing his good deeds. He never had a costume either, and preferred to work and fight evil in slacks, sweater, and tie. Once he did dress up like a chicken as part of a sub-chasing escapade.

THE SPECTRE   With the exception of CASPER, he was probably the most successful ghost in comic books. Co-created by the co-creator of SUPERMAN, the Spectre first materialized in DC's MORE FUN COMICS #52 (February 1940). He remained on the scene for five years the first time and has returned to haunt the newsstands several times since.

Jerry Siegel wrote *The Spectre*, Bernard Baily drew it. "When I was there at DC, Siegel came up with the Spectre," Baily once explained. "The look of the character I created, the scripts he wrote." Intended for stardom, the spectral superhero was featured on all but 2 of the next 15 covers after #52. He ceased to be showcased after that, and heroes such as DR. FATE and THE GREEN ARROW were given the cover spot. Perhaps the Spectre's failure to gain superstar status was due to his grim personality and the downbeat and unsettling nature of his early adventures.

According to the origin story, which took two issues to unfold, a hard-boiled, redheaded cop named Jim Corrigan was murdered by gangsters by being dumped in the river in the traditional barrel of cement. He returned as a spirit, cloaked in green and sporting a pasty white complexion. He had the ability, shared with Little Orphan Annie, of making the pupils of his eyes disappear. In some unexplained but obviously supernatural fashion, Corrigan could cause his spirit to look like his former body. Early on, he would turn himself into the Spectre, but later the Spectre was a projection that left the defunct cop's body to sail off and fight crime. Originally the Spectre operated in the city of Cliffland, quite obviously a surrogate for Siegel's hometown of Cleveland.

The Spectre's early adventures were decidedly odd. He had frequent conversations with the Almighty and made occasional trips to the hereafter to get clues from departed souls. Once he even stalked a supernatural villain "into the depths of infinity," which turned out to be a void made up mainly of clouds. He could walk through walls, turn crooks into skeletons, and grow as tall as a downtown office building. A grim, uniquely talented fellow, he didn't just catch criminals, he enjoyed himself by destroying them. After one instance of spectral vigilantism, he observed, "One less vermin to peril decency."

Not an especially likable character, the Spectre never achieved the popularity of Superman or BATMAN. At the end of 1941, he was eased to the back of *More Fun*, and newer heroes vied for the top spot. Baily took over the scripting and attempted to lighten up the Spectre's caseload. He invented a humorous sidekick named Percival Popp the Super Cop and he had Corrigan serve in the Army. This last change, as *Amazing Heroes* has pointed out, "left the Spectre behind as an invisible spirit. For the remainder of his series' run, the Spectre was reduced to a subordinate role in his own strip, serving as a sort of guardian angel to the bumbling Popp." A ghost of his former self, he hung on until *More Fun* #101 (January–February 1945) and then was gone. That was the same issue that introduced SUPERBOY. In his prime the Spectre had also been a member of the JUSTICE SOCIETY, appearing in ALL STAR until #23 (Winter 1945).

The Spectre had to remain in limbo for over two decades. The SILVER AGE was well under way when he finally made his comeback in SHOWCASE #60. Corrigan, a bit older, was alive now and shared his body with the Spectre. Gardner Fox wrote the scripts and Murphy Anderson provided the drawing. As Alan Stewart has observed in *Amazing Heroes*, this was a somewhat tamer character and "despite occasional references to the character as a 'dread figure,' or renderings of skulls for pupils in his eyes, the revived Spectre was essentially a typical DC superhero of the period—a comfortable establishment figure." He was awarded a book of his own late in 1967. Various artists and writers worked on it, including Fox, Neal Adams, and Jerry Grandenetti. The title made it through only 10 issues.

When he next returned, the Ghostly Guardian was much nastier and meaner. He came back in ADVENTURE #431 late in 1973, in a story written by Michael Fleisher and drawn by Jim Aparo. Corrigan, "the toughest cop on the New York force," was dead again, but was capable of assuming both a red-haired human form and a ghostly avenger form. He had a *Death Wish* outlook and was determined to destroy "the vermin of the underworld." The Spectre had no qualms about killing and was, in fact, quite fond of turning his opponents into skeletons. He addressed them in such colorful phrases as, "Stare into my eyes, evil one—and we will walk into the valley of death— TOGETHER!"

The vermin-exterminating Spectre lasted for roughly two years. Since then his career has waxed and waned, and he's appeared in such titles as THE BRAVE AND THE BOLD, *Ghosts*, *All Star Squadron*, and *Swamp Thing* (see SWAMP THING). In 1987, he was back in his own book, drawn by Gene Colan. That run lasted until 1989.

SPIDER-MAN His publishers call him "the world's greatest non-mutant superhero," and he's been the most successful and popular of all the characters introduced by Marvel since the beginning of the SILVER AGE. Spider-Man first spun his web in the summer of 1962. After auditioning in *Amazing Fantasy* #15, he moved into his own title, *The Amazing Spider-Man*, early in 1963. Spidey has been at the top of the sales charts and the popularity polls just about ever since. Long an industry icon, his image even appears on Marvel's business cards and stationery.

Several people were involved in the conception, gestation, and birth of Spider-Man, including Stan Lee, Steve Ditko, Jack Kirby, Joe Simon, and C.C. Beck. According to Lee, who wrote the scripts and edited the magazines, he came up with Spider-Man because he wanted "to try something different. . . . a strip that would actually feature a teenager as a star . . . a strip in which the main character would lose as often as he'd win." As for the name, it was Lee's homage to "one of my favorite pulp magazine heroes . . . a stalwart named the Spider." Jack Kirby, who drew the cover for *Amazing Fantasy* #15, has told a different story and claims Spidey as his idea. "Spider-Man was not a product of Marvel," he has said. "It was the last thing Joe Simon and I had discussed. We had a strip called *The Silver Spider*. *The Silver Spider* was going into a magazine called *Black Magic*. *Black Magic* folded . . . I believe I said this could become a thing called *Spider-Man*, see, a superhero character. So the idea was already there when I talked to Stan."

According to Joe Simon, he and a writer named Jack Oleck came up with the idea in the mid-1950s. Working with longtime CAPTAIN MARVEL artist C.C. Beck, they'd created a character first called Spiderman and then the Silver Spider. The story involved an orphan lad named Tommy Troy who became a superhero by way of a magic ring. The feature was submitted to Harvey, but turned down. Later in the 1950s Simon, working again with his erstwhile partner, showed Kirby the old Silver Spider material and they turned it into THE FLY, which the Archie Comics folks bought. In his book *The Comic Book Makers*, Simon contends

that Kirby's "never-dependable" memory was at fault and that the Silver Spider character was never intended for the *Black Magic* comic. Simon further states Steve Ditko revised the Lee–Kirby version of Spider-Man when drawing the story that appeared in *Amazing Fantasy*. It's possible, then, that Spidey had six fathers.

The origin story introduced mild-mannered high school student Peter Parker (like Billy Batson and Tommy Troy, he had an alliterative name), who lived with his Uncle Ben and Aunt May. Clean-cut, hardworking, and bespectacled, Peter was a brilliant science student but was shunned by his fellows and labeled a "bookworm." After being bitten by a radioactive spider at a science exhibit, he gained "spider powers" that included superhuman strength and agility, and the ability to cling to any surface. Peter donned a costume so that he could pursue a career in show business doing stunts of the sort then popular on "The Ed Sullivan Show," but when his Uncle Ben was murdered, he went after and caught the killer. He became convinced that "in this world, with great power there must also come—great responsibility," and he set out to become a dedicated crimefighter. Following in the footsteps of Clark Kent, Peter got a job on a newspaper. He worked on the *Daily Bugle* as a freelance photographer, serving under the irascible editor J. Jonah Jameson. Readers enjoyed both Spider-Man's flippant heroics and Peter Parker's adolescent angst, and he quickly became one of Marvel's bestselling characters.

Spidey's been fortunate in that the villains he's encountered have been, for the most part, a vile and colorful lot. They've included such recurring favorites as the Green Goblin, the Kingpin, Doc Octopus, the Vulture, Kraven the Hunter, the Scorpion, and Morbius. There have also been various ladies in Peter Parker's life, among them Gwen Stacy, Betty Brant, and THE BLACK CAT. But *the* woman is Mary Jane Watson. His relationship with the redheaded model-actress began in the mid-1960s and, after a courtship that waxed and waned over 20 years, the two were married in 1987. Marriage hasn't slowed him down or affected his popularity and the sales on some of the *Spider-Man* titles in the early 1990s have been in the millions.

Among the other artists who've drawn the old web-spinner have been John Buscema, Gil Kane, John Byrne, and Todd McFarlane.

THE SPIRIT A truly unsinkable masked man, Will Eisner's phantom detective has been at it now for well over 50 years. The Spirit is one of the very few characters to have appeared in a weekly comic book and perhaps the only one to have remained available for decades now, chiefly through reprints of his 1940s and early 1950s adventures.

As the 1940s began, comic books were selling in the millions, a fact that had not gone unnoticed by newspaper syndicates. *Superman* had branched out into a newspaper strip in 1939 and by the following year ready-print comic books were being offered for insertion in Sunday papers (see SUPERMAN). The enterprising publisher Victor Fox tried to launch one, the *Chicago Tribune* introduced a *Comic Book Magazine*, and the Register & Tribune Syndicate, a silent partner in Everett "Busy" Arnold's Quality comic book line, brought forth a 16-page weekly *Spirit* booklet. The first one appeared June 2, 1940.

In addition to Eisner's hero, it featured LADY LUCK, originally drawn by Chuck Mazuojian, and Bob Powell's *Mr. Mystic*. Although The Spirit somewhat resembled a traditional comic book character, he differed sharply from the brightly costumed superheroes. For one thing, he refused to take his job seriously. "Sartorially the Spirit was miles from the other masked heroes," Jules Feiffer has observed in his *The Great Comic Book Heroes*. "He didn't wear tights, just a baggy blue business suit, a wide-brimmed blue hat that needed blocking, and, for a disguise, a matching blue eye mask."

Once The Spirit had been Denny Colt, a private eye. But after the world came to believe he'd been murdered by a villain known as Dr. Cobra, Colt went underground to become a

The *Spirit*™, Will Eisner, © 1988 Will Eisner.

masked avenger. He took up residence in a roomy crypt in Central City's Wildwood Cemetery and, aided by a young black man named Ebony White, he waged war on crooks, con men, criminal masterminds, and shady ladies. The grumpy Inspector Dolan and his lovely blonde daughter Ellen both knew who The Spirit really was.

Eisner quite obviously learned on the job and had a great deal of fun doing it. His stories got better, trickier, and less melodramatic. His layouts moved further and further away from the traditional. Nobody has equalled him in incorporating his logo into the splash panel and few have come close to capturing the look and feel, the shadows and smells, of urban life.

Eisner entered the service in 1942, turning the weekly Spirit story over to others, chiefly

Lou Fine. He returned in 1945 and, aided by such artists as John Spranger, Jerry Grandenetti, Wally Wood, and Feiffer, turned out six more years of *The Spirit*.

Arnold's *Police Comics*, which starred PLASTIC MAN, started reprinting a Spirit story in each issue from #11 (September 1942) onward and the rumpled crimefighter remained in the magazine until #93 (November 1950). A separate title devoted exclusively to *Spirit* reprints began in 1944 and continued until 1950. The stories, which Eisner owns, were reprinted regularly in the United States and around the world through the early 1990s. In this country, Fiction House issued a five-book series in the early 1950s and Harvey produced two issues in the mid-1960s. Warren Publishing launched a black-and-white reprint series in the mid-1970s. In the 1980s and early 1990s Kitchen Sink published a long-running series of reprints in black and white.

STEEL STERLING   *See* Zip Comics.

STRAIGHT ARROW   He was yet another radio hero who branched out into comic books. Aimed at kids, the *Straight Arrow* program was heard on the Mutual network from 1949 to 1951 and sponsored by Nabisco Shredded Wheat. Magazine Enterprises (ME) brought out its comic book version in 1950 and it outlasted the show by several years.

Sheldon Stark created the radio show and wrote the scripts. It was based on the then-popular (and still politically correct) gimmick of having a white man dress up as an Indian. In this case it was Steve Adams, a rancher who'd been raised by Comanches, who became "a mysterious, stalwart Indian, wearing the dress and warpaint of a Comanche, riding the great golden palomino Fury" whenever danger threatened or evildoers plotted.

The ME comic book adaption was drawn by Fred Meagher, who'd earlier done the Tom Mix comic books used as premiums by Ralston.

The setup of the program was carried over into the magazine, including the post–Civil War setting and Steve's grizzled sidekick Packy. Unlike many Western comics, *Straight Arrow* offered a positive and sympathetic—though somewhat patronizing—view of native Americans. Even in his everyday phase, Steve was always ready to boot any citizen who made trouble for "our Indian neighbors."

In its early days, the magazine also contained Nabisco ads for assorted Straight Arrow premiums. One of them was a booklet about Indian crafts, touted as being full of secrets of "Injun-uity." *Straight Arrow* lasted through 55 issues before heading back to the corral early in 1956.

STRANGE TALES   This was originally one more of Marvel's 1950s horror comics, purveying grim tales of vampires, voodoo, witches, grave robbers, and other accepted staples of the genre. In the early 1960s, however, it became a showcase for superheroes, successively introducing DR. STRANGE, NICK FURY, and Warlock.

Begun in the spring of 1951, *Strange Tales* initially went in for standard horror fare and employed such artists as Joe Maneely, Bill Everett, and Bernard Krigstein. It grew less ghastly in the mid-1950s, especially after the Comic Code was established. In the late 1950s, like its sister *Journey into Mystery*, the magazine was dominated by a succession of Jack Kirby's giant monsters. Steve Ditko provided backup stories of science and fantasy.

With the 101st issue (October 1962), things changed. Editor Stan Lee introduced adventures of the new Human Torch, with Kirby supplying the artwork (see ALL WINNERS COMICS). "One day, having nothing better to do, I decided to attempt to tie the whole Marvel line more closely together," Lee once explained. "Since the Human Torch was tremendously popular in *The Fantastic Four*, I thought it would be a good idea for him to appear in another strip as well—a shorter story in which he would be the solo star. . . . The idea seemed to catch on. Sales increased by leaps and bounds" (see THE FANTASTIC FOUR).

As a backup feature, Lee introduced Dr. Strange in #110 (July 1963). Ditko did the drawing. The Torch left after #134 and by that time the magical doctor was an established star. *Nick Fury, Agent of S.H.I.E.L.D.* came along in the following issue, drawn by Kirby. The magazine went on hiatus in 1968 and by that time it had also launched Warlock.

STUNTMAN He was a creation of Joe Simon and Jack Kirby who debuted and retired the same year. The first issue of Harvey's *Stuntman* appeared in the spring of 1946, the second and final issue two months later. After a guest appearance in *All New* that same year, the red-clad crimefighter left the scene. He made a very brief comeback in 1948 and was then seen again in 1955 by way of reprints in a magazine called *Thrills of Tomorrow*.

The costumed hero was in reality Fred Drake, a former circus acrobat who worked in the movies as both a stuntman and a double for handsome leading man Don Daring. Besides being a conceited dolt, Daring fancied himself as heroic in real life as he was in his swashbuckling screen roles. This caused him to blunder into assorted trouble, and Drake usually became Stuntman in order to save his boss from various murderers and madmen. Daring's co-star was lovely blonde Sandra Sylvan, who idolized Stuntman and never tumbled to the fact he was actually stuntman Fred Drake.

The feature was handsomely done, displaying more humor than Simon and Kirby had hitherto used, and they also returned to using the impressive double-page splash panels they'd first experimented with back in 1941 on *Captain America* (see CAPTAIN AMERICA). Simon has said, "Kirby and I thought we did some of our best on the comic books we pro-

Stuntman, Joe Simon–Jack Kirby, unpublished, 1946.

vided for Harvey." Unfortunately, the immediate postwar years were not a good time for costumed heroes. Further, there was a glut of new titles. "Bundles were returned, unopened," Simon has explained. "The Simon and Kirby titles were canceled after we had completed two issues."

SUB-MARINER The most successful aquatic character in comic books, Prince Namor made his first big splash in 1939 and worked, on and off, for MARVEL COMICS through the early 1990s. He was the creation of artist-writer Bill Everett and after a single appearance in the short-lived *Motion Picture Funnies Weekly*, Sub-Mariner was reintroduced in *Marvel Comics* #1 in the autumn of 1939.

The prince was born in an undersea kingdom, the result of a misalliance between his royal mother and an explorer named McKenzie. Because of his mixed genetic code, he was able to live on both the land and in the sea. For good measure, he was incredibly strong and could fly. An angry young man, the pointy-eared Namor arrived in Manhattan from his decimated undersea home in the second issue of *Marvel*. He was bent on revenge. "You white devils have persecuted and tormented my people for years," he explained to policewoman Betty Dean, who eventually became his closest friend. Once in Manhattan, he went on a rampage of destruction.

"He was an angry character," Everett reflected some years later. "He was probably expressing some of my own personality."

With the Sub-Mariner cutting up in New York City and the Human Torch freshly arrived in the Apple to work as a cop, a confrontation was inevitable. "That was an idea Carl [Burgos] and I dreamed up," Everett once said. "We considered the fact that the two characters and their opposing elements had separate stories and wondered what would happen if we got them together as rivals to fight each other." What happened was a battle royal that raged through #8 and #9 before winding up in a standoff in #10, when Betty Dean was able to arrange a truce.

When next the representatives of fire and water met, they were "fighting side by side!" As a caption in the 26-page team-up saga in *Marvel* #17 (March 1941) explained, "The Human Torch and the Sub-Mariner are together again. Not to destroy each other but to form an alliance that will stop the gigantic plans for an invasion of these United States!"

The prince calmed down somewhat after that, and with Betty often acting as his conscience, he concentrated on quieter capers. In addition to frequent fantasy elements and pretty women, Everett's stories always provided readers with numerous examples of Sub-Mariner's colorful aquatic expletives. Namor's favorite, spoken in times of stress, surprise, or amazement, was "Sufferin' shad!" He was also fond of "Jumpin' jellyfish!" and "Great pickled penguins!"

The popular Sub-Mariner also appeared as a backup in the *Human Torch* comic book that started in 1940 and got a book of his own in 1941. He showed up as well in ALL WINNERS and assorted other Marvel titles. When Everett entered the service, a succession of artists carried on his feature. The best of them were Carl Pfeufer and Jimmy Thompson. Sub-Mariner was very active during World War II, fighting both the Nazis and the Japanese.

Everett returned in 1947 and stayed on with Namor until the prince sank from sight in 1949. Betty Dean became a newspaper reporter in those postwar years and Sub-Mariner's cousin Namora surfaced. One of several superheroines introduced by Marvel at the time, she aided her quick-tempered cousin and soloed briefly in a magazine of her own.

Prince Namor, along with the Torch and CAPTAIN AMERICA, was one of the three 1940s heroes that Marvel resurrected and attempted to reestablish in the mid-1950s. The trio first showed up, in separate yarns, in YOUNG MEN #24 late in 1953. Early the following year, the *Sub-Mariner* magazine returned, picking up with #33. Like his colleagues, Namor now added the Red Menace to his list of targets. His anti-Communist stand was especially noticeable on the covers of most issues, where his opponents prominently displayed the hammer and sickle and copy lines such as "The Commie Frogmen vs. Sub-Mariner!" and "Sub-Mariner Fights Commies and Crooks!" were to be seen. Namor fared somewhat better than the other returned heroes and his magazine lasted through 10 issues before ceasing late in the summer of 1955. Everett wrote and drew most of the new adventures of his underwater avenger. Betty Dean, who seemed to be living with Namor, was on hand, and Namora returned in several of the stories.

After an absence of several years, Sub-Mariner rose again in 1962. After assorted guest appearances, including some in *The Avengers*, he settled into his own magazine in

Sub-Mariner®, Bill Everett. All Marvel characters and the distinctive likenesses thereof are trademarks of Marvel Entertainment Group, Inc. and are used with permission. © 1992 Marvel Entertainment Group, Inc.

1968. Among the artists who drew the new series were John Buscema, Marie Severin, and Gene Colan. Everett drew him again in 1972 and 1973. During that period Betty Dean, now a plump gray-haired matron, appeared again and Namora's daughter Namorita was introduced. The prince has sunk and resurfaced several times since, serving for a time as part of the Invaders superhero team. Early in 1990, he came back again in *Namor, the Sub-Mariner*, written and first drawn by John Byrne. He was billed as "Marvel's first and mightiest mutant."

SUGAR AND SPIKE This unusual and highly original kid feature was drawn and written by Sheldon Mayer. DC published the first issue of *Sugar and Spike* in the spring of 1956 and the magazine reached nearly 100 issues before coming to a halt in 1971. Its team of toddlers, who seemed as meant for each other as Romeo and Juliet or Nick and Nora, hadn't reached the age where they could communicate with grown-ups. They could talk to each other with ease, however, and together they participated in a decade and a half of wild-and-woolly adventures that ranged from the domestic to the fantastic. Mayer kidded not only middle-class suburban life but, being a man who wasn't reluctant to bite the hand that fed him, many of the characters and concepts that were being treated seriously in the other DC titles of the day.

At first Mayer devoted the magazine to four- and six-page stories about the two preschool next-door neighbors. The blond Sugar Plumm was clearly the dominant member of the pair, continually dragging the hapless, red-haired Spike Wilson into trouble. The adventures that unfolded as Sugar and Spike explored the wonders of the everyday world were shot at kid level. Parents and other obtuse adults were usually shown from the waist down. Intended originally for a young audience, *Sugar and Spike* began to reach a somewhat wider readership. Mayer encouraged reader participation and introduced a letters column in the third issue. The letters, as Jack C.

Harris pointed out in *Amazing World of DC Comics*, came "from three-year-olds and grandparents and every age group in between."

Mayer eventually began doing "complete novel-length" stories that ran to 20 or more pages. He allowed adults to appear fully and his plots made fun of everything from superheroes to South American dictators. In #72, he introduced a toddler named Bernie the Brain, a scientific genius whose precocious inventions unfailingly got Sugar and Spike and him into complex messes with alien invaders, giant robots, monsters, growth elixirs, and other sci-fi annoyances. Mayer had always had a vigorous, appealing cartoon style and on the longer adventures he did some of his best work.

Sugar and Spike ended with #98 in the fall of 1971. Mayer continued doing the feature in the 1980s for publication overseas, and some of that material, with new covers by him, was reprinted in a series of DC digests. Throughout the years the parents never understood what the kids were really saying, and all they heard were phrases like "Glx sptzl glaah."

SUPERBOY Although the Man of Steel had been introduced in 1938, it was not until late in 1944 that DC got around to expanding the SUPERMAN family. The first addition was Superboy, who was introduced in MORE FUN COMICS #101 (cover-dated January–February 1945). The new feature was credited to Superman's creators Jerry Siegel and Joe Shuster, but they had nothing to do with it.

Superboy was introduced without much fanfare. There was no mention of him on the covers of #101 or #102. *More Fun* #103 carried the line "What was Superman like when he was a boy?" and, finally, on #104, Superboy himself actually appeared on a cover. Initially he was a little boy, no more than nine or ten, but within two years he had turned into a teenager and remained at that stage of development. The feature named Smallville, a quintessential Midwestern town, as the spot where the tiny rocket ship from Krypton had

landed. Soon the Superboy stories filled in the numerous details about Smallville's citizenry and geography. Occasional tales revolved around Superboy's adoptive parents, Ma and Pa Kent, or around his best friend Pete Ross. It was in Smallville that young Clark Kent first met Lana Lang, a redhead who was destined to be an important woman in Superman's life.

When *More Fun* was converted to a humor title in 1946, Superboy moved into ADVENTURE. He was better treated there and from his first appearance, in #103 (April 1946), he appeared on every cover for years to come. In 1949, a *Superboy* title was added. The cover of the first issue, drawn by Wayne Boring, showed Superman and a group of kids. One of them asks, "Superman, what were you like when you were a boy?" He replies, "If that's what you'd like to know, look inside." Among the artists who drew the adventures of Smallville's favorite son were Stan Kaye, John Sikela, George Papp, and Curt Swan.

In the spring of 1958, in #247 of *Adventure*, Superboy first became involved with the Legion of Super-Heroes, a future-based organization that seemed to have more members than a family of cockroaches. Young Clark met the group when, as the official DC history puts it, "three time-travelers appeared in Smallville, introduced themselves as members of a far future Legion of Super-Heroes, and invited him to visit their century and join their club. Superboy did so, and continued to make periodic journeys for several years to let loose among other super-powered young people." The membership list included Ultra Boy, Shrinking Violet, Mon-El, Saturn Girl, Cosmic Boy, Star Boy, Colossal Boy, Element Lad, Invisible Kid, Brainiac 5, Chameleon Boy, Light Lass, Sun Boy, Elastic Lad, Phantom Girl, and Bouncing Boy.

Eventually the Legion eased Superboy out of the top spot in *Adventure*. In the late 1970s, they went further, moving into the *Superboy* magazine and taking it over, too. The youthful superhero next showed up in *The New Adventures of Superboy*, which went through 54 issues between 1980 and 1984. The start of a syndicated television show based on the character prompted a new comic book, *The Adventures of Superboy*, in 1990.

SUPERGIRL   She was introduced in a story of her own in DC's ADVENTURE COMICS #252 (May 1959). Supergirl was a pretty, blonde teenager who arrived on Earth by way of a small rocket ship similar to the one used by the Man of Steel two decades earlier. SUPERMAN happened to be on hand at her arrival and was understandably perplexed when the girl, clad in a costume very much like his own, popped from the wreckage. "Great guns!" he exclaimed. "I seem to see a youngster flying, dressed in a super-costume. I . . . uh . . . must be an illusion!" But, no, it wasn't a hallucination—simply his long-lost cousin, Kara. After adopting a mousy secret identity and the name Linda Lee, she went to live in an orphanage in a town named Midvale.

The writer and co-creator of Supergirl was Otto Binder, who had devised the earlier adventures of MARY MARVEL. Editor Mort Weisinger had suggested the new character to him, but never mentioned CAPTAIN MARVEL'S kid sister as a source of inspiration. "It was kind of weird in a way," Binder once remarked, "like reliving the past." The chief artists during Supergirl's career were Jim Mooney, Bob Oksner, and Kurt Schafenberger, who'd previously drawn all the members of the Marvel Family.

DC tried two separate *Supergirl* titles, once in the mid-1970s and once in the mid-1980s, but she was only moderately popular and was killed off in 1985 during the *Crisis on Infinite Earths* series. In 1991, however, she was brought back to life.

SUPERMAN   He was the first superhero and the most important comic book character ever created. Superman was conceived in Cleveland in the early 1930s by author Jerry Siegel and artist Joe Shuster, who'd met in high school. It took Superman several years to find a publisher. In 1938, he finally got a break and started appearing in DC's ACTION COMICS. He single-handedly turned the fledgling comic book business into a major industry, changing the look and the content of the four-color magazines forever. He made several people associated with him impressively rich and for nearly a decade even his creators prospered.

The 13-page story that introduced the Man of Steel in *Action* #1 (June 1938) was mostly cobbled together from Siegel and Shuster's unsold *Superman* newspaper strip. It offered a one-page introduction to the new hero, listing his birthplace only as "a distant planet" and making no mention of his real or adoptive parents. Page two began in the middle of the story, with the costumed Superman carrying a pretty nightclub singer through the air. It managed to introduce mild-mannered Clark Kent and his newspaper co-worker, Lois Lane, who was already giving him the cold shoulder.

By the fourth issue, *Action*'s sales had leaped forward. They quickly rose to 500,000, and by 1941 the magazine was selling 900,000 copies a month. The *Superman* magazine, begun in 1939, soon reached a circulation of 1.25 million and grossed $950,000 in 1940. These impressive figures didn't go unnoticed by other publishers, and by the time the 1940s started, a full-scale superhero boom was under way.

When DC bought *Superman*, business manager Jack Liebowitz had explained that Siegel and Shuster had to sign a release giving all rights to the feature to the publisher. "It is customary for all our contributors to release all rights to us," he wrote. "This is the businesslike way of doing things." As the years passed and the kid from Krypton continued to pile up profits, the team grew increasingly unhappy. In 1947, when their joint income dropped to $46,000, they decided to go to court. "In New York Supreme Court in Westchester County they had filed suit seeking (1) to regain the rights to their brainchild, (2) to cancel their newspaper syndication contract with McClure and their contract with [DC publisher Harry] Donenfeld on the ground that they have been violated, and (3) to recover about $5,000,000 they say *Superman* should have brought them over a nine-year period," reported the April 14, 1947, issue of *Newsweek*. There was also a conflict over the SUPERBOY character. "When Siegel was in the army, Superboy made his debut under the double byline. Siegel claims he never authorized such use of his name and has never received a cent for the strip." The partners did not do well. While the court ruled that "Detective Comics, Inc., had acted illegally" as far as *Superboy* was concerned, DC did indeed own *Superman*. Siegel and Shuster were paid for *Superboy* in a settlement rumored to be around $50,000, but they were fired by DC publisher Donenfeld. *Superman* was no longer theirs. It would be almost 30 years before they would see any further compensation for having created one of the most valuable characters of the 20th century.

Superman continued, drawn by former Shuster ghost Wayne Boring and several others. Editor Mort Weisinger, who felt that Superman was "invulnerable, he's immortal. Even bad scripts can't hurt him," oversaw the Man of Steel in the 1950s and 1960s. He seemed determined to test his theory about bad scripts and during his era Superman suffered through innumerable strange, bizarre, and downright silly adventures. When Weisinger departed DC in 1970, the immortal hero wasn't nearly as popular as he'd once been.

In the years since, DC has worked to boost Superman's popularity. In the mid-1980s, with considerable publicity, they brought in Marvel star John Byrne to rejuvenate the character. That didn't especially work. More recently, Lois Lane, after a half century of conspicuous density, was finally informed by Clark Kent that he was Superman. Late in 1992, in an attempt to boost sales, the company pretended to kill the Man of Steel.

SUPERSNIPE One of several kidders of the basic tenets of the superhero profession, the feature began in 1942. Koppy McFad, also known as the Boy with the Most Comic Books in America, was an imaginative, well-meaning lad. Driven by dreams of glory that were fueled by the enormous quantities of comic books he read, Koppy longed to be a superhero. Undaunted by reality, he put together a costume from his father's lodge cape, his grandfather's red-flannel longjohns, and his own tennis shoes. Thus attired, he set out to fight crime as Supersnipe.

Supersnipe was written by Ed Gruskin and drawn by George Marcoux, who'd assisted on the *Skippy* newspaper strip before doing a kid strip of his own called *Toddy*. Their feature had trial runs in *Shadow Comics* and *Doc Savage Comics* (see THE SHADOW, DOC SAVAGE) before graduating to a bimonthly title of its own in the fall of 1942.

It poked fun at the whole idea of costumed heroes and youthful aspirations to adventure. Often the situations that Koppy perceived to be dire crimes turned out to be far less than sinister, and when he did encounter real crooks, they were small-timers far removed from the evil masterminds of his imagination. Most of the stories had an undertone of the sort of smalltown-America humor found on radio shows such as *Fibber McGee and Molly* and *The Great Gildersleeve*. Now and then, Koppy would have a dream-sequence adventure in which Supersnipe was a real, grown-up superman, complete with rippling muscles, skintight costume, and flowing cape. These sequences were usually illustrated by C.M. Payne, another newspaper veteran.

Supersnipe enjoyed a respectable run of 44 issues before ceasing publication in 1949.

Another kid who dressed up in a costume of red flannels was Herbie Popnecker. But when he did it, he became a real superhero known as the Fat Fury. Created by editor-writer Richard Hughes and drawn by Ogden Whitney, Herbie was introduced in ACG's *Forbidden Worlds*. In the spring of 1964, a *Herbie* bimonthly was launched and made it through 23 issues before expiring early in 1967.

Herbie was a fat, bespectacled boy with a fondness for lollipops and lethargy. Even before becoming a practicing superman, he possessed unusual powers and was, as his father pointed out "a little . . . well, strange." In the eighth issue of his magazine (March 1965) he decided to become a costumed hero and, after flunking out of American Hero School, he fashioned his own costume and set up as the Fat Fury. A broad, slapstick sort of affair, *Herbie* took a dim view of both heroics and family life.

SWAMP THING This particular caring monster owed a great deal to Theodore Sturgeon's short story "It" and to the 1940s comic book character known as the Heap. Swamp Thing first appeared in DC's *House of Secrets* in the summer of 1971 and was promoted to a book of his own the following year. Never a major hit despite two movies and a television show, Swamp Thing nonetheless has managed to hold out in comic books, with some vacations, for over 20 years.

The initial creative team consisted of writer Len Wein and artist Berni Wrightson. They concocted sentimental horror tales about a scientist who was transformed into a muck-encrusted horror after being doused by chemicals when his bayou lab was destroyed by criminals.

Wein's scripts worked at being touching, even philosophical, but the real selling point on the early issues of *Swamp Thing* was the spidery, vaguely disturbing artwork of Wrightson, a young man under the spell of fantasy illustrator Frank Frazetta and EC horror artist Graham "Ghastly" Ingels.

The most recent title devoted to the forlorn bayou monster began in 1982 as *Saga of the Swamp Thing* and later became simply *Swamp Thing*. It has attracted some of the more innovative and controversial artists and writers in the field, among them Steve Bissette, Alan Moore, John Totleben, and Rick Veitch.

Supersnipe, George Marcoux, © 1944 by Street & Smith Publications, Inc.

TALES FROM THE CRYPT The first of the EC horror titles, it began as *Crypt of Terror* in the spring of 1950. After three issues, the name was changed to *Tales from the Crypt*. Edited by Al Feldstein, with publisher William Gaines looking over his shoulder, the magazine presented gruesome horror tales illustrated by such artists as Jack Davis, Graham Ingels, Johnny Craig, Wally Wood, Reed Crandall, and Feldstein himself. It was a fairly literate comic book, influenced by the horror and suspense radio shows of the 1940s, and it influenced the dozens of horror comic books that followed. Its eventual excesses, along with those of its sisters, contributed to the ultimate downfall of the entire EC line.

Under the two titles, the magazine made it through 30 issues before ceasing operations in 1955. Jack Davis drew the majority of covers, with Craig, Wood, and Feldstein taking care of the rest. The favorite subject was the reanimated corpse, with the living dead in various states of decay displayed on eight different covers. Burial, premature and otherwise, was also a recurring theme. Frequently used props included axes, coffins, tombstones, and, on two different covers, guillotines. From issue #22 on, portraits of the three hosts—the

Crypt-Keeper, the Old Witch, and the Vault-Keeper—appeared in a stacked row along the lefthand side of each cover.

The magazine began in the spring of 1947, shortly before the death of EC founder M.C. Gaines. In its first incarnation it was an adventure book called *International Comics*. The next summer it became a true-crime book under the name *Crime Patrol*. In issue #15 (January 1950), a section called *The Crypt of Terror* was added, offering a single "terror-tale" in the midst of the gangbusting. Feldstein provided it, saying later that he and William Gaines had decided "that we were no longer going to follow, but we were going to go out on our own and let them follow us if we hit it right." Two issues later, the crime book became a horror book.

Eventually each yarn, in the tradition of such radio programs as *Inner Sanctum*, was introduced by a host who was fond of cackling and indulging in macabre puns. The Crypt-Keeper, a repellent fellow with a wart on his nose and long, unkempt white hair, always narrated the leadoff tale in each issue. Feldstein relied on the pulps, movies, and radio for his inspiration, also borrowing from the likes of Ray Bradbury on occasion. He wrote stories about severed hands that took on life, about werewolves, vampires, walking mummies, and all the other staples of the weird genre. One of the magazine's stars was Graham Ingels, who always signed his work with the pen name Ghastly. He was especially good at drawing rotting corpses, malformed humans, blade-wielding fiends, and decaying architecture.

Like many a horror and crime comic, *Tales* fell victim to the anticomics crusade of the mid-1950s. Late in 1954, after the major comic book publishers formed the Comics Magazine Association of America to administer the new Comics Code, Gaines (who didn't join the organization) announced he was killing all his crime and horror titles. He later said that the distributors had caused his decision. "I'd been told that if I continued publishing my magazines, no one would handle them," he explained. "I had no choice."

The Crypt-Keeper, Jack Davis, © William M. Gaines.

THE TARGET Although *Target Comics* hit the stands early in 1940, the Target himself didn't arrive until late in the year. Not until the tenth issue (November 1940) did he show up to share the magazine's 64 pages with such heroes as the White Streak, the Chameleon, and Basil Wolverton's Spacehawk. A hero with a big bull's-eye emblazoned on the front of his tunic might seem to be asking for it. And in a way the Target was, smug in the knowledge that bullets would bounce off him.

Bob Wood, who a couple of years later would join Charles Biro in editing BOY COMICS, DAREDEVIL, and CRIME DOES NOT PAY, was responsible for the feature. He used some Biro touches in the early stories. In the first adventure, for instance, the identity of the Target was kept a secret and in the final panel, Wood asked, "Who is the Target? And how can it be that he has been seen in 3 different places at the same time??? And in different colored uniforms???"

In the second episode readers learned that the Target was actually Niles Reed, who'd been a metallurgy major and a four-letter man while at college. After his older brother—who happened to be Manhattan's district attorney—was killed as a result of a gangland frame-up, Niles decided to use "this flexible bulletproof metal I've discovered" to fight crime. He designed a suit of bulletproof underwear and a yellow-and-black costume and became the Target. At the same time, two young men who were equally ticked off at crime, Dave and Tommy by name, joined him and got bulletproof suits of their own. They called themselves the Targeteers.

Each subsequent story ended with a teaser and numerous provocative questions: "Who pretended to be Colonel Cushing? Who impersonated the bellboy at the hotel? Will the TARGET and the TARGETEERS catch up with the midget, 'MIGHTY MITE,' and the mysterious foreign agent before they can complete their sinister mission against the American government???" So it went, one thing after another: Murderous midgets, crazed scientists, a green-faced madman known as Dr. Time, etc.

After Wood, a succession of artists took turns. Sid Greene did an interesting and highly individual job. He was followed by Edward Ryan, W.M. Allison, and others less gifted. The Target and the Targeteers were last seen in the fall of 1948.

The Target, Sid Greene, unpublished, 1942.

TARZAN The undisputed king of the jungle, Edgar Rice Burroughs's apeman was first seen in 1912 in the pulp magazine *All-Story*. After that, Tarzan branched out into books, movies, radio shows, and a comic strip. The first reprint comic book appeared in 1929, the first original-material *Tarzan* comic was published in 1947.

The daily newspaper strip, adapted from the first novel, *Tarzan of the Apes*, began in January of 1929. Late that same year Grosset &

Dunlap reprinted a sequence of the strips, handsomely illustrated by Hal Foster, in a hardcover book that sold for 50¢. The *Tarzan* Sunday, which was also drawn by Foster after the first few months, started in 1931. When the United Features Syndicate started *Tip Top Comics* in 1936, the Foster pages were among the features reprinted. *Comics on Parade*, launched in 1938, included reprints of the dailies, first by Foster and then by the less-gifted Rex Maxon. A 1940 *Tarzan* one-shot comic book reprinted an impressive Foster Sunday sequence and in 1941 the *Tarzan* Sundays of Burne Hogarth were part of the lineup in United's new *Sparkler Comics*. In addition, Dell's *Crackajack Funnies* had run Tarzan text stories, with spot drawings by such artists as Bill Ely, from 1939 to 1941. In 1947 it was Dell that introduced an original-material comic book devoted to the famous apeman.

Dell's first book, *Tarzan and the Devil Ogre*, was written by Gaylord DuBois and drawn by Jesse Marsh. It appeared early in 1947 and was followed a few months later by *Tarzan and the Fires of Thor*. In 1948 Dell started a regular *Tarzan* bimonthly, with scripts by DuBois and the majority of the artwork by Marsh. Marsh was an unconventional choice to illustrate the jungle-man saga, since he worked in the lushly inked realistic style developed by Milton Caniff and Noel Sickles rather than the heroic, larger-than-life manner favored by Foster and especially Hogarth. Comic book readers accepted him, however, and he stayed with the book for more than 150 issues.

One of the areas where Marsh excelled was in his settings—the jungles, forests, veldts, the lost cities, and the hidden valleys where prehistoric monsters roamed. His Africa wasn't the fantasy land of the Sunday funnies and the movies, but a real place, albeit rich with romance and mystery. Nobody drew Africans as well as Marsh or with such an eye for variety and individuality. And his women were distinctive and real. The character who gave him trouble was Tarzan himself. Alex Toth, a friend and great admirer, has commented that "Tarzan was, it seems, a chore for him."

The Dell/Gold Key *Tarzan* continued until 1972. DuBois remained the chief scriptwriter. Among the other artists were Doub Wildey, Paul Norris, and Russ Manning. A companion book, *Korak, Son of Tarzan*, was also published by Gold Key between 1964 and 1972. Art was by Manning and Warren Tufts.

In 1972, DC licensed the Tarzan property from Edgar Rice Burroughs, Inc. and brought out its comic book version. Getting back to basics, their first issues featured an adaption of *Tarzan of the Apes*. That was followed soon after with continuities based on *Jungle Tales of Tarzan* and *The Return of Tarzan*. Joe Kubert, who also edited the magazine, did much of the early drawing. The adaptions were interspersed with some odd-looking issues that blended old art from 1930s Sunday pages by Hogarth and Foster with new panels by Kubert.

DC also took over *Korak* from Gold Key, but only stuck with it for 14 bimonthly issues. Kubert provided all the covers and Frank Thorne was the first artist. Burroughs's Carson of Venus, drawn by Mike Kaluta, appeared as a backup feature. The magazine was retitled *The Tarzan Family* late in 1975 and John Carter of Mars was added to the lineup. Burroughs's swordsman of Barsoom had initially appeared in the first seven issues of DC's *Weird Worlds*.

By late 1976, DC had given up on all the Burroughs properties. The publisher had stayed with *Tarzan* the longest, for a total of 51 issues. Next Marvel took a turn and its first issue of *Tarzan, Lord of the Jungle* had a cover date of June 1977. John Buscema was the initial artist. While Marvel didn't try a Korak title, it did publish *John Carter of Mars* with Gil Kane drawing the early issues. Less successful at selling Burroughs than even DC had been, Marvel called it quits after only two years. It did, however, return to the jungle in 1984 with a two-issue adaption of the latest *Tarzan of the Apes* movie. In the early 1990s, Malibu Comics took a crack at a *Tarzan* comic book.

Tarzan was a very influential character, especially during the GOLDEN AGE. Numerous imitation jungle lords popped up in the 1930s and 1940s, including KA-ZAR, Jungleman, Kaanga, Oran, Tabu, Beebo, Samar, WAMBI, Kalthar, Jo-Jo, Zudo, Zago, Ty-Gor, and Zaan. The most successful Tarzan imitator in comic books was a woman, SHEENA.

TEEN-AGE DOPE SLAVES This one-shot comic book was an interesting artifact of the 1950s. While the title and the cover were somewhat sleazy and exploitative, the material inside was innocent and well-intended. Yet the magazine aroused the ire of anticomics crusaders and earned itself a place in Dr. Fredric Wertham's influential *Seduction of the Innocent*.

Published by Harvey early in 1952, it was merely a reprint of a *Rex Morgan M.D.* newspaper-strip sequence about the drug addiction of a once-clean-cut high school jock. Written by psychiatrist Nicholas Dallis and drawn by Marvin Bradley and Frank Edgington, the continuity included a nasty drug dealer, a dedicated narcotics agent, the helpful Dr. Morgan and his concerned nurse, plus perplexed parents and an unhappy teen girlfriend. The story was obviously intended as a strong antidrug statement and it was considerably more realistic than the other soap-opera strip narratives of the time.

Rex Morgan was a very successful strip. It ran in several hundred newspapers around the country, and when the dope sequence appeared in the comic sections, it elicited few or no complaints. When Harvey reprinted the material, it was apparently aiming at the buyers of the increasing number of violent true-crime comics. Since Harvey didn't actually have that type of material, it had to rely on packaging. In addition to the lurid title, the cover ran the overline "Shocking Dope Exposé" and showed the young addict begging the pusher for a shot from the needle. The back cover, on the other hand, contained a page of facts about the dangers of drugs and was headlined, "Warning! Dope Leads to Death!"

It seems obvious that Dr. Wertham was led astray by the front cover and didn't examine the contents closely or realize the origins of the material. In his book, he wrote, "When adolescent drug addiction had finally come to public attention, it led to publication of lurid new comic books devoted entirely to the subject, like the one with the title, *Teen-age Dope Slaves*. This is nothing but another variety of crime comic of a particularly deplorable character."

Because of its notoriety, *Teen-age Dope Slaves* is listed in Overstreet's *Comic Book Price Guide* as being worth between $45 and $315 per copy, depending on condition. Other *Rex Morgan, M.D.* reprint comics go for as low as $3.70.

TEEN TITANS   They were introduced by DC in 1964 as a sort of combination of THE YOUNG ALLIES and the ARCHIE gang. Robin, Kid Flash, and Aqualad, three teenage sidekicks of grown-up heroes, first made up the group, but the membership changed and expanded over the years (see BATMAN, FLASH, and AQUAMAN). In the 1980s, as the New Teen Titans, they become one of the most popular groups in comics. Writer Bob Haney and artist Bruno Premiani were responsible for the original team, Marv Wolfman and George Perez for the new, improved bunch.

When the trio of sidekicks first teamed up in THE BRAVE AND THE BOLD #54 (June–July 1964), they didn't have a group name. They got together to help some small-town teenagers who'd run afoul of a super-villain named Mr. Twister while trying to get the stodgy town adults to build them a clubhouse. The heroic trio returned to *B & B* a year later as the Teen Titans, and with Wonder Girl added. After an appearance in SHOWCASE, the group was promoted to a book of its own. The first issue of *Teen Titans* had a cover date of February 1966 and proclaimed, "They just couldn't wait to start THEIR OWN MAG!" Haney continued as

scripter, but Nick Cardy took over as artist.

This was a book that was striving mightily to be hip. It treated most adults, including Batman and the Flash, as hopeless squares and, as Lou Mougin has pointed out in *Comics Collector*, "You could hardly find a page without a 'Groovy!' or a 'Freaky!'" The membership of the titans fluctuated, with the GREEN ARROW's companion Speedy joining on in some issues and new characters such as Beast Boy (later known as Changeling) being added. Various artists drew the feature, including Gil Kane, Neal Adams, and George Tuska. The book halted with its 43rd issue in 1973, then returned for another 10 issues from 1976 to 1978.

The New Teen Titans were introduced in *DC Presents* #26 and were given their own title late in 1980. The new group included Robin, Kid Flash, an alien girl named Starfire, and a black youth called Cyborg. This title proved much more popular than the earlier ones and for a time in the mid-1980s *The New Teen Titans* was scoring close to the top in fan polls. It was in this book in 1984 that Dick Grayson, Batman's Robin for all those years, shed that alternate identity to become Nightwing.

The magazine continued until early in 1984, then returned in a more expensive format later that year. Late in 1988, it changed its name to simply *The New Titans*. In 1992 DC added two variant groups: *Team Titans* and *Teen Titans*.

TEK WORLD   One of the more successful science fiction comic books of the 1990s, its full title was *William Shatner's Tek World*. Published by Marvel as part of their Epic line, the magazine was based on actor–writer Shatner's bestselling series of novels. Lee Sullivan was the artist, Ron Goulart the scriptwriter.

The initial five issues of *Tek World* offered an adaption of the first novel, *TekWar*. The story unfolded in a hightech future, ranging in locale from the vast urban sprawl of Greater Los Angeles to the forest wilds of Mexico. The leading characters were private eye Jake Cardigan, a tough excop who bore some resemblance to Shatner, and his partner Sid Gomez. Tek itself is an electronic drug, tomorrow's version of crack and heroin, and a great many of Cardigan's opponents were involved in the Tek trade. The Tek world was also populated with an interesting mix of robots, androids, cyborgs, gadgets, and eccentric humans.

Subsequent issues offered brand-new adventures set in various spots in the future world. Stories were by Goulart, with input from Shatner.

TESSIE THE TYPIST   The first of the pretty girl characters who were to play an important part in Marvel's post–World War II lineup of titles, Tessie had her modest inception in JOKER COMICS #2 (June 1942). At first Tessie was the typical dumb blonde, working as a secretary for a series of grumpy bosses and dating a zoot-suited boyfriend named Skidsy. The feature concentrated on simple-minded gags. Gradually continuity was added, and within two years Tessie was the star of *Joker*, upstaging Basil Wolverton's Powerhouse Pepper and the rest of the magazine's "laff favorites."

As the popularity of superheroes waned in the mid- and late-1940s, publishers became interested in new types of characters and new kinds of customers. While girls had never made up a large percentage of the audience for the slam-bang adventure comics, they did seem to go for characters like Archie, Suzie, and KATY KEENE. Marvel decided to add more of that sort of thing to its production schedule.

In the mid-1940s, Marvel introduced Millie the Model, Nellie the Nurse, Hedy DeVine, and teens such as Patsy Walker. Tessie, the pioneer, had a title of her own from the summer of 1944 through the summer of 1949. She also shared *Comedy Comics* with Millie and Hedy from 1948 to 1950 and *Gay Comics* from 1944 to 1949. Harvey Kurtzman provided filler material for both these titles.

Artists on *Tessie* over the years included George Klein, Dennis Neville, and Morris Weiss.

THOR   The Mighty Thor debuted in Marvel's *Journey into Mystery* #83 in the summer of 1962. A cover blurb introduced him as "the most exciting superhero of all time!!" Based on an idea of editor Stan Lee, the origin story was written by his brother Larry Lieber and drawn by the dependable Jack Kirby. Their mixture of superheroics and Norse mythology proved effective and Thor, winged helmet and all, stayed on as a star. In 1966, the magazine's title was changed to *The Mighty Thor* and the Thunder God continued in business through the early 1990s.

The first adventure told how frail, lame Dr. Don Balke found the hammer of Thor in a secret cave while vacationing in Norway. As soon as he clutched the legendary implement, the spindly doctor was miraculously transformed into a muscular superman with shoulder-length blond hair and a form-fitting Norse costume. In subsequent stories the amount of mythology increased considerably. Lee—who'd taken over the writing early on—even added Thor's traditional nemesis, Loki, and also tossed in Balder and Odin.

Lee has said that when he started scripting, "Thor became the first regularly published superhero to speak in a consistently archaic manner. Call it a biblical style—call it neo-Shakespearean." Kirby departed the feature in 1970 and Lee stopped writing it in 1972. "Thor trundled along at a workman-like level through the 1970s," Gerard Jones has observed, "mainly under writer Roy Thomas and artist John Buscema."

The situation improved when Walt Simonson took over the writing and editing. *Thor* #337 (November 1983), the first issue written and drawn by Simonson, sold out in comic shops across the country. Simonson remained with the character until the summer of 1987, and Thor continued, though with somewhat diminished popularity.

THUN'DA   This character represented Frank Frazetta's homage to Hal Foster's version of TARZAN. The first issue of *Thun'da, King of the*

Congo was published in 1952 by Magazine Enterprises. The prolific Gardner Fox wrote the script and Frazetta provided the impressive drawing. The young artist left after that and the remaining five issues were illustrated by Bob Powell.

The initial issue dealt with the crash of pilot Roger Drum while flying over "the gorilla-infested jungles" of Africa during World War II. Drum found himself in a lost world where cavemen, dinosaurs, and other leftovers from the dim past still existed. After tangling with some surly club-wielders, he encountered a superior tribe of primitives. Among them was Pha, the beautiful young woman who became his true love. Drum quickly went native, toughened up and took the name of Thun'da. His subsequent adventures were all nearly pure Edgar Rice Burroughs.

At this point in his career, Frazetta was still very much under the spell of Hal Foster's *Tarzan* Sunday page of the 1930s. In his single issue of *Thun'da*, Frazetta did a creditable job of following in the footsteps of the older artist. His pages are full of admirable figure work and awesome vistas.

Columbia Pictures' 1952 serial, *King of the Congo*, was based on the comic book. Buster Crabbe portrayed Thun'da.

Thun'da, Frank Frazetta, © 1952 Magazine Enterprises.

T.H.U.N.D.E.R. AGENTS   This comic book, part of the mid-1960s boom in superheroes, was the first title issued by paperback publisher Tower Books in its attempt to set up a comics line. It was edited by Wally Wood, with artwork by Wood, Reed Crandall, Gil Kane, George Tuska, and Mike Sekowsky. Despite nicely drawn and competently written material, the magazine stayed in business for only four years. The other Tower titles—*Undersea Agent*, etc.—fared much worse.

The acronym stood for The Higher United Nations Defense Enforcement Reserves. Just before getting knocked off by the opposition, a scientist for this top-secret organization had invented "an electron intensifier belt which will make the wearer's body structure the consistency of steel," an invisibility cloak, and a cybernetic helmet that would "amplify a man's brain power many times." After finding candidates to try out these three inventions, the agency launched a trio of superheroes— Dynamo, NoMan, and Menthor. In early issues, each T.H.U.N.D.E.R. Agent starred in a separate story.

The Tower publisher was Harry Shorten, who'd been an editor and writer for MLJ on such titles as *Pep Comics*. According to an account Wally Wood once gave, "I was not only Tower's top artist, I created the characters, and wrote most of the . . . stories. Harry Shorten came to me and asked me to work up a super-hero book. I then functioned as a freelance editor and did as much of the art as I could."

In the first issue (November 1965), Wood drew two Dynamo stories, introduced not only the blue-clad wearer of the "thunderbelt" but his chief opponent, an armored lady known as the Iron Maiden. Crandall took care of the NoMan origin and Menthor was a Kane–Tuska joint effort. As the magazine progressed, other new heroes were added, including Lightning and the Raven.

In 1966 Tower branched out, publishing new titles that included *Undersea Agent*, *Dynamo*, *NoMan*, and a war book called *Fight the Enemy*. The most successful of these was

Undersea Agent, which lasted for six issues.

T.H.U.N.D.E.R. Agents #19 (November 1968) was the last issue to use all original material and #20 (November 1969), which ended the run, was made up mostly of reprints.

TOMAHAWK Offering historical fiction in comic book format, *Tomahawk* was a combination of James Fenimore Cooper's *Leatherstocking Tales* and the adventures of BATMAN and Robin. The feature began as a backup in *Star Spangled Comics* #69 (June 1947). Within two years, the frontier hero and his boy companion were the stars of the DC magazine and remained so until 1951. A separate *Tomahawk* comic book was started in 1950 and lasted until 1972. Not a bad run for a character who had no superpowers and who tried to teach a little American history on the side.

The leading characters in the saga were Tom Hawk and his young sidekick Dan Hunter. They wore buckskin clothes and coonskin caps and roamed Colonial America, encountering pirates, highwaymen, patriots, and historical personages such as George Washington and Daniel Boone. There were also many confrontations with Indians. At the start Tomahawk was antagonistic to most Indians, calling them "Injuns" and worse. Gradually, however, he mellowed and became an accepted friend of many tribes. He later married an Indian woman and his son Hawk took over the magazine for its final 10 issues.

The first artist to draw the feature in *Star Spangled* was Edmond Good. He was followed after a few months by Fred Ray, one of whose passions was American history. Ray stayed with the frontier feature for several years. Others who drew it were Bruno Premiani and Frank Thorne. Both Neal Adams and Joe Kubert contributed covers to the *Tomahawk* magazine.

TOP-NOTCH COMICS The second MLJ/Archie title had a cover date on its first issue of December 1939. The magazine boasted only one superhero when it started, but by the end of its first year *Top-Notch* housed several, including one fellow who would appear several times.

The only true superman in the first issue was the Wizard, also known as the Man with the Super Brain. At first he performed his deeds wearing black tie, tails, a cape, and a red domino mask. In that clean-shaven era he was one of the few comic book mystery men who sported a mustache. The Wiz's specialty was "plots against the government" and invasions. In civilian life he was Blane Whitney, polo-playing scion of one of America's first families. "With his super-brain and photographic mind the Wizard is able to visualize far-away happenings," explained a caption. "With these mental powers and his super-strength, he ferrets out plots against the U.S."

In #7, he got a new costume consisting of blue tunic and tights, red shorts, and cape. He kept the red mask and the mustache. In #8 he acquired a feisty young companion. A concluding blurb proclaimed, "The Wizard fights alone no longer! Now side by side with the Man with the Super Brain is Roy, the Super Boy, the most astounding youth in all history! Together these two fight all evil!"

Most of the other features in the early issues were lackluster. They included *Air Patrol*, *Lucky Coyne*, *Kardak the Mystic Magician*, and *Bob Phantom*. Another superhero was added in *Top-Notch* #8 (September 1940). The Firefly was the creation of writer Harry Shorten and artist Bob Wood. He became a crimefighter after he'd "discovered the secret of the tremendous strength of insects." While he was working on this in his private lab, the lights went out and some fireflies flickered in. "That's what I'll be," he told himself. "*A firefly!* Lighting up the darkness that shrouds the underworld!"

The next month brought yet another costumed hero. The Black Hood had to work long and hard to become what he did. While a uniformed cop, Kip Burland was framed by a sinister, green-faced villain aptly known as the

Skull. After being discharged from the force in disgrace, Burland was taken for a ride by crooks and left in the woods to die. He was found by a kindly old hermit, a self-taught scientist and philosopher who'd also been wronged by the Skull. He decided to turn Burland into a super-crimefighter, someone who would defeat the Skull and then use his "abilities against all crime and criminals!" Burland underwent months of rigorous training, "both to rebuild his strength and to learn all of science and all knowledge, in order to make himself the world's greatest fighter against crime!" Donning the hood that gave him his name, along with yellow tunic, black shorts, and yellow tights, he went forth. He finally confronted the Skull and, after several issues, succeeded in getting him sent to the hot seat. Al Casmy was the original artist.

Once the Hood came aboard, the Wizard was relegated to second-banana status. He, his super-brain, and Roy were dropped after #27 (May 1942).

In the summer of 1943, anticipating a trend that would sweep through comic books a few years later, the magazine converted to humor. With the bold slogan, "We Dare to Do It! A Joke Book That's Really Funny!", issue #28 (July 1942) appeared under the new title *Top-Notch LAUGH*. The Black Hood and Kardak were the only heroes who didn't get pink slips. The new star was a Li'l Abner simulacrum named Pokey Oakey. This was the creation of Don Dean, longtime ghost on the *Big Chief Wahoo* newspaper strip, and the first episodes looked as though they might be recycled samples of an unsold strip of his own.

Dean also contributed *Señor Siesta* and Bob Montana drew *Percy*, a teenage feature. Other additions included *Gloomy Gus*, *Suzie*, and *Dotty & Ditto*. This last was by Bill Woggon, the KATY KEENE creator.

With issue #30, the Black Hood became the only serious character in the book. He probably felt like a clergyman stranded in a boarding house full of carnival performers, but he stuck to his guns until #44 (February 1944). After one

more issue the magazine became just plain *Laugh Comics*. The sturdy Hood survived for another two years in his own quarterly. In his final days, drawn by Irv Novick, he shed his costume to work in civvies as a hard-boiled private eye.

The Black Hood has been brought back several times. He returned for awhile in the mid-1960s as part of the Mighty Crusaders group and also starred in a few issues of *Mighty Comics*. An updated version in the mid-1980s had Kip Burland as a motorcycle-riding Hood complete with black leather jacket. Both Gray Morrow and Dan Spiegle illustrated his short-lived new career. In 1991, DC licensed the name and created a completely different Black Hood.

TORCHY   The years following the end of World War II saw an influx of pretty girls into comic books, sometimes in rather unlikely spots. Torchy, a "tall, whistle-provoking blonde" who was frequently to be seen wearing nothing more than frilly black lingerie, moved into *Modern Comics* in the summer of 1946. Formerly MILITARY COMICS, the magazine was still the home of the macho BLACKHAWK and his gang. Torchy, created by cartoonist Bill Ward, remained in *Modern* until its final issue in 1950 and appeared in *Doll Man*, where she had debuted, from the spring of 1946 to the autumn of 1953. She also soloed in six issues of her own title.

Ward, a graduate of both the Pratt Institute and the Jack Binder art shop, had drawn Blackhawk before entering the service. When he returned, he drew the paramilitary hero again in the *Blackhawk* comic book. For *Modern*, however, he turned out *Torchy*, based on a comic strip he'd drawn for camp newspapers during the war. The six-page backup stories that ran in *Modern* and *Doll Man* looked something like storyboards for a sexy sitcom. Torchy and her girlfriend would become involved with the likes of gangsters, ghosts, and eccentric millionaires. While the plot unfolded, there would arise several opportunities for Torchy to appear in her underwear, in a negligee, or with her stocking tops showing. Like many cheesecake models of the day, she favored black spike heels.

The bimonthly *Torchy* magazine began late in 1949. Ward contributed the covers for two of the issues and drew one of the three stories in the fifth issue. The publisher, Everett "Busy" Arnold of Quality, assigned Ward to the nascent line of romance comics and all the rest of the Torchy work was handled by his capable colleague Gill Fox.

True Comics, Jack Sparling–Ed Smalle, © 1945 True Comics, Inc.

Torchy, Bill Ward, © 1947 Comic Magazines.

TRUE COMICS   This sedate, nonfiction publication was launched by *Parents' Magazine* in the spring of 1941 in an early attempt to counteract the wild, rowdy superhero comics. Its purpose was to offer comic book material that was "attractive, interesting, and worthwhile." For its stories, *True Comics* turned to "past and present history." The first issue, which included Winston Churchill, Simon Bolivar, and the Marathon Run among its topics, sold 300,000 copies within 10 days.

George Hecht, who headed the *Parents'* organization, was the publisher, and its first editor was a young historian named David Marke. Later, Al Capp's brother Elliot Caplin

served as editor. Though dull and stodgy, the magazine remained in business until 1950, covering everything from General MacArthur to Charlie McCarthy.

Although the field of nonfiction funny books never became a crowded one, several similar titles joined *True* on the newsstands in the 1940s. *Parents'* themselves introduced *Real Heroes*, showcasing Franklin Roosevelt, Eddie Rickenbacker, and Molly Pitcher in the first issue, in the summer of 1941. At the same time, the Pines publishing outfit brought out *Real Life Comics*, which included bios of Daniel Boone, Alfred Nobel, and Lawrence of Arabia in its premiere number. Late in 1941 Street & Smith tried both *Pioneer Picture Stories* and *Trail Blazers*.

1944 saw Pines' *It Really Happened* and in 1946 DC introduced *Real Fact Comics*. This latter title, which only lasted through 21 bimonthly issues, included artwork by Jack Kirby, Virgil Finlay, Howard Sherman, and Dick Sprang.

TWO-FISTED TALES   The earliest of the 1950s wave of war books was published by EC and edited by Harvey Kurtzman. The first issue was #18, dated November–December 1950. A well-drawn, well-written, and well-researched comic, *Two-Fisted Tales* was the least gung-ho of the combat comics of the decade.

Initially the bimonthly was intended to be simply a collection of adventure yarns. The first issue was not war-oriented.

"When we originally started," Kurtzman has said, "we were going to do blood and thunder tales and rip-roaring adventure." At about the same time that the magazine hit the stands, however, the war in Korea began. The second issue had a war cover drawn by Kurtzman, and the contents reflected his new preoccupation. He drew the next 10 covers, all of them forceful, violent, and downbeat, all devoted to servicemen in Korea. Not all the stories in each issue dealt with the Korean War, since Kurtzman tried for a balance between the present and the past.

He did most of the writing and layout. The chief artists were Jack Davis, Wally Wood, George Evans, John Severin, and Kurtzman himself. Unlike many of the war comics that followed, this one never went in for flag-waving or glorifying war and combat. Kurtzman once said, "All our stories really protested war." He went on to say, "The whole mood of our stories was that war wasn't a good thing. . . . You get killed suddenly for no reason."

Kurtzman also had an abiding interest in the Civil War and devoted two complete issues, #31 (January–Februrary 1953) and #35 (October 1953), to it. By the time the second one appeared, the Korean War was over and the remaining six issues of *Two-Fisted* turned to tales of combat and intrigue in other climes and times, ranging from the Old West to Victorian India. The final issue came out early in 1955.

EC's other war book was *Frontline Combat*, which went through 15 issues from 1951 to 1954. Kurtzman edited this one, too, and devoted considerable space to Korea. There was one Civil War number and assorted stories dealing with the World Wars. A number of other publishers, including DC and Marvel, went to war in the early 1950s. Among the many new titles issued were *Battle Action*, *Marines in Action*, *Our Army at War*, and *Star Spangled War Stories*.

Two-Fisted Tales, Harvey Kurtzman, unpublished cover rough, 1952.

WAMBI   The first and most successful jungle boy in comic books was found in *Jungle Comics* from the first issue (January 1940) onward. Wambi was a lad of about 11 or 12 who wore a red breechclout and matching turban and was described as a "mysterious child of the jungle" who "understands the language of the jungle beasts." His favorite friend among the animals was an elephant named Tawn. A product of the Eisner–Iger shop, the Wambi stories were drawn for the most part by Henry C. Kiefer.

Wambi operated in a sort of fantasy jungle world that mixed elements of Africa and India. Readers got the veldt, glimpses of tigers, encounters with black tribesmen, and intrigues

Wambi, Henry Kiefer, © 1946 Fiction House, Inc.

involving maharajahs. The jungle boy was clever and resourceful, dedicated to protecting his many animal friends and to preserving the ecological balance of the jungle. He found time to help girls in distress and to roust evil hunters. He also appeared in a now-and-then magazine of his own and was last seen in the early 1950s.

Among the other underage 1940s jungle heroes were Ty-Gor in *Blue Ribbon Comics*, Lion Boy in *Hit Comics*, and Beebo in *Shadow Comics*.

WAR COMICS   This was the first comic book devoted exclusively to the topic. It appeared in the spring of 1940 as World War II continued to spread across Europe. It was published by Dell, and sported a logo that showed the blood-red letters *W*, *A*, and *R* exploding across the page. *War* offered both fictional and fact-based yarns. The contents were not especially bloody, and most of the violence involved explosions and aerial warfare rather than hand-to-hand combat and civilian casualties.

War employed artist Alden McWilliams—one of the best planes, ships, and weapons experts in comics at the time—to handle its nonfiction, such as accounts of the Scapa Flow and Graf Spee incidents. Among the fictional characters were two war correspondents, Scoop Mason and Danny Dash, as well as a daredevil Navy pilot nicknamed the Sky Hawk (he was already unofficially fighting the Japanese in 1940) and a fellow called the Peace Raider, who fought a freelance seagoing war against the "warmongers of the world." The fourth issue introduced two chaps who dressed up in skintight, hooded black outfits and parachuted into enemy territory, where they operated as costumed commandos. Initially known as Black Wings, they later did business as Night Devils.

Apparently the public wasn't ready for a total war comic book even after America officially entered World War II, and *War* only appeared eight times in its three years of existence.

THE WEB   *See* Zip Comics.

WHIZ COMICS   This was the magazine that introduced the original CAPTAIN MARVEL. The first newsstand issue had a cover date of February 1940. In addition to the captain, Billy Batson, and SHAZAM, Fawcett Publications' initial venture into comics also launched such successful individual characters as Spysmasher, IBIS the Invincible, and the Golden Arrow. C.C. Beck contributed a goodly portion of the artwork and editor-writer Bill Parker did much of the scripting.

Whiz was one of the most popular titles of the 1940s and didn't cease publication until 1953, with its 155th issue.

WILBUR   One of the earliest teenage characters in comic books, the blond, crew-cut Wilbur had his coming out in MLJ's ZIP COMICS #18 (September 1941), a good three months before *Archie* Andrews's freckled face was seen anywhere. He was the invention of artist Lin

Spysmasher, C.C. Beck, © 1940 Fawcett Publications, Inc.

Streeter and a writer named Harvey Willard.

Wilbur Wilkins wore a high school letter sweater, bow-tie, and saddle shoes. He lived in a middle-class home, liked to play his "jive records," had a stuffy, businessman father, a plump mother who didn't quite understand him, and a pretty older sister who didn't think much of him. All the standard equipment, in other words, for the star of a teenage comedy strip. Wilbur existed in a milieu that was probably a bit more affluent than that of the average comic book reader and some of his misadventures took place at such leisure-class settings as country clubs and golf courses. What he lacked was a strong supporting cast of friends and sweethearts. Even when Archie creator Bob Montana took over the drawing, Wilbur's rather mechanical sitcom escapades remained stubbornly second-rate.

Nevertheless, as the popularity of teen characters increased in the 1940s, the lackluster Wilbur enjoyed a fairly successful career. He was given a title of his own in the summer of 1944 and the magazine went through 90 issues before shutting down in 1965. The popular KATY KEENE made her debut in *Wilbur Comics* in 1945.

WINGS COMICS The first comic book devoted exclusively to aviation, *Wings Comics* was introduced in the summer of 1940. Like several of the other Fiction House comics, it took its name from one of the company's established pulp fiction magazines. A line of copy over the title proclaimed that the book was devoted to "Fighting Aces of the War Skies." Each month's cover offered a scene of aerial combat. Most of them were drawn by Gene Fawcette. Eventually, as World War II progressed *Wings* began to take an interest in women as well as airplanes.

Among the characters featured in the early years were Clipper Kirk, the Skull Squad, Greasemonkey Griffin, Jane Martin—War Nurse, and Captain Wings. The stories offered airborne thrills and on-the-ground intrigue in such varied locales as Egypt, England, the Balkans, China, Germany, Malaya, and Libya. Scripts were credited to a batch of fictitious writers that included Major T.E. Bowen, Ace

Atkins, Capt. Derek West, and Capt. A.E. Carruthers. Early artists, real people all, included George Tuska, Klaus Nordling, Henry C. Kiefer, and Al Avison.

At the beginning of 1942, after America had officially entered the war and comic books were being sold to thousands of GIs through post exchanges, *Wings Comics* grew considerably sexier. Several artists who could draw not only planes but pretty women as well joined the staff. Among them were Nick Cardy, Artie Saaf, and Bob Lubbers. Hiked skirts and cleavage were seen as frequently as propellers and machine guns. Ladies started playing important roles in just about every story. Long-established Jane Martin started showing up in provocative attire and, on occasion, in nothing but her undies.

The postwar years found *Wings* in an especially girl-happy mood. Every monthly cover

Captain Wings, Nick Cardy, © 1942 by Wings Pub. Co.

from the spring of 1947 to the autumn of 1949 featured a pretty (and usually scantily clad) young woman. There was also, of course, at least one airplane on every cover. The dependable Lubbers did all 28 of these covers.

In the early 1950s, *Wings* grew more sobersided and most of the ladies were dropped. Realistic yarns dealing with the air war in Korea became common. The magazine ceased to be in the summer of 1954.

THE WIZARD   *See* Top-Notch Comics.

WONDER WOMAN   She was created by psychologist-turned-author William Moulton Marston, using the pen name Charles Moulton, and artist H.G. Peter, and was introduced at the back of ALL STAR COMICS #8 late in 1941. "At last in a world torn by the hatreds and wars of men," exclaimed a caption, "appears a woman to show the problems and fears of men are mere child's play."

The nine-page intro story began in the manner of some of the Dorothy Lamour sarong movies of the 1930s, with a handsome blond aviator crashing on the "shores of an uncharted isle set in the midst of a vast expanse of ocean." Captain Steve Trevor was seriously hurt in the crash and was nursed back to health by Diana, the daughter of the queen of Paradise Island. The island was an all-female enclave and the Amazons had been living there, immortal, since before the Christian era. Because of unfortunate past experiences, they were dedicated to keeping "aloof from men." But the power of love proved to be too strong for Princess Di and she left her island and forsook her immortality to escort Steve back to America.

When *Sensation Comics* #1 (January 1942) appeared, Wonder Woman was its leading character. She arrived in the United States with Steve, flying her transparent airplane. (Nobody ever explained the advantage of an invisible plane in which the pilot remains visible.) She assumed the identity of a lovelorn nurse named Diana Prince so that she could be close to Steve while he convalesced. The real Diana wanted to go off to South America to be married. "By taking your place," Wonder Woman explained to her, "I can see the man I love and you can marry the man you love." As with most dual-identity situations in comics, Steve never paid much attention to Diana and was enamored of Wonder Woman, whom he persisted in calling "my beautiful angel."

In the second issue of *Sensation*, readers met the sweets-loving Etta Candy and the other girls of the Holliday College for Women. The students all seemed to attend classes wearing sweaters and shorts, yet one of them criticized Wonder Woman's star-spangled costume for being too skimpy: "The Dean . . . insists on more above the waist." Aided by Etta and the girls, Wonder Woman went on to wage war on spies, crooks, and assorted bizarre villains. There was hardly a story in which women weren't tied up with ropes, manacled with chains, and spanked. Sheldon Mayer, editor of *Sensation*, has said that the stuff would've been even wilder if he'd allowed Marston to include all the plot elements and symbolism that he tried to sneak in.

Dr. William Moulton Marston, a psychologist who'd lectured and taught at Radcliffe, Tufts, Columbia, and the New School of Social Research, was nearly 50 when he assumed the pen name Charles Moulton (taken from his middle name and that of publisher Max Charles Gaines) to begin scripting the Wonder Woman stories for DC. The rationale he put forth made him sound like a pioneering feminist. "Women's strong qualities have become despised," he wrote. "The obvious remedy is to create a feminine character with all the strength of a superman plus all the allure of a good and beautiful woman."

As to whether boys would go for a strongwoman, the doctor asserted, "Give them an alluring woman stronger than themselves to submit to and they'll be proud to become her willing slaves!"

The early Wonder Woman yarns are rich with the sort of bondage-and-submission fantasies that had hitherto been seen only in under-the-counter publications. Moulton's scripts offered wartime readers some of the wackiest continuities to be found in funny books, a heady brew of whips, chains, and cockeyed mythology. H.G. Peter, the artist hand-picked by Marston, brought it all to life. He'd been a professional cartoonist since early in the century, and he gave the feature a slightly decadent, entertainingly unsavory feel.

Wonder Woman returned to *All Star* with #11 and became a member of the JUSTICE SOCIETY, staying with the magazine until it ceased publication early in 1951. In that more sexist era, however, she was sometimes called upon to remain at headquarters to serve as secretary while the men went out to combat crime and villainy. She was also a regular in the 15¢ COMIC CAVALCADE from 1943 to 1948.

Marston died in 1947 and Peter was fired late in 1949. With editor Robert Kanigher providing scripts and the team of Ross Andru and Mike Esposito doing the drawing, *Wonder Woman* became a slicker and less eccentric feature and the Amazon took to looking like the heroine of a romance comic. She was affected by the waning interest in superheroics, and late in 1951 she was dumped from *Sensation*. The magazine soon changed its name to *Sensation Mystery* and continued as a rather mild horror–fantasy entry until 1953.

The *Wonder Woman* magazine, begun in 1942, survived and served to keep the character alive. As Gerard Jones has pointed out, she "cruised through the 1950s and 1960s with directionless stories and little trace of her former depth and oddity." In 1968, Wonder Woman was revised by artist-writer Mike Sekowsky, given a new costume, and converted to a sort of comics version of Emma Peel of *The Avengers* television show. For good mea-

sure she worked with a wise Chinese mentor who called himself I Ching.

By the early 1970s, Wonder Woman was her old self again, decked out in red, white, and blue. The *Wonder Woman* title was suspended early in 1986, then revived a year later. George Perez produced the new book, returning to the earlier mythological elements and creating a livelier Wonder Woman than had been seen for many a year.

WONDERWORLD COMICS The flagship of the Victor Fox line and the home, briefly, of the very first SUPERMAN imitator, it began in the spring of 1939 under the title *Wonder Comics*. Included in the first issue were Dr. Fung, Shorty Shortcake, and, most importantly, Wonder Man.

Fox, a former accountant at DC, was one of the first to realize the financial possibilities of comic book superheroes. He formed his own company and he hired the Will Eisner–Jerry Iger shop to provide material. The one character he insisted on was Wonder Man. In everyday life, Wonder Man was a mild-mannered blond newsman named Fred Carson and the superpowers that he picked up in Tibet were fairly close to those enjoyed by the Man of Steel. Using the pen name Willis, Eisner wrote and drew the first and only adventure. As soon as DC got wind of the new character, they called in attorneys. Fox, not waiting for the courts to decide the case, retired his pioneering character.

Wonder Man was replaced in the second issue by Eisner's Yarko the Great, a turbanned magician, who was seen on the second cover hypnotizing a giant ape. With the third issue the magazine became *Wonderworld*. The new superhero star was Lou Fine's THE FLAME. Thereafter the yellow-clad mystery man was featured on every cover but one. Some of the later characters included the Black Lion, Lunar, and a superpatriot named U.S. Jones.

Spark Stevens was a comedy–adventure feature about a tough sailor and his equally tough sidekick. It ran for the life of the magazine and was drawn by a succession of artists who went on to better things. Bob Kane was the first, followed by such as Klaus Nordling, Sid Greene, and Bob Montana.

The magazine ended with issue #33 (January 1942).

WORLD'S FINEST COMICS The first regularly issued comic book to sell for more than a dime, it was an offshoot of the earlier *New York World's Fair Comics* and hit the stands in the spring of 1941. The initial issue was called *World's Best*. The title was then changed to *World's Finest*. Bound in cardboard covers and containing 96 pages, the fat magazine was priced at 15¢. It offered brand-new adventures of such established DC favorites as SUPERMAN, ZATARA, BATMAN, JOHNNY THUNDER, and THE SANDMAN and of characters created just for *World's Finest*.

Among the new heroes introduced were Lando, yet another magician, and Drafty, a less-than-serious soldier. Others who frequented the magazine in its early years were the Star Spangled Kid, THE GREEN ARROW, the Boy Commandos, the Wyoming Kid, and Tommy Tomorrow.

With its 71st issue (July–August 1954), *World's Finest* dropped its price to 10¢ and cut its page count. In another innovation, it teamed its headliners, Batman and Superman: "Your two favorite heroes together in one adventure!" Robin also joined in. The initial artist for these amalgamated yarns was Dick Sprang, who held on until 1963.

World's Finest continued until its 323rd issue (January 1986), fluctuating in price, page number, and lineup. As the magazine grew older, the Superman–Batman combo did not always appear and considerable reprint material was used. In 1990 DC used the title for a three-issue mini series teaming Batman and Superman, written by Dave Gibbons and illustrated by Steve Rude and Karl Kesel.

X-MEN A very important group, they were the first mutants to show up in Marvel comics. Yet another creation of Stan Lee and Jack Kirby, *X-Men* #1 appeared in the summer of 1963 and introduced Professor Xavier and his band of teenage mutants. They have continued, with considerable personnel changes and comings and goings, for three decades and have inspired other groups ranging from the New Mutants to the Ninja Turtles.

The wheelchair-bound Professor Charles Xavier, as explained in the *Official Handbook of the Marvel Universe*, "is the mutant son of nuclear researcher Brian Xavier and his wife Sharon. Even as a pre-adolescent, Xavier could use his powers to sense other people's intentions and emotions. Upon reaching puberty, Xavier's telepathic powers began to fully emerge. As a side effect, he began losing his hair until by high school graduation he was completely bald." Professor X also "possesses numerous psionic powers, making him the world's most powerful telepath." Among his knacks were the ability to read minds and to project his own thoughts within a radius of 250 miles. He could make others think he's invisible, sense the presence of another mutant "within a small but as yet undetermined radius," project his astral body, and control matter psychokinetically. For good measure, he was "a genius in genetics and other sciences."

Professor X gathered together his team of good mutants "to protect mankind from . . . evil mutants." The first such evil mutant they tackled was the red-armored Magneto. The initial X-Men consisted of "Hank McCoy, known to us as the Beast! Bobby Drake, nicknamed the Iceman! Slim Summers, our human Cyclops! . . . Warren Worthington the Third, who is called the Angel! . . . Miss Jean Grey . . . Marvel Girl!" The Beast was an apelike version of the Thing; Iceman could turn himself into a human icicle and toss deadly snowballs and ice bombs; Cyclops, who had two eyes, could send powerful rays out of them; the Angel had real wings growing out of his back and could fly; and Marvel Girl possessed powerful telekinetic powers. This collection of misunderstood misfits appealed to teenagers, many of whom feel like mutants during some stage of their development. After an initial success, however, *X-Men* began to fade and the original material was halted in 1970.

After the original X-Men had been in limbo for several years, existing only in reprints, Marvel issued an annual titled *Giant-Size X-Men.*

This introduced a new batch of teenage mutant heroes. They included Colossus, Nightcrawler, Thunderbird, Storm, Banshee, and a pathologically violent antihero named Wolverine. Len Wein was the writer, Dave Cockrum the artist. Starting with *X-Men* #94 (August 1975), the group began appearing in brand-new adventures in their own, revived magazine. Very shortly Christ Claremont took over as writer and made the X-Men his own. His intricate plots, ranging over many issues and mixing fantasy, science fiction, physical transmutation, adolescent anguish, identity crises, and topics of the day, won an increasing readership. The success of the new, improved bunch encouraged Marvel to add more mutant characters to its lineup over the years and inspired other publishers to do likewise. Among the many new mutants have been *New Mutants*, *The Defenders*, *Alpha Flight*, *X-Factor*, and *Dazzler*, dealing with one of the few mutant superheroines on roller skates.

X-Men®, Jack Kirby–Paul Reinman. All Marvel characters and the distinctive likenesses thereof are trademarks of Marvel Entertainment Group, Inc. and are used with permission. © 1992 Marvel Entertainment Group, Inc.

YANK AND DOODLE What you had here was two Robins in search of a BATMAN, a pair of boy wonders fighting crime with no adult supervision whatsoever. Yank and Doodle were billed as "America's Fighting Twins." The two wore red, white, and blue uniforms, identical except for a *Y* on the chest of one and a *D* on the chest of the other, and had no special powers. Their reason for being was explained in an early caption: "American youth shall not be denied their chance to safeguard American democracy. . . . With that in mind, the Walter Twins, Rick and Dick, too young for naval or military service, crusade against all un-American activities as Yank and Doodle."

Yank and Doodle commenced their crusade in *Prize Comics* #13 (August 1941) and were the creation of Paul Norris, who later graduated to such newspaper strips as *Jungle Jim* and *Brick Bradford*. The boys' most persistent antagonist was the Limping Man, "a master of disguise, who cannot be recognized except by his limp! The forces of law and order are helpless in the face of a villain who never looks the same way twice."

In *Prize* #34 (September 1943) another of the magazine's crimebusters, the Black Owl, got himself drafted. He explained his problem to his old school chum, the twins' father:

"While I'm helping take care of international gangsters abroad, who will keep crime in check

Yank and Doodle, John Giunta, © 1945 Feature Publications, Inc.

here?" Dad Walter agreed to take over the role and then teamed up with Yank and Doodle. He knew they were really his sons, but they didn't know he was the Black Owl. That made for a complicated but stimulating home life. Eventually the boys found out about their pop's alter ego and things ran a bit more smoothly for the "terrific trio." Among the other artists who illuminated this unusual *ménage à trois* were Jack Alderman, Fred Guardineer, and a youthful Gil Kane. The father and sons act took its final bow in *Prize* #68 early in 1948.

THE YOUNG ALLIES This was a patriotic kid gang whose membership mixed regular fellows with super-powered youths. Master-

minded by Joe Simon and Jack Kirby but written and drawn by others, the Young Allies were introduced by way of their own magazine in the summer of 1941. They roamed the war-torn world, battling the Nazis, the Japanese, and other enemies of the United States. Although they never quite adjusted to the post-war world, they remained in business until the summer of 1947.

The stars of the group were Toro, the flaming boy companion of the Human Torch, and Bucky, the scrappy sidekick of CAPTAIN AMERICA. The other four members were Jeff, the brainy one who wore glasses; Tubby, the fat one; Knuckles, the Dead End Kid surrogate; and Whitewash, the zoot-suited black. Simon has said that he got the name for the gang from

Young Allies®, Al Gabriele. All Marvel characters and the distinctive likenesses thereof are trademarks of Marvel Entertainment Group, Inc. and are used with permission. © 1992 Marvel Entertainment Group, Inc.

a series of juvenile novels about the Boy Allies that he read in his youth.

Each adventure took up nearly an entire issue, something that wasn't much done at the time. In their first outing, the new team battled Nazi spies as well as the evil Red Skull, a master villain borrowed from the Captain America saga. The second issue found them fighting Nazis again while discovering a lost civilization, and tangling with the Black Talon, another villain borrowed from Captain America. In that issue the boy buddies introduced their very own fight song:

"We fight together thru stormy weather—
We're out to lick both crooks and spies!
We won't be stopped—and we can't be topped—
We are the Young Allies!"

In addition to 20 issues of their own magazine, the lads also appeared in *Kid Komics*, *Amazing*, *Complete*, *Marvel Mystery*, *Mystic*, and *Sub-Mariner*. Among the artists who drew their adventures were Charles Nicholas and Al Gabriele; among the writers were Stan Lee and Otto Binder. The dependable Alex Schomburg supplied the majority of covers.

YOUNG MEN   This was one of the comic books used in Marvel's attempt to revive its top 1940s superheroes in the mid-1950s. *Young Men* began in 1950 as an anthology book offering assorted adventure tales, then at the end of 1951 it switched to war stories. After another brief fling at general adventure with an emphasis on hot rods, the magazine changed again.

Issue #24 (December 1953) showcased the famous flaming hero of the 1940s on the cover along with the headline "The HUMAN TORCH Returns." For good measure, the SUB-MARINER and CAPTAIN AMERICA were also brought back. Dick Ayers drew the Torch and Toro, John Romita drew Captain America, and Bill Everett took care of his creation, the Sub-Mariner. The Torch was apparently considered the most saleable of the old-timers and was fea-

tured on all five covers of the resurrection effort issues.

The time was not yet right for a revival, however, and *Young Men* and its gang of heroes ended with the 28th issue (June 1954). *Men's Adventures* was similarly used and issue #27 (May 1954) and #28 (July 1954) offered the same lineup. In addition, three new issue of *Captain America* appeared during this period, as well as three issues of *The Human Torch*. Everett's aquatic hero fared somewhat better and his revived magazine made it through 10 issues before sinking in the autumn of 1955.

YOUNG ROMANCE   This was the magazine that inspired one of the most lucrative postwar trends. It introduced the romance category and turned millions of girls into comic book buyers.

Young Romance, Joe Simon–Jack Kirby, © 1947 Feature Publications Corp.

Young Romance was invented by Joe Simon and packaged and produced by him and his long-time partner Jack Kirby. Published by the Prize Group, the first issue arrived in the summer of 1947.

Although the book initially ran the slogan "For the More ADULT Readers of COMICS" on the covers, what it offered was easier-to-digest versions of the type of material that had long been available in confession magazines like *True Story*. While the audience for *Young Romance* did include older readers, the majority of the customers were teenage and preteen girls, an audience that had never supported the now-fading superheroes in any great numbers. The first issue sold out a printing of 500,000 and soon the circulation climbed to a million per issue.

Simon recruited artists such as Bill Draut and Mort Meskin and has said that he and Kirby turned out the early scripts themselves: "We wrote the whole thing. We couldn't afford writers." Later, since they were getting 50 percent of the profits, they did hire authors. "All the stories were shamelessly billed as true confessions by young women and girls," Simon once confessed, "when in actuality, all were authored by men." Typical story titles were "I Was a Gangster's Moll" and "They Called Me Boy Crazy." The team followed their hit invention with *Young Love* late in 1948 and it, too, became a million-copy bestseller.

Other publishers began getting into the romance business and, according to comics historian John Benson, "at the height of the phenomenon there were nearly 150 titles being published simultaneously." Simon and Kirby eventually moved on to other things, but *Young Romance*, which was taken over by DC in 1963, survived until its 208th issue in 1975.

ZATANNA *See* Zatara.

ZATARA   The profession of magician was followed by quite a few comic book characters in the late 1930s and early 1940s. There were dozens of them, top-hatted or turbanned and decked out in opera capes and tuxes. In addition to combating crooks and criminal masterminds, most of them also did battle with a wide range of devils, demons, and monsters. Zatara was among the top-seeded mystics of the GOLDEN AGE. Though nothing was mentioned at the time, he also sired the lady magician Zatanna, who first appeared during the SILVER AGE.

Zatara came along in the first issue of ACTION COMICS (June 1938), along with SUPERMAN. He looked a great deal like Mandrake of the newspaper funnies and even had a giant sidekick named Tong to act as a Lothar surrogate. Zatara could do just about anything and there was never any pretending that his tricks were merely hypnotic illusions. He really could move buildings, turn crooks' guns into snakes, turn the crooks themselves into pigs, and then project his astral body to the moon.

Zatara was the joint effort of artist Fred Guardineer and writer Gardner Fox. During his early days, the magician explored areas of the weird and the occult that would have caused the urbane Mandrake to hide under his bed. A *Weird Tales* fan, Fox used a goodly amount of supernatural material in his scripts. Zatara met up with the mummy of Cheops; he visited Atlantis and battled sea serpents and a giant octopus. While hunting for a fountain of youth in Brazil, he encountered a zombie queen—"I have been dead a thousand years, rash stranger! You are doomed!"—whose throne was surrounded by huge slithering snakes. He defeated a hooded villain who trained giant condors to murder people on the moors; tangled with with another ancient evil queen who exchanged her withered old body for that of a lovely young girl; and conquered a mad scientist who had created an army of intelligent gorillas.

Zatara's immense magical powers stemmed from his discovery that words said backwards had unfailing effect. "Emoc nwod!" he'd order and something or somebody would come down. His reversed commands often had a nice ring, as when he told someone who'd just lassoed him to "Ossal flesruoy!" Once, annoyed with some unruly gorillas, he instructed them, "Sallirog llaf ot ruoy htaed!" By the early 1940s, Zatara's adventures had

Zatara, Fred Guardineer, © 1939, renewed 1967 DC Comics, Inc. All rights reserved.

require the currently deceased magician to be resurrected.

Eventually, Zatanna abandoned the stage magician's outfit she'd worn (complete with black net stockings), became a regular member of the Justice League, and adopted a blue-and-red crimefighter costume. She has soloed a few times in one-shots, where she went back to wearing the magician outfit, but according to a recent DC *Who's Who*, she's retired now and has "given up adventuring in favor of a quiet life, buying a home in San Francisco and performing when the mood strikes her." Her mother was Sindella, a resident of Atlantis whom Zatara met during one of his adventures in the undersea kingdom.

become much less spooky and he took to combating gangsters, murderers, bank robbers, and other mundane sorts. Zatara left *Action* early in 1950 and he took his final bow in WORLD'S FINEST #51 the following spring. Among the other artists to draw the feature were Joseph Sulman, W.F. White, and Joe Kubert.

Zatanna was also the creation of Gardner Fox, with an assist from DC editor Julius Schwartz. She first appeared as a guest in *Hawkman* #4 in the summer of 1964 and was drawn by Murphy Anderson (see HAWKMAN). The notion was that she was looking for her long-lost father Zatara. This quest took her through various other titles, including *Atom*, and *Green Lantern*, until she finally found the missing mystic in *Justice League* #51 (see ATOM, GREEN LANTERN, and JUSTICE LEAGUE OF AMERICA). Zatara was later killed while trying to save his daughter in a continuity that appeared in *Swamp Thing*, but he resurfaced in the late 1980s in *Young All Stars* (see SWAMP THING). Those stories were set in the 1940s and didn't

THE ZEBRA   Though not as ominous a creature as, say, a bat or a spider, a zebra does happen to have stripes. And that was the reason unjustly imprisoned John Doyle decided to call himself the Zebra when he began his crime-fighting career in POCKET COMICS #1 (August 1941).

The digest-sized *Pocket* marked publisher Alfred Harvey's entry into comics. Among its other characters were the Spirit of '76, the Phantom Sphinx, and THE BLACK CAT. The kid public of the early 1940s wasn't ready for the digest format and the new title folded after four issues. The Zebra, however, survived, and after a hiatus of a few months, he became a regular in *Green Hornet Comics* (see GREEN HORNET).

According to the origin story, handsome young John Doyle was framed for murder by crooked politicians. A scant two days before his scheduled execution, he managed to escape from death row. Once free, he decided to devote his life to combating "all crime and evil where justice fails." He fashioned a black-and-white striped costume that looked quite a bit like his prison outfit, donned a black mask and a red cape, and christened himself the Zebra. By the end of his first adventure, as might have been expected, he succeeded in clearing his name. But he continued to go after crooks and grafters. Doyle, an attorney by day, also found time to combat Nazi spies and an occasional madman.

He was last seen in 1946. Among the artists who drew his adventures were Pierce Rice, Arturo Cazeneuve, and Bob Fujitani.

ZIGGY PIG   He was one of the earliest creations of MAD regular Al Jaffee. Ziggy and his partner Silly Seal were first seen in Marvel's *Krazy Komics* #1 (July 1942). Though not the most popular porcine character in comic books, Ziggy appeared in more than a half dozen different titles in the 1940s. These included *All Surprise*, *Silly Tunes*, *Animated Movie Tunes*, and *Ziggy Pig–Silly Seal Comics*.

Unlike the pantless Porky Pig, Ziggy usually appeared fully clothed. He favored a sweater with a *Z* emblazoned on the front. He was not especially courageous, was quick to anger, and had little patience with his partner. Silly Seal spoke with a lisp in the early stories.

The team led an adventurous life, tangling with Japanese spies, murderers, crooks, con men, and an occasional mythical monster. After Jaffee departed for wartime service, several anonymous artists carried on.

Ziggy and his cohort were last seen in *Animal Fun 3-D* in 1953.

ZIP COMICS   This was the fourth of MLJ's monthly GOLDEN AGE titles and the premiere issue had a cover date of February 1940. In its four-plus years of existence, *Zip* introduced nearly two dozen characters. Two of them, Steel Sterling and the Web, outlived the magazine and have recurred several times over the past half century or so.

Over in ACTION COMICS, SUPERMAN himself was known as the Man of Steel, but that didn't keep *Zip* from introducing its own Man of Steel. His name was Steel Sterling and he could be seen on the cover, red-costumed and over-

Ziggy Pig, Al Jaffee, © 1942 U.S.A. Comic Magazine Corp.

muscled, ripping up enemy airplanes while bullets bounced off his broad chest. Steel Sterling was drawn by Charles Biro and written by the magazine's editor, Abner Sundell. The hero had an origin that was traumatic enough to have caused the average superhero to call it quits right then and there. An early caption explained it thusly: "To avenge the death of his father, who was murdered and robbed of all his wealth by gangsters, and to avoid a similar end for himself, John Sterling devoted every minute of his youth to dangerous experiments! In one final experiment, the result of which would be success or death!—he hurled himself into a tank of molten steel and fiery chemicals! The test realized his life ambition. He emerged 'Steel Sterling,' with all the attributes of this sturdiest of metals!!"

Zip offered two more costumed heroes, neither of whom had any superpowers. The Scarlet Avenger wore a bright-green business suit and a scarlet cloak and mask. He was "the man who never smiles" and had "dedicated his life to the extermination of crime, and for the accomplishment of this purpose he has brought into play his super-scientific brain." Most of his early troubles were caused by an extremely tall red-haired villainess named Texa. Irv Novick drew the feature.

Edd Ashe illustrated the adventures of Mr. Satan, a chap who did his gangbusting in a cape and skintight costume that was topped with devil horns.

Rounding out the lineup were a masked cowboy, a jungle man, a matched pair of daredevil aviators, a soldier of fortune, and a magician. In #10, a somewhat violent kid fantasy by R.L. Golden was added. *Dicky in the Magic Forest* took place "in the realm of fancy and at no particular place, at no particular time." MLJ introduced WILBUR, its first teenage character, in #18 (September 1941). Black Jack, a red-costumed crimefighter with an ace of spades on the front of his costume, made his debut in #20. Appropriately enough, his favorite opponent was a hooded rascal known as Poker Face. By this time, MLJ's comics had moved into a

bloody phase and the Black Jack stories were full of bloodshed and sharp weapons.

An even bloodier hero showed up in #27 (July 1942) in the person of the Web. He was a red-haired fellow who wore a green-and-yellow costume that included a cape resembling a giant spider web. In everyday life, he was a bespectacled professor of criminology named John Raymond. The professor operated in various parts of the war-torn world. He was especially fond of torture chambers, locales where one encountered "the shrill agonizing shrieks of terrible suffering and the low piteous moans of those praying for death." The Web first retired after #38 (July 1943). Mort Leav was the original artist and Bob Montana depicted the Web on several covers.

By the time the Web left, *Zip* was a different magazine than before. Humor had crowded out many of the serious features. The Slaphappy Applejacks, Ginger, and Señor Banana, all by Harry Sahle, had been added. Issue #39 saw the arrival of Red Rube, a red-haired mock superhero who was a heavy-handed spoof of CAPTAIN MARVEL. Instead of "SHAZAM," he shouted "Hey, Rube!" The entire magazine shut down with its 47th issue in the summer of 1944.

Steel Sterling, looking not a year older, returned in the mid-1960s in both *Mighty Comics* and *The Mighty Crusaders*. Archie Comics, formerly MLJ, also gave him another chance in the mid-1980s in a revived *Blue Ribbon Comics* and eventually in a short-lived title of his own. In neither case did he catch on. The Web, too, returned in the mid-1960s and the mid-1980s. He made a third comeback try in 1991. Retaining only his name, and looking now like an aging hippie biker, he had his own title in DC's Impact series.

ZORRO   The veteran mystery man began life in a pulp fiction magazine in 1919. The following year, he jumped into silent films and in the 1930s and 1940s he fenced his way through both serials and feature films. Zorro first appeared in a comic book in 1949. Disney got hold of the masked swordsman of old California in 1957 and made him a television star. More comic books resulted from that. A 1990 cable TV show brought Zorro back into public ken and, briefly, into the comic shops.

Johnston McCulley, a one-time newspaper reporter from the Midwest, created Zorro in a serial that appeared in Munsey's *All-Story Weekly* in the spring of 1919. Eventually McCulley would write more than 60 novels and stories about the mild-mannered, foppish young man who donned a mask to become a fearless avenger. In 1920, the story served as the basis for Douglas Fairbanks, Sr.'s *The Mark of Zorro*. It was remade by 20th Century Fox in 1940 with Tyrone Power as the dueling hero. Republic Pictures also bought partial rights to the character and that resulted in a 1936 movie titled *The Bold Caballero* and such chapter plays as *Zorro Rides Again* in

1937 and *Zorro's Fighting Legion* in 1939.

In 1949 Dell issued the first Zorro comic book, a one-shot titled *The Mark of Zorro*, with artwork by Bill Ely. Dell returned to the character several times in the early and mid-1950s, offering such titles as *The Return of Zorro* and *The Challenge of Zorro* as part of its Four Color series. Early in 1958, Dell began a new series of Zorro comic books based on the Disney TV show. These used photos of actor Guy Williams, in costume, on the covers. The interior artwork was first done by Alex Toth. Warren Tufts later drew the character.

The magazine outlasted the show, which went off the air in 1959, and didn't cease until the autumn of 1961. Between 1966 and 1968, Gold Key offered a nine-issue series, reprinting from the earlier Dell issues. In 1990, to tie in with the new Family Channel cable *Zorro*, Marvel published a short-lived series of comic books. Toth drew some of the covers.

Bibliography

Bails, Jerry. *Collector's Guide: The First Heroic Age*. Detroit: Panelologist, 1969.

Bell, John. *Canuck Comics*. Montreal: Matrix Books, 1986.

Cox, J. Randolph. *Man of Magic and Mystery: A Guide to the Work of Walter B. Gibson*. Metuchen: Scarecrow Press, 1988.

Dunning, John. *Tune In Yesterday*. Englewood Cliffs: Prentice-Hall, Inc., 1976.

Gerber, Ernst and Mary. *The Photo-Journal Guide to Comic Books*. Vols 1 and 2. Minden: Gerber Publishing Co., 1989.

Gifford, Denis. *The International Book of Comics*. New York: Crescent Books, 1984.

Goulart, Ron. *Great History of Comics*. Chicago: Contemporary Books, 1986.

—, ed. *The Encyclopedia of American Comics*. New York: Facts On File, 1990.

Horn, Maurice. *The World Encyclopedia of Comics*. New York: Chelsea House.

Jacobs, Frank. *The Mad World of William M. Gaines*. Secaucus: Lyle Stuart, 1972.

Jacobs, Will, and Jones Gerard. *The Comic Book Heroes*. New York: Crown, 1985.

Keltner, Howard. *Index to Golden Age Comic Books*. Detroit: Bails, 1976.

Lee, Stan. *Origins of Marvel Comics*. New York: Simon and Schuster, 1974.

—. *Son of Origins of Marvel Comics*. New York: Simon and Schuster, 1975.

Lupoff, Dick, and Thompson Don. *All in Color for a Dime*. New Rochelle: Arlington House, 1970.

Maltin, Leonard. *Of Mice and Magic*. New York: McGraw-Hill, 1980.

O'Neil, Dennis. *Secret Origins of the DC Super Heroes*. New York: Warner Books, 1976.

Overstreet, Robert. *The Official Overstreet Comic Book Price Guide*, No. 21. New York: House of Collectibles, 1991.

Simon, Joe. *The Comic Book Makers*. New York: Crestwood/II, 1990.

Wertham, Fredric. *Seduction of the Innocent*. New York: Rinehart, 1954.

The author also made use of numerous back issues of *Amazing Heroes*, *Comic Reader*, *Comic Scene*, *Comics Buyer's Guide*, and *Comics Journal*.

About the Author

RON GOULART, long recognized as one of the leading historians of comic books and comic strips, is also a well-known science fiction and mystery writer. He has twice been nominated for an Edgar Award by the Mystery Writers of America. Among his books on comics are *The Great Comic Book Artists* and *The Encyclopedia of American Comics*.